the
HEAVY
ART of JOY

the

HEAVY
ART of JOY

How I Encountered God in the
Midst of Mental Illness

NANCY CRAIG ZARZAR

Author photo by Tanya Hurter Photography

ISBN 978-1-7361050-3-0
EPUB 978-1-7361050-5-4

DEDICATION

To my beautiful daughters:
EVA ELISE
ABIGAIL MARYAM
MORIAH HOPE
Through whom Jesus has always poured out on me
"grace upon grace." (John 1:16)
May you be "pillars in the temple of God,
and never again may you leave it." (Revelation 3:12).

And to all those who, like me,
have found that the mind
can have "frightful mountains."
May we meet in eternal *shalom* on Mount Zion.

CONTENTS

Prologue

*J*UST AFTER HER twentieth birthday, my youngest daughter, Moriah Hope, had the words "no turning back" tattooed in Arabic right above her left ankle. The tattoo represented the spiritual strength and resolve of her Arab grandmother, Alice Zarzar, who at the time was dying of ALS. As a young woman in Bethlehem, where she grew up, Alice had knocked on every door in town to spread the news that the Jewish carpenter, the man Jesus, was the Deliverer of humanity. Her very being reverberated with the gospel. Alice emigrated to the United States in 1978 and eventually had several grandchildren, my three daughters among them. She taught them to sing Arabic worship songs, and their favorite was the chorus "I Have Decided to Follow Jesus," which they would sing in lilting Arabic:

> Sumumtu ani atba'a yesu'a[1]
> Sumumtu ani atba'a yesu'a
> Sumumtu ani atba'a yesu'a
> Atba'a yesu'a
> Bilaa reju'a

---

[1] I have decided to follow Jesus,
   I have decided to follow Jesus,
   I have decided to follow Jesus,
   No turning back,
   No turning back.

When Alice was dying, my daughters would flutter around her bed like three wood-nymphs and sing this refrain that would fill the air like an unction of light from a sacred parallel universe. Her body by then was useless baggage, yearning to be at once discarded and baptized with Forever. But she could still move her right hand a few inches off the bed that imprisoned her, so she would lift her wasted limb in worship every time they sang and whisper, "no turning back." Alice's story intersects mine in numerous ways; I too have suffered from a wasting disease that has attempted like a wicked archer to rob me of life, and barring that, to curse my soul to limp through life in silence. Yet I have resolved not to be silent, and my words rain down like meteors on the enemies that are always in the process of thrusting a gag into my mouth. Depression is a shameful word. And so is its evil consort, anxiety. Whenever I dared to confess them aloud in a room, silence would explode, and all the occupants would suddenly look down at their cell phones or begin picking at a piece of lint on their clothing. Yet so many have suffered as I have, as I still do, and made the obligatory pact with Silence. However, there is one sound, another Word really, that speaks itself in the valley of weeping and makes it a place of springs. That Word is the Incarnate Son, Creator and Sustainer of all that is.

So, this is and is not a happily-ever-after story. Some days I can only lift two fingers or a hand toward heaven, but lift them I do, in praise of the crucified and risen Christ, in defiance of all the nihilism that threatens those with mental illness. Yet I live in hope of the resurrection, when all wounds will go backwards into unscarred flesh and the mouths of the voiceless will bloom with violent glossolalia. Until then, like Alice I will lift my two or three fingers that are still alive with motion and paper the walls of my temporary prison with the name of Jesus. This book is the wallpaper, in hopes that some who suffer may decipher the scrawled words, confront the utterly exquisite face of the Creator and find that they too have voices. So, until the *Parousia,* when evil will miscarry its dark fetus of suffering, may I, like Ezekiel and the apostle John, ingest a scroll, this one stamped in blood with the words "no turning back." And as it was for Alice, "may the lifting up of my hands be like the evening sacrifice."[2]

---

[2]   Psalm 141:2b (NIV).

When Stones Become Bread

I stood by the bed that held your twisted alter ego,
A body frozen like a deceptive photograph
That can no longer shout out its black-haired beauty.
But I know still who you are
Though your lips that long to speak of love
Have sold you into the servitude of silence.
You are the woman at the well
Who abandoned the wicked water of her jug
To plunge into the perpetual pouring
From the side of a Jewish nobody
Whose body held everything.
Your own body may be stone
But your zeal is stonier,
A perpetual resolve to thrust the Gospel
Into every passerby:
"I met a man who told me everything
I ever did.
Can't you see He's the One?"
And what have you done but waste all your perfume,
Then waste some more
On the body of your Lover who died
But loved death into a plaything.
Your children's children in the pallor of your sickroom
Dress your God and theirs
in praise like shimmering scarves,
And you lift the two or three obedient fingers left to you
To bless the One who emasculated death.
"No turning back,
No turning back" they sing
And your face indeed
Has ever been fixed on a perpetual Canaan
Like a resolute mask that you would die before removing.
I see death attempt to feed on you
Like a myriad of wasps poised to sting

But you whisper to me
Above the bitter beating of their wings: "Don't be afraid."
Those were your last words to me.
The wasps are wasting their work
Because your body is bathed in irresistible light
That pierces them with their own swords.
Death has been eaten with nothing left to fill a basket.
Its wings are whirring a dark refrain
But your Lover tells you they are lies, and you believe Him.
The Jordan undulates with holy blood
And you will at last go under,
Suffocating into life
And death will choke on the torrents of your praise.
"Well done," your Lover whispers.
Your body and lips thaw from the sound
And you pour yourself into His arms
And whisper at last against His skin:
"No turning back."

1

Hotel California

*I*T HAS BEEN TWILIGHT all day long. In the beginning was this room, and this room was with silence, and this room was silence. I am lying on the gray bed, narrow in the half-light, and staring at the tile floor and toilet through the open bathroom door. How did it come to this, that I find myself in a place of padlocked doors and windows covered with grating? When I was ten years old and seeing a psychiatrist, my mother told me not to tell any of my friends about it or else their parents wouldn't let them play with me. What about this? Should I tell them about this? When I was ten, the sky went gray, and my heart went gray, and the whole year happened without sound. By my eleventh birthday, the sounds and colors had returned with no explanation or apology. But now, at twenty-three, I found myself alone again in a silent film, a black-and-white daguerreotype. How curious, that the world is not colorfast. Nor sound fast, because the silence has come back too. I cannot move. My body has petrified to gray stone. On the table is a plastic jar with my name on it. "Reseal jar tightly," it admonishes on the lid so the nurses won't pick it up and spill something unpleasant on themselves. They wanted my blood, too. They have analyzed all my body fluids to determine which chemical stirred up my fears. I am not chosen.

That is it. God has mercy on whom He will have mercy. I am not included. That thought had possessed me this morning as I watched my fingers typing at work. I began to think with my very entrails about predestination. *I am a minute point that infinity consumes like a whale straining plankton. What if heaven lasts too long for me and starts spinning around in my head? What indeed?* How dare such a thought come to me. I don't understand God. Sometimes I try to fit all of Him into my brain and He lodges there like a blood clot threatening to choke it. What else could I do, sitting there at work watching my fingers typing as if they belonged to someone else, but go to Sunoco and fortuitously find single-edged blades? This isn't me thinking now. It's someone else. Remember that throughout, please. I watched her do all these things but couldn't stop her. I opened the razor blades while driving home. Sobs were rasping out of my throat. Tears fell everywhere. The package told me there were five blades enclosed, but there were only three. I counted them several times. I felt an impending irony but couldn't quite grasp it. The two missing blades were significant. I noted how neatly they were wrapped in blue paper. Just like tiny Christmas gifts. I rewrapped the blades and put them back in the box. Cutting and driving are incompatible. At home the dog sniffed me curiously. I think she can smell fear on me.

Tears are hot in my eyes. I can't see, but I know the way by heart. No one is home, and no one will be home. In my bedroom I put on an audiotape, a singing monk crooning the poetry of St. John of the Cross to a trembling guitar. The poems sound like running water—a kind of almost sound. I don't think about the beauty of his voice; I only know the words will intensify my pain. He sings that Christ has wounded his soul. I am going to wound mine, if I can cut deeply enough to find it. Under the translucent skin of my wrists are veins strung like taut blue cords. I spread a towel on the bed and unwrap one of the blades. The monk's song fills the air like tiny golden ornaments strung from an invisible thread. The cutting itself is no longer in my mind. Perhaps it took five minutes—perhaps twenty. I don't know. I remember the startling absence of pain and the release of fear like air from a balloon. I cut deeper, searching for a wellspring of blood. Blood drips on the white ribbons that hold on my shoes. I am still crying. I am pacing the floor, bleeding on everything around me. I am kneeling beside the bed, my head bowed. *Father, forgive me. Father, forgive.*

I look at the bright gaping mouth on my wrist. It is trying to speak.

"What have you done?" it accuses.

Suddenly, the Speaker changes. "Don't you know that your blood cries out to Me from the ground?"

"No," I reply.

"What has SHE done?"

I wrap my wrist carefully in a towel and go to the phone to call him.

"I'm bleeding," I say when he answers.

"How much?"

"A lot."

"I'm coming over; stay there."

"No, no, no, don't come, don't come." I wait for him to save me. Something has vivisected my soul. That's why I did it. Isn't that logic? I don't want to die. Dying isn't the issue. I have to let the demon escape through my wrist. Nothing makes sense in my mind. It's all chaos and I must cut a line of demarcation. Everything will be orderly now that I have a plumb line.

When my boyfriend, Issa, rang the doorbell, I crept to the door in my white-ribboned, now-stained, shoes. Blood was pooling up slowly in the towel. My brother had told me that I could sever an artery when I cut myself and bleed to death before I could get to the phone. But I wasn't afraid. Death haunted me, but somehow, I believed that it couldn't claim me before my purpose had been fulfilled. I belonged to the Father, the Father who had allowed my mind to stalk and pursue me like a bird of prey. I could feel its relentless stare as I typed at work, chatting casually with my co-workers as if I were not a hunted thing, as if I did not have the mark of Cain on my head. I had been driven from the presence of the Lord for some reason I could not comprehend, driven to slash at myself as if I were Dorian Gray attempting to destroy the portrait of himself that had taken on all his wickedness, and finding instead a knife in his heart.

I opened the door and all Issa said was "Let me see it." I unwrapped the towel gingerly as if it were the swaddling of a newborn. He stared at the wound for a few seconds, and I almost expected it to speak, to bring forth an oracle.

"It's deep," he said. Then, "I can't be here for the rest of your life to take care of you when you do these things." Later I would recognize the irony of this statement, for he would indeed take care of me again and again. I don't know if he knew then that I had attacked myself instead of him, that I wanted to punish him for not loving me the way I wanted him to. He had awakened my desire to love, then moved quietly away leaving me with the hot lava of an emotion that must flow out or explode, catapulting pieces of myself in all directions.

"I'm taking you to the doctor," he said, and he motioned for me to follow him.

I sat silent in his car, half demon, half wood nymph, eviscerated by emotion, but still aware of the theatrical effect of my situation. In the waiting room I clutched the towel like a small child would cling to a favorite blanket. It covered the gaping mouth so it wouldn't start prophesying there in front of everyone. I vaguely wondered if anyone was curious about the towel. I was mulling over this conundrum when the nurse called my name, and I obediently followed her as she ushered me into an exam room.

"This could use a few stitches," the doctor muttered to himself in a tone of mild boredom when he had surveyed the damage. I watched as he numbed my wrist and silenced the terrifying mouth with black thread. It looked almost respectable then. Afterwards a nurse wrapped my wrist with an endless length of gauze until I felt like Lazarus being prepared for burial. I sat there, naively assuming that I could be taken home, neatly stitched up like a rag doll that had sprung a leak of sawdust, and that I would be at work typing nonchalantly the next day. Then the doctor announced my destiny, a handful of words only, but pregnant with endless repercussions: "I can't let you go home."

My psychologist had been begging me to go to the hospital for months. During one session he even offered to call me a taxi to take me there. I was determined not to go. The hospital was for strange people with drooling mouths and protruding teeth. It represented to me a violation of myself, an imprisonment relegating me to the ranks of the insane. I had not thought of this complication as I had taken in the monk's lilting voice and completed my sacred ritual.

"What do you mean?" I stammered, suddenly realizing that I was no longer the director in this drama. The plot had been manipulated by someone else.

"I'm sending you straight to the hospital," he said.

"I won't go," I retorted with all the vehemence of a rebellious teenager. I had just turned twenty-four the week before.

"If you won't go voluntarily, it will be easy for me to have you committed," replied the voice, which in my mind had become disembodied, a floating echo of doom. I realized there was no way out.

"Can I go home and pack some clothes?" I queried.

"I can release you into Issa's custody. He seems to be a responsible person."

A responsible person, I mused. How true. I did not realize then my own culpability, how I had returned his kisses with a dangerous fever, luring him to the edge of an emotional cliff and expecting him to jump. He didn't. I had felt a sudden frost in our relationship, and inside me something ruthless as a scimitar of ice had pricked my shriveled sense of self-worth. We left the doctor's office, and my mind drifted back to my tenth year, when I had been forced to see a psychiatrist at the state mental institution. Every week my mother would take me to an ominous red brick building with black-shuttered windows reminiscent of an Edgar Allen Poe story. I remembered being swallowed by an endless hallway with alternating black and white tiles on the floor. The pattern seemed to crawl, as if it were made of swarming insects. All the doors looked the same—gray with crinkled glass that I couldn't see through. Later I remember thinking that the walls could have been pink or yellow or any color, and I would have seen them as gray. My eyes no longer responded to color, it seemed. There were never any people in that hall, just my mother and me, both of us being brutally painted into that wasteland. I wondered if anyone else ever came there, or if the whole huge horrible building existed to torment me alone. But no one ever told me anything. There was a shameful glare of mystery surrounding my situation; I had no frame of reference, no trellis for the thorny weeds of emotional and physical bedevilment that harassed me. They all told me I wasn't dying. Why had no one had the courage to break it to me that I was dying? How could they have just handed me, or handed my parents, slips of paper and released me? How could such a malady not be fatal? And yet there I was, cheating death, it seemed. Again. The prescription was for Valium, which I took every day for six months when I was ten. It gave me headaches. I obediently carried one yellow pill in a bottle with me to school each day and swallowed it with lunch. I never thought of asking anyone why. I just accepted it as part of the unspeakable mystery that I was told not to reveal to anyone. When I was released by the psychiatrist, he told my parents he didn't think I would ever have problems again. But now I marveled at his naïve myopia. *Why couldn't he see that I still carried the cryptic mark on my forehead that set me apart as one chosen for suffering?* I considered all this as I packed my clothing for the hospital, with Issa standing beside me rather too closely, like a sentinel. I sifted through my wardrobe, still conscious of what looked best on me. Even in a tragedy, I figured it would pay to look pretty.

The only book I packed was my oversized leather study Bible that I had bought for seventy dollars. I had not even flinched at the price, although I had, as my mother would say "Scottish blood" in me. That was her term for stinginess. The Bible was a royal purple, with delicate onion skin pages edged with silver. I nestled it carefully among the clothes so none of the pages would be crumpled. I loved the beauty of the book as much as its content and would sometimes run my hand over its cover as if that alone were a devotion.

"Okay," I finally murmured, and Issa walked with me to the car, carrying my bag. I tried to imagine what music should be playing for that kind of trip, but nothing came to mind for such a fierce and final journey. The hospital was located on Sunnybrook Ave., a rather ironic location for a mental hospital, I thought. A large, overdressed woman met us at the door, and then Issa left, promising to visit me later. As he left, I felt the last vestiges of civilization abandoning me. The woman looked formidable, so I squelched my sudden inclination to bolt for the door. She fired questions at me, typing blandly on the computer. Finally, she took me upstairs to the ward. She had to ring a buzzer beside the door so someone would unlock it. Against my will, the lyrics of "Hotel California" began to flood my mind. I followed the woman into a small room, where she opened my bag and began to inspect every item in it. She sifted through my purse, too. I began to feel like the naked Eve, ashamed in the garden, with God calling out her name. She took away everything considered dangerous: makeup, shampoo, hair dryer, mirror. *But I'm still dangerous,* I thought. *My thoughts are murderers.* The unnamed woman suddenly noticed the elaborate wrapping on my wrist, and her manner became abrupt.

"What's that?" she demanded.

"A bandage," I replied helpfully.

"What did you do?" I also wondered what I had done. Why should my mind have pursued me with such ferocity, attempting to destroy me?

"I cut myself." The woman became visibly agitated.

"Do you have any blades somewhere? Is there something hidden in your bra?" I had a horrible feeling that she was going to check, but she didn't.

"No," I replied, trying to sound convincing. She seemed satisfied and escorted me to the nurses' station. The head nurse was a matronly looking woman with tightly permed hair. Her name was Brenda. At least it wasn't

18

Bertha or Hulga. Those seemed like appropriate names for nurses in a place like this.

"Why don't you go around and meet some of the other patients, dear?" Brenda said in a patronizing voice, her lips like the two pink halves of a mollusk, opening and shutting.

Other patients? I thought with horror. For some reason, it hadn't occurred to me that there would be others trapped in here with me. All day it had seemed that the world contained only me and my gigantic, overbearing, murderous mind. But slowly my eyes began to perceive haunted-looking figures darting in and out of the TV room and hallways, pale as ghost crabs on the beach, their eyes just as startled and strange, except they weren't on stalks. *Maybe that will happen to me also, with time,* I thought wryly. I wasn't too keen on running into any of the crabs, so I found an abandoned table with a few empty chairs arranged neatly around it, and I sat down. I didn't know what else to do.

What does one do after being unceremoniously dumped in a mental hospital against one's will? Was I properly dressed? I was wearing a girlish pale blue blouse with an enormous bow on the front. My makeup was perfect since I had touched it up at home after the crying fit.

I must have looked too good, because an unwary male inmate wandered up to me and said, "Who are you visiting?"

"No one," I murmured. "I belong here." The words slipped out before I caught their import. "I mean...I'm a patient."

"You don't look like one."

I basked for a moment in the glory of the compliment. I didn't look like one. Surely that must count for something.

"My name's Roland." Roland looked to be about twenty years old, with colorless eyes and a shock of whitish-blond hair. "When I was at the state mental institution in Butner, I escaped, and it took the hound dogs a whole day to find me," he continued. I pretended to examine my pearl-colored nail polish as I considered what to make of this information.

"You wanna see my guitar?" he asked. I nodded my head, not knowing what else to do, and I found that my feet were moving to follow Roland. The rest of me went too, to my chagrin. The first thing I noticed was that the room door had no lock on either side. The bathroom door didn't either, I later discovered. Roland found his guitar and began to twang out what he told me was a Bob Dylan song: "All I really wanna doooo is baby be friends with you."[3] I wondered if his choice of songs had significance. The music ended with a final mournful moan. Roland stared at me with a doleful, dog-like expression.

"What you like to do?" he asked.

"I write poetry."

"I bet I could write poetry. I'm gonna write you a poem."

"Okay." I decided to extricate myself from Roland. "Uh, it was nice meeting you...." I lied.

"I need to go...." I wondered if it had occurred to him that I had nowhere to go. His face began to wilt slightly, but I turned away and left the room. I wandered back into the TV room, considering whether I should take my chances with some other patients. I discovered that Roland had padded down the hall after me. He shuffled up to a deep-cushioned chair that almost swallowed a slight young man with spiked black hair and acne scars. He wore a black AC/DC tee shirt and black jeans.

"Hey Chase," exclaimed Roland. "Come meet Nancy." He took my arm and half dragged me to the figure in the chair, whose leg was jittering back and forth like a bat's wing.

"Hi," I ventured in a quizzical voice. He looked like the kind of boy my mother had warned me about. "Nice boys don't wear black or earrings," she had said. I took a quick inventory of his ears. They were bare. I felt somewhat relieved.

"You wanna play Scrabble?" Chase inquired.

"Okay." We moved to a table in the middle of the room where the Scrabble board was set up and commenced playing. I had an X, a Q with no U, and a Z, that I had no idea what to do with. Chase, on the other hand, quickly configured words like "quark" and "qi."

"You're pretty lame," he finally concluded.

"I have a degree in English," I announced with indignation.

"That must be the problem." Fortunately, at that moment an orderly ambled over and handed me a covered gray plastic tray.

"You're eating up here tonight because you're on restriction for at least the first twenty-four hours," he informed me.

I was aware that a nameless shame was wearing away at my soul like sandpaper. I opened the dinner tray hesitantly. It contained a plate with some unidentified fried meat, a few abnormally long green beans,

---

[3]   Bob Dylan, "All I Really Wanna Do," *Another Side of Bob Dylan*, Released August 8, 1964.

and a bleached-looking roll. A tiny bowl to the side boasted a blob of chocolate pudding topped with some anemic whipped cream. I felt odd eating while people fluttered in and out like disoriented moths, but I managed to tackle about half the food on the plate. I left the tray on the coffee table afterward. Exhaustion began to creep over me like a dank fog. My mouth started to droop from its piquant smile. I suspected I was beginning to look as if I belonged there. A nurse showed me my room, and I met my roommate, a perky Irish woman who told me she was thirty-three years old and bi-polar. She couldn't pronounce the "th," so it sounded as if she said "tirty-tree."

"I really embarrassed myself when I first came here," she told me. "I put on my headphones to look like antennae and told everyone I was an alien, which was technically true, I guess. I'm not an American citizen. Then I sat on Dr. Annabale's lap and said, 'Let's talk about the first thing that pops up.'"

Her name was Fiona O'Brian. She had just had a baby, and her husband came the next day bringing the baby and four other impossibly red-haired children. After being in the hospital a few days, I had a startling revelation about Fiona, and about most of the other residents: they were human. There was a man about fifty-five who was dealing with grief over his dad's death, a woman whose husband just left her, and a lawyer going through financial troubles. Except for two or three people who had seemed to make a career of going from one hospital to another, like Roland, these men and women led fairly normal lives punctuated by moments of agony. I realized that mental illness affected people of all types and ages seemingly indiscriminately, marking them as I had been marked, with an invisible sign of torment. Slowly the shame I felt began to diminish, although it would never go away completely. These rather ordinary people, including myself, could not have all committed some unpardonable sin that made our minds detonate like bombs. I longed to find the secret behind the suffering, to crack the code in the brain that would explain the fear, the haunting, distorted thoughts, the urge to hurt myself. But I thought of none of this that first night.

My interest in the other patients faded quickly, and I became overwhelmed with horror that I was there, in a virtual prison, and also imprisoned in my malfunctioning mind. I had the impression that my mind was separate from my true self, that it inhabited my body like a malignant spirit bent on destroying me. I believed this because I was always aware of a sane, objective presence in myself that observed everything that went on inside me, giving relevant commentary when needed, such as "that thought isn't normal." This observer kept me from total insanity, and even though mental illness would stretch on for years, this benign presence never left me. Because I felt the influence of the Observer, I concluded that this was my real self, my spirit, which could not be affected by my illness, or perhaps it was the Holy Spirit. Even so, I knew that my mind had mutinied and was now in open warfare against me.

That night I lay awake for hours, which were punctuated every fifteen minutes by a nurse who popped through the door like the wooden cuckoo of an overly vigilant clock. I could hear my roommate's slow, regular breathing. It didn't seem to be coming from her, but from the ceiling, the walls, the carpet. The room seemed like an organic thing that had swallowed me. I was Jonah in the guts of a whale for an unknown act of disobedience. I could see the huge rib cage enclosing me. I suddenly jumped out of bed and grabbed my Bible, taking it into the bathroom. I closed the door and turned on the light, situating myself on the closed toilet seat. I opened the still-new pages to Psalm 88, my favorite one because it ended on a note of despair. I read the last few verses:

> From my youth I have been afflicted and close to death;
> I have suffered your terrors and am in despair.
> Your wrath has swept over me;
> your terrors have destroyed me.
> All day long they surround me like a flood;
> they have completely engulfed me.
> You have taken from me friend and neighbor—
> darkness is my closest friend.[4]

I felt a deep kinship then with the author, Heman the Ezrahite, whoever he was, though he had been dead for thousands of years. Heman and I just sat there together for a while, mulling over the darkness that had become our best buddy. I tried to pray, but the words stuck in my throat.

---

[4] Psalm 88:15-18 (NIV).

A silent prayer wouldn't do either. *God had abandoned me. I wasn't chosen.* The thought began to spin inside my mind again, the way it had earlier that day, until the floodgates burst open and I felt driven to cut myself again. I crept into the room and walked over to the bedside table with a lamp on it. I stared at the dingy brown shade for a moment, then carefully unscrewed the bulb and took it out. I knew I had to hurry before the nurse came back.

I picked up one of my shoes, a brown penny loafer with a hard heel, and took it and the bulb into the bathroom. I put on my shoe, put the bulb on the floor and stomped on it as hard as I could with the heel of the shoe. Nothing happened. I tried again, with the same result. Then in frustration, I threw the bulb violently into the sink. It shattered into bright shards. As I was about to pick one up, the door opened and the nurse stuck her head in like the periscope of an enemy submarine.

"What do you think you're doing?" she asked.

"I don't know," I sobbed.

"We can't watch you every minute, you know," she said as she pushed me aside and picked up the pieces of glass, tucking them gingerly into the pocket of her uniform.

When all the fragments were removed, she ran some water in the sink and said, "Don't try that again, honey. Go on back to bed." I silently obeyed her. She slipped noiselessly from the room. A few minutes later a man opened the door, leaving it open with light from the hall streaming in, and walked over to the lamp. I saw that he was replacing the bulb. I languidly lamented the fact that my brain could not be thus unscrewed and easily replaced with a more satisfactory one.

After the man left, I began to hear some muffled howling noises that seemed to come from down the hall. I understood them. My soul spoke that language too. I found out later that the howls were emanating from the "quiet room," a dreaded place that was empty except for a bed. Apparently disorderly patients were relegated there. After about fifteen minutes the silence returned, except for the predictable whoosh of my breathing. I assumed someone had drugged the unfortunate creature, and I returned to my repartee with Heman the Ezrahite until sleep at last separated us. For a few moments my mind hovered over thoughts of who he might have been, and what stories he could tell. Then sleep at last fell like a dismal rain on the smoldering wasteland that my mind had become.

Asylum

Sometimes our voices here
Slip through chinks in the wall
Like those tiny blue lizards,
Their yellow stripes thin
As if painted with an eyelash.
Where they go after that,
I don't know,
But they never come back;
No olive branch, or even a slip of grass
In that mouth just barely a mouth.
I don't know if they've drowned
Or if the waters are receding.

Sometimes at night
My walls become cypress wood
And I count the days of rain
With notches in the doorpost.
There are sounds in the hull
No longer human.
Two elephants bellow,
Mourning their dead
In the everywhere ocean;
The hunger of lions becomes audible.
We are the sons and daughters of Noah,
Or the last two crocodiles,
Or mice huddling in straw.

We are all here for building arks
At the bidding of gods who speak to no one else,
For toting lumber and nails when the sky is cloudless.
I wonder then,
Are we the saved or the damned?
Do wood and pitch outsmart the malignant water,
Or just keep us imprisoned?

Nurses hover here like moths
That migrate in shifts,
Walking away on water that strangely
Turns to a sidewalk when they leave.
They gorge us on pills and concoctions,
In hopes that the flood will abate.
But still, sometimes, we pay with blood.

I wonder which god those outside heed,
Or if they listen at all.
But I know when I emerge
The sky will bend into a colored bow
Seen only by my eyes.

But I will remember the drowned ones' cries.

Love in the Mental Ward

She sits transfixed in the dark gold stretches of sun
Like a scarab caught in amber,
A girl half-mad, half-seraph,
Her wings spread over the ark of a potent god.
I approach her, barefoot,
Startled as I move by a vase of orchids that seem
Insect-like, large.
She is laughing, a sound like cool porcelain beads
Flung from a snapped string.
I bring her little offerings of language
Like the two pigeons asked from the poor.
Words arabesque between us, golden spiders
Pearling sticky ropes on her lips
My wrist
Her calf
Mine.
Hers.
I dream their silk surrounds us in a chrysalis
And we grow together in its slow womb.
By the third day I cannot tell my mouth from hers;
Our hearts couple together in a glistening thorax.
After forty days we emerge, a seamless moth,
Our wings flecked with eyes that see as if through prisms—
Yet she is not lost, nor am I.

"Stephen?"
My name on her lips unweaves us,
Draws me back into the box of my self.
I remember what she told me once—

"We can't go visiting when we're selves, Stephen.
We aren't made with doors
Though we still try to force things through
Or let things in."

I laughed at her then,
Believing the self could follow the body wherever it went,
Forgetting that night after night I never found her.

Next morning she hung a prism by the window
And I watched her through it.
She suddenly had twelve faces, connected like petals;
Her hair seemed everywhere,
the twelve unbraiding ropes of it.
"She has no need of me now," I thought.

But I knew she could press me simultaneously with her
dozen mouths,
So I returned, and still return,
To be drawn deep into her apparitions.

Today she is golden in the gathering of her selves,
And I choose one and give myself.
But I long to be many, to smudge the square of thought
that delineates,
Assigning me to oneness.
She calls me to her, her voice a delicate orchestra.
"I love you, Stephen," she says in the half-light,
In the delirium of orchids.
But holding her,
I feel her other arms still groping outward.

2

The First Vision that Set Fire to the Stars

*T*HE NEXT MORNING the Inquisition began. I started my day off by taking a voluminous mental health inventory of true/false questions such as "I like to hurt small animals," "I hear God speaking to me," "I like flowers," "If I had a flower, I would give it to my mother." I answered "true" to the one about God, thinking that I was probably sealing my fate. After an hour of this, I was whisked away to Dr. Valentine's office, where he showed me a series of colored ink blots and instructed me to tell him what I saw in them and why. Then I had to draw an endless series of pictures. I remembered the stick figure with the corkscrew hair that I had drawn for my psychiatrist at age ten. *These masterpieces aren't much better than that,* I thought with embarrassment. I longed to know what the doctors could possibly learn from my rudimentary drawing of my house. I figured it couldn't be anything good. Once all the testing was completed, I had a call from my parents, who had put an abrupt end to their vacation in the mountains due to my hospitalization.

"Do you know how it feels," my father began, "to have to clean up your daughter's blood off the floor?"

I didn't answer. There was nothing to say. "I need some more clothes," I finally muttered. "Can you bring me the black and pink striped top and my teal sweater dress?" They agreed, and I quickly made some excuse to get off the phone. In the hallway I met Roland, who was sporting a rather absurd grin. I couldn't avoid him, so I faced him head-on.

"Good morning, Roland," I said, trying not to sound too friendly.

"Hey Nancy, guess what? I wrote a poem about you! You wanna hear it?"

"Sure. I guess."

"Okay. Here goes. I once knew a girl named Nancy, and she was very fancy." Roland's grin seemed to expand until it included his whole face.

"Uh…that's a good start."

"I have something else in my room that I wrote 'bout a year ago. It's called 'The Love Biography.' You wanna read it?"

"No thanks, Roland. I really don't have time right now…." I tried to make a smooth exit from the conversation, but Roland would have none of it.

"Can I play you s'more Bob Dylan?"

As I was considering my reply, a bewildered nurse appeared and announced in a loud voice, "There are ten people outside with guitars who want to come in. Where can we put them?" As I was considering who these mad minstrels might be, the head nurse unlocked the door and my entire Bible study group walked down the hall. Two of them carried guitars.

"They can go in the group therapy room," said the head nurse. I was speechless, but I led the group into the room, where we all stared at each other awkwardly.

"How did you find out I was here?" I finally managed to say.

"Issa called us and told us you tried to kill yourself," said Tracy, a heavy-set girl with large black-rimmed glasses. I silently chafed at this untruth, but I didn't bother to correct her. Gary, the leader of the group, handed me a mug covered with sketches of non-descript cats, with a distinctive-looking cat in the middle holding a balloon. The mug read: "You're one in a million." *That's probably true,* I thought wryly.

As I was reaching out to take the mug, which I noticed was filled with multi-colored jellybeans, the nurse, who had followed us into the room, grabbed it and droned sweetly, "I'll just keep that up at the desk for you, honey." Another dangerous item, I supposed. She left carrying the mug, and immediately Roland came in toting his guitar, followed by Naomi, another patient I had met that day. Gary, who was always cracking jokes, tried to cheer me up by telling me about the prank James and Jordan had played on him last winter.

"They took a whole package of Oscar Meyer wieners and pushed them down onto my car antenna. The wieners froze overnight, and the next day they wouldn't even budge. I had to wait for them to thaw out!" Everyone laughed a little too loudly. Another awkward silence.

"Well, let's praise the Lord," said Sundar, a young Indian friend of mine who stood there clutching his guitar so tightly his knuckles were turning white. We all sat down in a circle and began to sing one of my favorite hymns:

Long my imprisoned spirit lay
Fast bound in sin and nature's night;
Thine eye diffused a quick'ning ray,
I woke, the dungeon flamed with light;
My chains fell off, my heart was free;
I rose, went forth and followed thee.
Amazing love! How can it be,
That thou, my God, should die for me.[5]

These eloquent words at once began to coax my spirit into a holy flame, but the flood of Darkness, sensing an enemy, doused the incipient fire with ferocity. The light in the dungeon was quenched. I sang a few more songs half-heartedly with my friends. During a lull, Roland started strumming violently, singing:

How does it feel,
How does it feeelllll
To be without a home
Like a complete unknown
Like a rolling stone.[6]

"Stop that, Roland," said Naomi from the corner. "I want to sing about the Lord." Naomi was a devout Catholic woman who was bi-polar. She told me she had hallucinations in which Lucifer appeared to her and told her to jump out a window.

"Roland," the nurse piped up, "Why don't you let Nancy visit with her friends now?"

A rather disgruntled Roland put away his guitar, closed the case with a thud, and squeezed past the chairs into the hallway. There was a collective

---

[5]   Charles Wesley, "And Can it Be, that I should Gain?" in *Hymns and Sacred Poems*, 1739.

[6]   Bob Dylan, "Like a Rolling Stone," from the album *Highway 61 Revisited*, released June 15-16, 1965.

sigh of relief. At that moment, another nurse came in and announced it was time for "vital signs." Vital signs was a daily humiliating ritual in which one sat in a chair while all the other patients stood around waiting, so a nurse could take one's temperature, pulse, and blood pressure. After these were completed, the nurse would ask "Are you a 'yes?'" which was a euphemism for "Yes, I have had a bowel movement today." The crowd always stared with bated breath, eager to hear everyone's answer to this all-important question. Woe to those who said "no." Images of strange concoctions and enemas went through all our heads when this shocking scenario occurred.

"I guess I have to go now," I told the Bible study group. "Thanks for coming," I said sincerely. "It really means a lot to me." The group nervously stood up and made a speedy exit. They probably didn't like the sound of "vital signs." Naomi and I headed toward the TV room to meet our fate. Once vital signs was over, I was told that the psychiatrist wanted to meet with me. I was beginning to wonder if one ever escaped from feverish activity in the hospital.

I met the psychiatrist in a windowless room that seemed to be constructed with claustrophobia in mind. I sat across from him at a small table.

"Major depression, pre-psychotic," he announced, without greeting me.

"Excuse me?"

"That's your diagnosis." I wanted to ask what pre-psychotic meant, but I was afraid to. I figured it meant I was about ready for the "quiet room."

"We're going to put you on 150 milligrams of imipramine and four milligrams of Trilafon daily." To me, the drugs sounded like diseases themselves, strange maladies that preyed on unfortunate victims.

"Okay," I acquiesced. Then I added, "When can I get out of here?"

"I can't tell you right now, but not for a while. You're pretty depressed."

A slight pause. "Any questions?"

Yes, I thought. *Why has God abandoned me? Why is my mind pursuing me with murderous intentions? What have I done to deserve this? Do I get extra credit on Judgment Day?*

"No," I said.

"Good. I'll see you again in a few days." I realized the interview was over, so I extricated myself from the coffin-like space and walked down the hall to my room. My roommate wasn't there, so I lay down on the narrow bed.

31

In the silence thoughts began randomly blowing through the desert of my mind like a cloud of black hallucinogenic mushroom spores. I tried in vain to assemble them into some kind of order. Finally, I whispered, "Lord, how did I end up here? Don't I belong to You? I thought You were going to get me out of this." As I groped in the half-light for answers, memories of the past year somehow drifted off the shelves of my brain into my hands like unopened boxes. I eased the lid off the first box, and saw myself the autumn before, buying a plain black NIV Bible at a bookstore in Montreat, North Carolina. I didn't know what had possessed me to do it. I only knew I felt a sense of urgency that I had never felt before, a sense that my destiny was somehow inextricably linked with the secrets of that book. I had never liked the Bible in the past. Every day of my life, it seemed, my mother had admonished me, "Now be sure to read in your little white Bible." I had hardly ever obeyed her. I would stare at the white leather cover with my name embossed in gold, the letters looking almost alien, as if they were in a foreign script. Sometimes I would read a few Psalms, or Song of Solomon, which I liked because it was a love poem, but other than that, I had no curiosity about what the pages contained. I had received the Bible as a birthday gift when I was ten years old. My mother told me much later that I had requested it, that it was the only gift I wanted that year. But whatever embryonic desire I had then had long since dissipated.

Yet there I was at twenty-three, determined to navigate the waters of what had somehow now become a scintillating mystery to me. I surveyed some of the other books, finally pulling off the shelf a huge, impressive looking volume entitled *Abingdon's Bible Commentary*, which I decided to buy also. My parents and I drove back to our vacation home up the street from the bookstore, and I sat in the ancient white rocker on the porch and surveyed my purchases. I felt a quiver of inexplicable delight. The porch seemed an appropriate setting to read such a book. The house was built on a hill, and the porch was level with the tops of a glorious group of trees. In the summer we had a perfect view of a hummingbird nest tucked between two branches. The birds would buzz over our heads to reach the nectar in our bird feeder, sometimes sword fighting with their long, belligerent beaks, or so it seemed to me. The mountain lay in front of me like the back of a sleeping dragon, armored with trees like bright scales.

I opened the Bible and read, "In the beginning God created the heavens and the earth. Now the earth was formless and empty, darkness was over the surface of the deep, and the Spirit of God was hovering over the waters."[7] I was astonished. Surely my life was "formless and empty," and darkness was brooding over it like an unwelcome, carrion-eating bird. But I was guarded, my sensors ready to detect approaching danger. God might still be boring. Hadn't years of church and Sunday school alerted me to that possibility? And what if He wanted me to be boring too, all in the name of holiness? I felt a slight shudder tingling down my vertebrae. Or He might be a dominating male with a staff and a long white beard like Charlton Heston, waiting to pounce on overly independent females. But I read for the rest of the afternoon, soaking in truth for the first time in my life. The silver trill of a towhee accompanied my biblical sojourn like a delicate harbinger of redemption. In the weeks that followed, I read voraciously, carefully checking the commentary on each passage. I was especially astounded by Ecclesiastes. I opened the Bible one day, unsuspecting, and read:

> Meaningless! Meaningless!
> says the Teacher.
> Utterly meaningless!
> Everything is meaningless....
> All things are wearisome,
> more than one can say.
> The eye never has enough of seeing,
> nor the ear its fill of hearing.
> What has been will be again,
> what has been done will be done again;
> there is nothing new under the sun.[8]

For a moment I thought I was mistaken. The Bible couldn't say that. Surely it only contained sweet, nice things. I was shocked to find verses that could have come from my *Norton Anthology of Modern Poetry.* I

---

[7] Genesis 1:1 (NIV).

[8] Ecclesiastes 1:2; 8-9 (NIV).

knew that I felt the ugly stare of meaninglessness in my own life, and that many others in the twentieth century had also, but surely not Solomon in 1000 B.C.! I reread the words. Yes, they did say that everything is meaningless! That day I gained a profound respect for the truth of scripture and its startling relevance to my life. I felt that the words held up the shard of a mirror to my psyche, and in it I saw a murky, bottomless pool. *Like Loch Ness,* I thought, remembering my first glimpse of those black waters a few years ago. Yes, perhaps aquatic Minotaurs dwelt in me as well. After several months I finished reading the Bible, but I still hovered at the edge of commitment, kicking stones fearfully over the cliff. It seemed to be a long way down. Could I be sure there was a net down there, or a trampoline, or maybe, counterintuitively—waiting arms of rescue? I could not bring myself to plunge wholeheartedly into the life of God. But a few months later, a greater fear would compel me to take the very step I dreaded.

The process began with a night of terror when I awoke in the middle of the night with my heart racing, seemingly ready to burst from my chest. I was choking on my scanty breaths. Waves of fear began in my stomach and swept up into my head. I tried to get out of bed, but the covers seemed to have sprouted arms that held me down. I finally extricated myself and ran from my bedroom into the living room of the apartment that I shared with my roommate, Emily. She had fallen asleep on the couch.

"Emily, wake up!" I shouted. She awoke, startled.

"What's wrong?"

"I think I'm having a heart attack. I can't breathe."

"I'll call 911," she said, surprisingly level-headed for someone awakened so violently. I fixed my eyes on her pale, heart-shaped face that was etched with lines of worry, and frantically wondered why the call seemed interminable. I began to pace the floor, mechanically moving back and forth between two faded stains on the carpet, certain that I was dying, but feeling too awful to care.

"I have to go outside," I said, sensing that the room was growing narrower and would possibly crush me.

"I'll go with you," Emily said. I ran out the door onto the front steps with Emily following me. I sat down on the top step and buried my face in my hands. But remaining still proved too torturous, so I paced back and forth on the sidewalk that led to the entrance to our apartment. Time seemed to be crawling like a reluctant slug. Finally, I heard the oscillating screaming of a siren close by, and a moment later an ambulance with its pulsating light pulled into the nearby parking lot. The light's red color alarmed me somehow, as if my senses had been heightened to an intolerable degree. The choking feeling began to diminish somewhat as I saw three men in blue uniforms emerge from the ambulance.

One of the paramedics walked up to me and rested his hand on my back, while another reassured me gently, "We are here to help you. Can you tell me what's going on?"

"My heart is racing and I can't breathe." My supply of air seemed so scant that I could barely gasp out the words.

"Okay," he said soothingly. "Since it seems like you're having a hard time breathing, we are going to check your oxygen level. My partner is going to put a clip on your finger. You will barely feel it." I held out my hand submissively, and the other paramedic slipped the small instrument on my finger.

As he was doing this, the first man said, "I need to ask you some questions, okay?" As I nodded my assent, I began to feel sheepish because my heart had ceased its rampaging and was now beating normally.

"Can you tell me your name?" said the paramedic.

I suddenly realized that I was wearing the ridiculous-looking Grinch pajamas I had received for Christmas, and that I had on no makeup. But I swallowed my embarrassment and muttered, "Nancy Craig."

"Do you know what day it is?" I suddenly entertained a suspicion that they thought I was crazy, but I brushed it aside.

"Saturday." Humiliated, I tried to avoid eye contact.

"Who is the president?" As the other paramedic began taking my blood pressure, I recalled that I had not bothered to vote.

"George Bush."

I could see the ghost of morning illuminating the trees in the distance. Then, to my horror, I noticed my elderly neighbor Mr. Stufflebeam with his black and tan Yorkie emerge from his apartment across the parking lot. The dog nonchalantly lifted his leg against a holly bush.

"Okay, Ms. Craig, your vital signs all look normal. Has this ever happened to you before?" The ghost of a recollection suddenly encircled my memory like a penumbra but wouldn't come into focus. I brushed the feeling aside.

"Nnno," I muttered.

"Are you on any medications?" I began to wonder what I could do to make the paramedics leave.

"No." I felt an overwhelming urge to yawn, but I decided that might be rude.

"We are going to let you get back to bed, but be sure to make an appointment with your doctor as soon as possible, all right?" I nodded. As the paramedics turned to leave, I remembered that Emily had been standing by the door the whole time. I stared at her for a moment, speechless. She gave me a sympathetic look.

"Do you think you can sleep?" she asked.

"I guess so," I mumbled, suddenly associating my bed with the nameless terror. There was an awkward silence as we both avoided referring to what had just occurred. Then, since there seemed to be nothing else to say, both Emily and I returned to our apartment and went back to bed. I finally fell into a stuttering kind of sleep punctuated by images of red pulsating lights and blood pressure cuffs. I did not call my doctor. I tried to avoid doctors whenever possible. But two weeks later I found myself again feeling as if I were choking on my own heart.

I was shopping in the mall, staring at the floor as I was walking, when suddenly the colored tiles seemed to move up toward my face and then down again with a sickening, swimming motion. I felt as if all the people were enemies, and that if anyone touched me my body would shatter. Then began the now-familiar racing heart and choking sensation. I ran through the crowd to my car and drove to the hospital, so overcome with fear that at one point I opened the car door while I was driving so I could jump out. I drove with the door open for a few seconds, watching the glistening asphalt moving like a conveyor belt beneath me. Then I regained enough composure to close the door and continue driving. I reached the hospital parking lot, almost running into a large tree surrounded with pansies. I didn't know where the emergency room entrance was, so I ran through the automatic doors of the main entrance, almost colliding with a huge white marble statue of Jesus with outstretched arms.

"Yeah, right," I whispered sarcastically.

I wandered desperately through the hospital corridors, not knowing where to go, until an orderly in pale green scrubs saw my stricken face and asked me if I were lost.

"Where is the emergency room?" I gasped, feeling as if the white floor were coming up to meet me.

"I'll show you," he said. I followed the orderly down a maze of hallways until we reached two double doors.

"Right through here."

I rushed in, not bothering to thank him. There were only a few other patients there, so I was quickly thrust behind a white curtain. As the ER doctor examined me, I was beginning to wish I hadn't come, because I was almost breathing normally. The doctor reassured me that I wasn't going to die and sent me out the door with a prescription that he said would prevent my heart from racing. As I drove home, I felt that my world had somehow become alien and threatening—a mutated version of the life I had known, with unrecognizable vestigial growths of uncertainty and absurdity. Desperate, I made an appointment to see my doctor, the one who would later stitch up my wrist, and he scheduled me for an echocardiogram. During the procedure later that week, I saw my heart on the monitor. The image reminded me of a gray, gyrating alien. The doctor told me I had mitral valve prolapse, a usually benign condition of the heart that can cause racing heartbeat.

"You also have panic disorder," he added. "But don't worry," he piped up cheerfully. "These symptoms are perfectly harmless and tend to improve over the years."

Years? I thought with horror. Then the doctor nonchalantly handed me a prescription slip with Philippians 4:6 written on it. "Do not be anxious about anything...." I remembered the gasping for breath in the middle of the night, my heart racing like a freight train plummeting down an incline. The verse seemed to mock me, as if I could unplug the blinding fear like a toaster. As the weeks passed, the panic attacks indeed ceased, but in their wake emerged a foe that I had no resources to combat.

Slowly, insidiously, my thoughts became distorted. I would be driving and begin to imagine myself bleeding on the side of the road. At a restaurant once I was transfixed by the cord of the blinds across the window next to me. It was tied in the shape of a perfect, tiny noose. My whole field of vision went black except for the noose and the circle of light around it. My mind fixated on this image, interpreting it as a sign of impending destruction. When I wasn't struggling with irrational thoughts, I felt numb, "as if I'm made out of Styrofoam," as I told a friend. I became more and more isolated as these feelings encroached on my sanity. One evening I noticed the disposable razor on the bathroom sink. I suddenly thought of a way to alleviate the numbness. If I could just feel again.... I stepped on the razor with my shoes on to break the plastic, and I was able to extract one of the blades. I stared at my wrist for a moment, then drew the blade cautiously across it. A red line appeared. As the blood formed little dots on my wrist, I began to cry until my whole body ached with emotion. The rush of feeling gave me an enormous sense of relief. I could still feel, after all. Thus began what was to become a nightly ritual, enacted in secret on my bathroom floor. When I was around other people, I carefully fastened my watch around the wound to hide it. I thought a lot about God during these weeks, and I finally decided He was giving me a vision of hell as a warning, perhaps. I had believed in God all my life, in theory, but I never understood until then the gravity of living one's life in rebellion against Him. I began to see that forces beyond my control were now shaping my life, and that they would soon destroy me if no one intervened.

One night as I stood by the mirror drying my hair, I came to a decision. I would choke down my pride and fear, throw myself into what seemed an abyss, and wait for Jesus to break my fall with His body. I thought of the expressionless stone Jesus I had seen in the hospital lobby and shuddered. But what did I have to lose? I had discovered that my fabricated worldview was a magician's illusion—no, a pool of pernicious quicksand. I turned off the hair dryer, although my hair was still half wet, and I sank to the bathroom floor where I had spent so much time during the last few weeks. Stanzas from "Just as I am" began to reverberate in my head but I ignored them and began to speak into the room, into the night, into the silent, expectant presence of God.

"Okay, God," I began. "I give up. I can't live this way any longer. If You get me out of this, I'll serve You for the rest of my life." Although it sounded like a bargain, it wasn't. I simply knew that I could not serve God or even seek Him in the condition I was in. My mind had degenerated into a maelstrom of irrationality. I felt that I barely existed. After the prayer there were no drastic changes, no "dungeons flooding with light," but that night I slept without nightmares, without waking to sudden, appalling terror. The next day I wrote this in my journal:

I have come at last into the knowledge of Him, and the thought of turning away has no bearing. I can say with Peter, "Lord, to whom shall we go?"[9] There is no other voice in the universe but His, although it seems to the anxious heart that He is silent, and other voices entangle and prevail. But beyond these illusory, chaotic sounds lie a blankness that has no expression, that is nothingness infinitely removed from nothingness. I can say so with the conviction of a witness—this is no fashionable cliché—it is truth. I have sat alone in a room and have cut my wrists repeatedly to entice feeling into my body. But the soul remained unmoved—I wanted the razor to penetrate my soul. But instead Christ pierced my soul with his love, and I have become real at last. My reality accrues hourly as I feel myself flowing in tribute toward its source. I am a tributary of the Father, wishing to be lost in His sea.

> "And taken by light into [his] arms
> At long and dear last
> I may without fail
> Suffer the first vision that set fire to the stars."

> —Dylan Thomas
> "Love in the Asylum"[10]

And so I moved into a season of reprieve. That day I opened up the Yellow Pages and found the church listings. I moved my finger down the page and settled on a Presbyterian church that I had heard good reports about. I became heavily involved in the church, attending Sunday worship services and a young adult Bible study. My mind had been healed of its aberrations, or so it seemed. Then, I was catapulted back to the present reality: I had just been forcibly admitted to a mental institution. "What happened?" I moaned silently on my hospital bed as my long reverie was broken. Although I did not know it then, my agonizing journey through

---

[9] John 6:68a (NIV).

[10] Dylan Thomas, "Love in the Asylum," in *The Poems of Dylan Thomas,* ed. Daniel Jones (New York: New Directions Publishing Company, 1971), 169.

mental illness was just beginning. But in the years to come the memory of "the first vision that set fire to the stars" and the ever-startling presence of the triune God would never abandon me. These would sustain me like an unseen Eucharist, a table prepared for me in the presence of my enemies: a heavy bread and pungent wine spread before me by God in the midst of my soon-to-be relentless foes.

My First Prayer

Wrestling in this slow light,
You would touch my hip,
Wrench my life from its socket.
Night has always been a writhing of spirits—
My soul takes on sinew and bone,
Pins me down with arms muscled by my own thoughts.
But we had reached an easy stalemate
Until one night You swindled me,
Slipped in like Leah for Rachel.
Now Your hands nail me to the bed
And my name seeps like sweat from my skin.

Perhaps the tomb became Your mother, unwilling,
Aborting her holy Firstborn from a stone belly,
But I saw You dead again,
Nailed to the hymnal and the prayer book.
Though You feed on being devoured,
They starve You by rote with wine and wafers.
That tomb, at least, I thought would carry You to term.
But they killed an imposter, an effigy limp on a cross,
Stuffed with manger straw.
Now You come back from the convenient dead
To impale me with Your God-awful love.

You are not so different from the old gods
Who hungered after mortals,
Bursting like a bull into my cell, or an amorous swan.
If there were anyone left to entreat,
I would beg to become a laurel like Daphne.

But You stand there tinctured with beauty,
Nourished in the amnion of light
And I cannot wrench You from the womb of my soul.
So I wait like a reluctant Lazarus

Curved in the mouth of the tomb—
A fetus torn away slowly
By God's dismembering voice.

Kitchen Fires

My mother's maid has visions
While scrubbing floors—
On her knees she sees me
In my wedding gown.
She has seen my children's children.
(I am sixteen. I hate both men and kids.)

My mother is on her knees, too,
Scrubbing and praying.
I am playing up my better features
In front of the mirror.

I go out half-dressed,
Intending to become less so,
But my mother's prayers hover
There like a chemise,
Like clothing sewn by God
For the naked Eve.

I do not believe—But I still think Jesus
Is standing in our kitchen
With an old black woman
And an old white woman
Shelling peas and saying prayers.
I give Him a sullen hello
When I return,
Avoiding the holy burn of His eyes.
In my bed I try to brush away
The prayers as if they were mosquitoes,
Though at times I try to hold them
And see how many bear my name.

It is hard to be lost.
It is harder still to stay that way,
Since God is a God of old women,
Who pray and scrub and weep and pray.

3

The Castaway

I SPENT THAT NIGHT with Silence as my companion, a haunting shade that hovered over my bed and taunted me with his blank stares. The morning came not as a relief, but as extension of the Silence made even more maddening because of the sunlight that promised joy, but could not deliver it. I spent my day in a haze, attempting to fill up the hours that seemed to crawl forward like a slug after a heavy rain. I painted my nails carefully, a light gold color, focusing on covering every trace of pink flesh that lurked beneath the hard-outer covering, like an exoskeleton harboring the delicate body of a sea creature. I had to check out the nail polish from the front desk and promptly return it when I was finished. I surveyed my hands and felt a brief pang of pleasure at the result. Surely someone would be impressed with such hands, smooth and white with shimmering nails.

My admiration was interrupted by a nurse, who announced dully that I had a visitor in the TV room. I got up unenthusiastically, holding my hands gingerly in front of me so as not to disturb the drying polish. When I reached the TV room, I saw the pastor of the PCA church I attended sitting in one of the overstuffed chairs. I immediately felt like a fox pursued by hounds and riders. What story had he heard about me? What would a pastor think of someone who claimed to be a Christian and still cut her wrists with razor blades?

I moved toward him, trying casually to hide my heavily bandaged wrist behind me. The bandage was so big it looked as if my hand must be nearly severed beneath it. I sat down beside him, squirming inwardly, and tried to look him squarely in the face. I failed. My eyes focused on his right ear.

"Hello," I said stupidly.

He had yellow hair and an innocuous-looking beard of the same color. I couldn't tell if I saw compassion or pity in his eyes. They held the same serene blueness that I had noticed on many occasions. I began to doubt my theory that he was shocked. After we exchanged some brief pleasantries, he gave me a few sheets of paper that looked as though they had been photocopied from a book.

"I wanted to give you this information about a poet named William Cowper who lived in the 18th century. He was a Christian who suffered from severe mental illness and wrote some famous hymns. I thought you might be interested in this since you're a poet."

I stared at him in astonishment. Where was the sermon? Where were the religious clichés? I glanced at the first paper, which contained a short biography of Cowper. It began: "There are no saner poems in the language than Cowper's, yet they were written by a man who was periodically insane and who, for forty years, lived with the possibility of madness in full view."[11] I felt my spirit quickening within me, attempting to reach across the centuries and touch the spirit of this fellow poet. The rest of the interview passed in a fog, as all I could think about was reading the biography and the attached poems and hymns. I continued to marvel at the pastor's placidness. He did not speak of what I had done, but I knew he didn't need to. The gift of the photocopies was an offering of peace to me, a reassurance that I had not abandoned God, nor had He abandoned me.

After the pastor left, I hurried to my room to peruse the papers. I read that Cowper had an attack of madness that convinced him that he was hopelessly damned for committing the unpardonable sin—blasphemy against the Holy Spirit. He attempted suicide during his illness but recovered and eventually was comforted by his conversion to Evangelical Christianity as a result of his doctor's witness. Cowper began to believe that he was indeed saved by the "healing and sustaining power of divine grace freely extended to him."[12] He was later befriended by John Newton, and together they wrote the well-known Olney Hymns. However, Cowper soon suffered another episode of insanity, which left him with the lifelong belief that he had been rejected by God and eternally damned.

---

[11] M.H. Abrams, ed. "William Cooper," in *The Norton Anthology of English Literature*, vol. 1, 4th edition (New York: W. W. Norton & Company, 1979), 2498.

[12] Ibid.

He continued to write until his death, because "despair could suppress neither his humor and gentle wit nor the religious side of his nature."[13] Fascinated, I began to read the attached poems. My eye was engaged by the title of one of the poems, "The Castaway." It told of a man on board a ship who is washed overboard during a storm and deserted by his shipmates, who are eager to escape the storm. The man drowns after several hours of shouting for help in vain. In the last stanza, Cowper compares himself to "the castaway:"

> No voice divine the storm allayed,
> No light propitious shone
> When, snatched from all effectual aid,
> We perished, each alone,
> But I beneath a rougher sea
> And whelmed in deeper gulfs than he.[14]

The words reverberated in my mind as I recalled my own "deep gulfs," and how no "divine voice" had allayed my storm. I silently marveled that I could connect with a figure so removed by time, just as I had marveled at my kinship with the writer of Ecclesiastes and Heman the Ezrahite. I continued reading and found a beautiful hymn of unyielding faith called "God Moves in a Mysterious Way." Cowper described how we cannot judge the circumstances of our lives by "feeble sense," but must trust that God "hides a smiling face" behind a "frowning providence." He wrote:

> His purposes will ripen fast,
> Unfolding every hour;
> The bud may have a bitter taste,
> But sweet will be the flower.[15]

I considered the "bitter taste" of my own life and wondered how such a bud could ever have a "sweet" flower. Cowper, as revealed in his

---

[13] Abrams, 2505.

[14] Ibid.

[15] William Cowper, "On the Receipt of My Mother's Picture out of Norfolk," *The Poetical Works of William Cowper,* ed. William Michael Rossetti (London: William Collins, Sons and Co., n. d.), 292.

biography and poetry, was such a blending of sanity and madness, of trust and despair, that he became for me a soul mate, the thought of whom would comfort me in the many desperate days that I would encounter in the years to come. I never forgot the haunting voice of "the castaway," or his terrible conviction that God had damned him. As I mused on Cowper, I was reminded of Christopher Smart, another poet of doubtful sanity that I had studied in college. Also living during the 18th century, Smart was apparently "seized by a religious mania and a preternatural excitement to prayer."[16] He would kneel down in streets, parks, and other public places to pray. According to his biography, he was so fervent that he "became a public nuisance, and the public took its revenge." Smart was confined for seven years, first in a hospital, then in a public madhouse, where he was cut off from his family and friends. After his release, his mounting debts landed him in debtor's prison, where he died, alone and forgotten. I remembered that he had written a delightful, though strange, account of his cat, Jeoffry, in the poem "Jubilate Agno":

> For I will consider my Cat Jeoffry.
> For he is the servant of the Living God duly and daily serving him.
> For at the first glance of the glory of God in the East he worships in his way.
> For this is done by wreathing his body seven times round with elegant quickness.
> For by stroking of him I have found out electricity.
> For I perceived God's light about him both wax and fire.
> For the Electrical fire is the spiritual substance, which God sends
> From heaven to sustain the bodies of man and beast.
> For God has blessed him in the variety of his movements.
> For, though he cannot fly, he is an excellent clamberer.
> For his motions upon the face of the earth are more than any other quadrupede.
> For he can tread to all the measures upon the music.[17]

---

[16] M. H. Abrams, ed. "Christopher Smart," in *The Norton Anthology of English Literature*, vol. 1, 4th edition (New York: W. W. Norton & Company, 1979), 2454.

[17] Ibid., 2455.

Years later, after Issa and I were married, a gray striped stray cat would show up every day at our door, and we would feed him. We named the stray "Jeoffry" in honor of Smart's cat, although we found out later that she was a female. Smart believed that "the spirit that informs poetry is praise and celebration, an intense vision of the divine presence shining through ordinary life." The world had been formed to "pay homage to its Maker," and the poet should be a "minister of praise at large" to "provide a voice of prayer for the whole creation."[18] I always wondered if Smart were really insane, or if others merely misunderstood him. Perhaps, I reasoned, the same could be said for myself.

What if I were correct in assuming that God had given me a vision of hell, of life separated from his grace? What if the madness I experienced was not madness at all, but the awful, horribly sane truth of life without God? If so, why was I chosen to bear such a message? In light of my own experiences, I could no longer decipher madness from sanity, nor could I decide what "normal" was. More than anything, life had become strange to me. I thought of Shakespeare's line from Hamlet, "There are more things in heaven and earth, Horatio, than are dreamt of in our philosophy."[19] My philosophy had been stretched to the breaking point, and would continue to be stretched for many years as I struggled to understand the bizarre malady that had come upon me in a swift, inexorable, and inexplicable descent. I felt as if I were periodically forced underwater by an invisible intruder and held down until my breath gave out. I always survived, but was left alone, bewildered and dripping on the shore, wondering when the next onslaught would be. My mind drifted back to Cowper and the mellow encounter with my pastor. As compassionate as the latter had been, I was reminded of how I had later witnessed the dark side of his theology, and how it had opened up in me a chasm of fear similar to Cowper's, that I was indeed an outcast from the grace of God. This thought had first assailed my mind on a beautiful spring day a few months earlier. I had flounced into church dressed in a knit dress the color of a daffodil,

---

[18]   Abrams, 2505.

[19]   William Shakespeare, *Hamlet,* in *The Norton Shakespeare,* 2nd edition, ed. Stephen Greenblatt (New York: W. W. Norton and Company, 2009), 1099.

which I knew complemented the golden highlights in my hair. I was radiating joy, the joy of a God whose mercies were unfailing and whose compassion was limitless.

Unsuspecting, I was perplexed as I overheard the pastor asking for prayer because he was going to preach on "predestination" that morning. I had never heard that word before, or if I had, it had made no impression on me. I sauntered down the sidewalk, into the church, and sat down in my customary seat behind the members of the singles' Bible study. I greeted them cheerfully, then settled down as the service began. We sang our first hymn, "There is a Fountain," written by William Cowper, although I had never heard of him at the time and did not notice the author. I was, however, compelled by the words:

> There is a fountain filled with blood
> Drawn from Immanuel's veins;
> And sinners, plunged beneath that flood,
> Lose all their guilty stains;
> Lose all their guilty stains,
> Lose all their guilty stains;
> And sinners plunged beneath that flood
> Lose all their guilty stains.
>
> Dear dying Lamb, Thy precious
> blood shall never lose its pow'r
> Till all the ransomed church of God
> Be saved to sin no more;
> Be saved to sin no more;
> Till all the ransomed church of God
> Be saved to sin no more.
>
> E'er since by faith I saw the stream
> Thy flowing wounds supply,
> Redeeming love has been my theme,
> And shall be till I die;
> And shall be till I die,
> And shall be till I die;

Redeeming love has been my theme,
And shall be till I die.[20]

I had never heard the words before, but I was overcome by the imagery of Christ's love like a fountain that washed away all stains. I knew I could never find redemption in the shedding of my own blood, as I had attempted to. Only the blood of the "dear dying Lamb" could accomplish salvation for me. I, like Cowper, believed then that "redeeming love" would be my theme until I died. I exulted in the words as I sang them, sure of my favor in the sight of God because of His endless mercy. After we sang a few more worship songs, the pastor rose and stood at the lectern and placed his sermon notes on it. He wore the same halcyon smile as he would later wear at the hospital. The smile never abandoned his face throughout the sermon. I moved forward slightly, eager as always to hear the word of God. He began:

> "What if there were a giant asteroid flying through space and heading toward earth? What if it hit the earth and destroyed it? Then God's plan for the earth and mankind would be thwarted. So, we know that God must be in control of all events, or else things would not happen according to His will. Chaos would reign on the earth. If all events on earth must be caused by God, as we have seen, this must mean that God is even in control of all human decisions. This includes the salvation of mankind. Jesus told His disciples in John, 'You did not choose me, but I chose you....'[21] The belief that God has chosen whom he wants to save and has caused them to believe is called "predestination." There are five points to this doctrine, which can be remembered by the acronym TULIP. The points are as follows: total depravity, unconditional election, limited atonement, irresistible grace, and perseverance of the saints. TULIP has been rightly called 'the fairest flower in God's garden.'"

---

[20] William Cowper, "There is a Fountain Filled with Blood," in *Conyer's Collection of Psalms and Hymns*, 1772.

[21] John 15:16a (NIV).

The pastor went on to explain each point in detail. I was beginning to squirm slightly in my chair. A mist of sweat appeared on my upper lip. I was especially horrified by his quiescent quotation of a verse from Romans chapter nine to clench his point:

> "Not only that, but Rebekah's children were conceived at the same time by our father Isaac. Yet, before the twins were born or had done anything good or bad—in order that God's purpose in election might stand: not by works but by him who calls—she was told, 'The older will serve the younger.' Just as it is written: 'Jacob I loved, but Esau I hated.' What then shall we say? Is God unjust? Not at all! For he says to Moses, 'I will have mercy on whom I will have mercy, and I will have compassion on whom I have compassion.'"[22]

I had read these verses before, of course, but never interpreted them to mean that God had loved Jacob and therefore had saved him but had hated Esau and had therefore sent him to hell. The implication was that He uses this kind of procedure with us also. At that moment, God grew strange to me. I began to question the "redeeming love" I had just sung of so heartily. I knew that if God had chosen beforehand whom He was going to save, then that meant He had created some people for the sole purpose of damning them. I shuddered inwardly as the pastor closed his sermon:

> "Billy Graham has written a book called *How to be Born Again*. Let me tell you that this is a contradiction in terms. There is nothing you can do to be born again. There is no prayer that you can pray. Apart from the converting work of the Holy Spirit, you are lost. If you want to be saved, I would suggest that you frequent places where the word of God is preached and take it in. Perhaps God will have mercy on you and save you. And remember also that you can believe you are saved when you are actually not. Satan

---

[22] Romans 9:10-15 (NIV).

can deceive you with a false assurance. So, as Paul says, 'examine yourselves to see whether you are in the faith.'"[23]

The pastor made a few closing remarks that I didn't hear due to the buzzing anxiety in my head. Then his voice broke through my terror, and I heard him say "Let's close our worship today by singing hymn number 334, 'Blessed Assurance, Jesus is Mine.'" I did not even attempt to sing, but the words stung me like a horde of mad bees:

Blessed Assurance, Jesus is Mine!
Oh, what a foretaste of glory divine!
Heir of salvation, purchase of God,
Born of His Spirit, washed in His blood.
This is my story, this is my song,
Praising my Savior all the day long;
This is my story, this is my song,
Praising my Savior all the day long.[24]

The repercussions of this sermon did not occur immediately. My mind was behaving properly at the time, and I was only aware of a new, vague coldness in my relationship with God. I felt as if I had found and eaten a whole box of gourmet chocolate, enjoying every bite and glorying in it, and then someone had told me that it might be poisonous. I stood there in shock, as though waiting for the first signs of illness. I carried a slight uneasiness with me everywhere, as if the world were starting to revert back to that distorted and terrifying place it had been during my depression. But it didn't. Not yet.

Then, enter the dangerous catalyst, would-be-prince: Issa Zarzar, six-foot-one, swarthy, born in Bethlehem (the original one) on Christmas Eve. Surely that was a sign, in addition to the fact that "Issa" is the Arabic word for "Jesus." On our first date he asked me, "So, what's God doing in your life?" and I had poured out the story of my struggles with

---

[23] 2 Corinthians 13:5 (NIV).

[24] Fanny Crosby, "Blessed Assurance," 1873.

depression. I was usually such a reticent person that I couldn't fathom why I was vomiting up such things to a virtual stranger. But he was so full of compassion that I succumbed, and thus the story was told. In him I began to see a view of God that I had never seen before, one that belied the sermon back in the spring. In him I began to realize, as if for the first time, that God is love. I had known this all my life, and yet I had never known a human love that could show me the incarnation of such a concept. All the "loves" I had known before had been performance-based or one-sided or colored with cruelty, and I had wandered through my life with a twisted view of this concept. So we began our relationship, climbing trees at two a.m. in a city rose garden. Issa commented that the trees were "clapping their hands," and I was impressed by such a poetic image until he admitted that it came from Isaiah.

One night on the sidewalk in front of his apartment he kissed me, and I thought I had found my own salvation as well as the secrets to world peace, global warming, and household mildew. I reasoned that all who had come before were imposters, and that finally I had found the ideal love portrayed in all the romance novels I had read. Love appeared before me like a celestial vision, a door into another universe or a taunting mirage. I didn't know which. Subconsciously I believed that my life lay scattered like metal shavings on a concrete floor, and that marriage to Issa would act like a giant magnet to draw them upward and unify them. Thus I activated all my feminine wiles and pursued my prey like a sleek leopardess. As we continued to date, it became clear that I was more invested in the relationship than he, and fear of rejection sparked a new round of panic attacks. So I panicked, and I flirted. Issa would be momentarily drawn in by my charms, then would back off and run for cover. Our relationship became a dangerous pendulum drawn this way and that by conflicting emotions. Finally, Issa admitted he did not have the "love of commitment" for me. Then the abyss in my mind opened up, the abyss where I had buried the sermon on predestination. In my irrational logic, rejection by Issa was only a symptom of another possible rejection, this time by an infinite being: God. The words of the sermon spun in my mind like a swarm of locusts, devouring every green leaf of sanity that sprouted in me. I was not chosen. I had prayed a prayer, but prayers didn't matter. It had all been determined from eternity past, and there was perhaps no hope. The clouds gathered in my soul until the storm broke, black and unforgiving, on that day when I cut myself with the single-edged blade and found myself at 222 Sunnybrook Rd., against my will.

> No voice divine the storm allayed,
> No light propitious shone,
> When, snatched from all effectual aid,
> We perished, each alone;
> But I beneath a rougher sea,
> And whelmed in deeper gulfs than he.[25]

---

[25] William Cowper, "The Castaway," in *The Norton Anthology of English Literature,* vol. 1, 4th edition, ed. M. H. Abrams (New York: W. W. Norton & Company, 1979), 2505.

Depression

You don't want to know this man.
He gives your heart a beating
Then turns it into sand,
That beating box that makes you tick.
He steals your blood; he makes you sick.
He takes the you from you;
He shuts you up until you're through
Then shoves his silence in your gut.

You don't want to know this man,
But he demands an introduction.
He'll rape your mind
Then rain on your production.
You know his kind.
He drapes all the furniture in your heart
Then shuts it down and makes it smart.

And what can you do
When his blue fingers tease your hair,
When he invites you in his chair
And you're compelled to go?
You're under his spell and so
You move to his dance
And he breaks you in his arrogance.
What to do?
No chance.
You're through.

An Attempt to Mourn

There are not enough tears;
Though we send our sorrow
Down the given channels
Still the world-ache swells its banks
And we shake until our dry grief rattles.

There are not enough tears;
That is why we shrink with need
As old age blooms on our face
Like dead flowers gone to seed.

There are not enough tears;
That is why we talk on in the dark
Though our lovers are asleep
And have been long asleep.
That is why we don't bother to weep.

There are not enough tears;
That is why Lot's wife turned to salt
When she saw Sodom burn
And Echo's beauty dried up to a stutter
When she grieved.
That is why God had to bleed.

4

The Mind has Mountains

MY BRAIN HAD BECOME a whirlpool of thoughts. Eternity haunted me like a specter as I considered Cowper and his obsession with damnation. Where did we belong, Cowper and I? To a special class of mad prophets, to the reprobate, to those destined for heaven but doomed to live a life of insanity? In years to come I would find that others had often asked these same questions, with various conclusions. I read books in which authors said that a depressed Christian was a "contradiction in terms." Others would say that depression was only self-pity, or the result of sinful thoughts. At the time I was not aware of these opinions, so I had not yet moved into the devastating guilt that the assertions of well-meaning Christian leaders would bring. I only knew that I was having an encounter with darkness, such as I had never known before, and that my soul was crumbling before it. Yet the Spirit of God was ebullient within me, though I did not feel him. His presence somehow sanctified the suffering and imbued me with the wisp of a hope that the Lord would deliver me. This hope was strengthened by a verse that Issa's roommate, Paul, read to me when he had visited me the day before. He said very little while he was there, but the silence did not disturb me. I understood it. We sat there on my bed while the Darkness seemed to bark at us like Cerberus, warning that we were approaching the underworld. Finally, Paul pulled out his pocket-sized Bible and began to read:

> Here is my servant, whom I uphold,
> My chosen one in whom I delight.
> I will put my Spirit on him
> And he will bring justice to the nations.

He will not shout or cry out,
Or raise his voice in the streets.
A bruised reed he will not break,
And a smoldering wick he will not snuff out.[26]

I did not know the Bible well, so I did not remember having read those verses before. Their effect began to fall on me like delicate snow out of season, and thus unexpected. I knew myself to be a "bruised reed" and a "smoldering wick," and I was indeed terrified of being broken or snuffed out. Here was assurance that my fragile state was respected and sheltered by the Lord. He would not allow me to feel the brunt of His consuming power. As Moses was shielded from the overwhelming glory of God by the Lord's hand, I, too, would be treated gently. I would treasure those verses for years afterward, never forgetting their astounding promise, or the Lord's nurturing care that they proclaimed.

This peaceful visit was in sharp contrast to that of my parents, who had also come that day, after having returned from the mountains. They marched into my room, their arms laden with paper bags full of clothes, cookies, a letter from a friend, and my favorite pair of gold shoes. The bags hid their faces. When they laid the bags down on the bed, I saw the startled, almost shrunken look around their eyes and mouths. Shame stung me like a surprised scorpion as I caught them glancing at my bandaged wrist. I felt somehow defective in their presence, as if I had a limb missing. We talked of trivial subjects, then they gave me detailed information about my insurance coverage. I knew they felt comfortable hiding the screaming truth behind a soundproof wall of business. They never asked me why I had cut my wrist. I neatly suppressed my turbulent emotions during their visit, as I had been implicitly taught to do while growing up. When they left, a nauseating hollowness welled up inside me, and I spent several hours incapacitated on the bed, wondering why a visit that had seemed so innocuous had been so traumatic. I was beginning to wonder how I was going to fill up the rest of the day when my two older brothers walked into the room. I was caught off guard. We had not really grown up together, because they were much older than I was. They lived two hours away, and I hardly ever saw them. At Christmas our whole family

---

[26]   Isaiah 42:1-3a (NIV).

would usually come together like an odd assortment of mismatched shoes, and we would endure hours of superficial conversation, during which I, at least, was screaming on the inside for someone to say something truthful and shocking. Other than this, we lived largely separate lives.

After I overcame my surprise, I got up and moved the two chairs in the room close to the bed so we could sit down and talk, though I wasn't sure about what. I sat back on the bed and waited. For the first time, they began to speak to me plainly and honestly. They asked me what medication the doctor had put me on, and I told them.

"But you know," said John, the younger of the two, "that medication just covers up problems. You need to get to the root of this."

I decided then that his mind must have never harbored anything awful that needed covering up. If so, he would have known that even a mere superficial deadening of pain is welcome to one who is dying, to one who can hardly bear to take the next breath. I wondered what he meant by "root." My psychologist had said that the unconscious mind is like a closet. If you keep stuffing more and more into it, one day everything will fall out on your head. That's why I was having panic attacks, according to him. I moved closer to my brothers without knowing it, in anticipation of an oracle. John began to speak again:

"Are you aware that our upbringing was, uh…, somewhat abnormal?" he began.

I wasn't aware.

"What do you mean?" I murmured, reviewing quickly in my mind how nothing unusual had ever happened in our family, not realizing that this was because nothing at all went on in our family. Period.

"Well," he continued, "don't most parents hug their children? Don't most parents say 'I love you' to their children?" he continued.

"I don't know," I replied, because the thought had never occurred to me that parents should do such things. A question began to grow in my mind like some alien life form. I spoke it out loud. "Is that what they're supposed to do?"

"Of course," said John. "Did they ever do those things for you?"

"Nnno," I stuttered. There was a terrible silence, like the silence in heaven before the seventh seal is broken and God's judgment is poured out on the earth. Finally, John proposed a question.

"Don't you think it's possible that if people never say they love you, and they never act like they love you, that maybe they really don't?"

I couldn't answer this question. It was too appalling. Then I thought of my parents standing in that very room, where I sat with my bandaged wrist, and dryly discussing my insurance policy. I couldn't hear most of what my brothers said after that. My mind was gnawing on what if's, and the taste was violently bitter. As my brothers left, I was aware of a strange feeling in both mind and body, a feeling I did not recognize. My jaws grew tight, my head felt as if my skull were encroaching on my brain, and my heart began to beat wildly in my chest. "Am I having a panic attack?" I thought. No, that wasn't it. Suddenly the feeling identified itself, as a huge wave of emotion overcame me. I knew what it was. It was anger. I began a mental inventory, racking my brain for memories that might unlock the door to some bitter secret. My search was rewarded with a plethora of images from childhood, all showing up at once like the squares of a crazy quilt—some non-sensical, some beautiful, and others too dangerous to be incarnated into thoughts. One by one I examined them, scrutinizing them with new, critical eyes. Still the anger rumbled in my heart like an approaching tank.

> She came to be at the age of three,
> For that was when memory gave birth to her.
> She began in Winn-Dixie,
> Holding up three fingers to a stranger
> Who asked her age.
> A hand-me-down green-checkered dress
> Hung on her, barely defying gravity,
> And black patent leather shoes worried her toes.
> She clutched a Shirley Temple doll stuffed with straw
> (which her brother later dissected with a piece of broken
> Coke bottle).
> This was the first moment that had survived in thought
> To take root in the tiny brain.
> Much later, she wondered what cruel amnesia
> Had clouded her beginnings.
> What if, she thought,
> Before she was conceived,
> The constituent parts of herself
> Waited in fragmented agony to be born?
> Sometimes she lay awake at night,

Feeling for those pieces of herself.
Perhaps in that first darkness her selves
Like scattered stones ached for each other across time,
Where an almost-child fingered the clock of the universe.

I saw my mother speaking for me, as she always had throughout my childhood. The woman asked me how old I was, but I was too afraid of the sound of my voice, as usual. I was fumbling with my sweating fingers, trying to hold up exactly three, but before I was successful, my mother exclaimed, "She's three. She's very shy." I put my fingers hastily down, since there was no need for them. I wondered what "shy" meant.

It is October of my first-grade year, and autumn is cauterizing the trees with red and yellow fire. My heart was galloping with anticipation because our class was going to dress up as leaves and sing a special song in honor of autumn. The teacher was addressing our class amid the whisperings and giggling of an overstimulated classroom of six-year-olds high on Kool-Aid that the room mothers had brought in as a treat. She adjured us to stand tall and straight as oak trees on the silver metal risers in the library, where we were to perform. The chorus was to be sung "gleefully," according to our teacher: "I'm just a pretty autumn leaf, dancing gaily down the street." "Okay everyone—let's go over the song one more time." "And no monkey business," she added. "Monkey business" was a veiled reference to some of my classmates' penchant for belting out a parody of the song composed by one of the more precocious boys: "I'm just an ugly rotting toad, squashed and flattened on the road." The teacher, Mrs. Earp, raised her hand high, counted to three, then dropped her hand briskly to signal us to begin singing. I was trying to belt out the chorus as commanded, but my voice was naturally soft and would not cooperate. I was looking down, staring at my black patent leather shoes—Sunday attire—that my mother had allowed me to wear since it was a special occasion.

Suddenly I heard a sharp voice: "One-two-three, eyes on me, Nancy!" I blushed to the roots of my blonde hair, and I could feel the unwelcome heat disfiguring my face. I immediately snapped my head up and held it there, stiff and motionless as a tree trunk. We sang the song *ad nauseam* until the teacher was satisfied with the result, then she announced that it was time to put on our costumes for the performance.

"Okay boys listen up!" she ordered with a truly military zeal. "Line up in front of the door to go to Mrs. Dozier's room to get dressed."

The boys were to wear dark brown pants and shirts that represented a tree trunk, on which some of the room mothers had glued gold and red leaves. But the girls' costumes were more subtle, and truly glorious in my opinion. We were to wear dark green leotards with a spectacular skirt fashioned from a length of wide ribbon, to which were sewn gossamer, transparent gold and rust-colored scarves. Mrs. Earp was going to supervise the boys in the music room while they changed clothes, and Mrs. Dozier was to oversee the girls' transformation in our classroom. As our teacher was leaving, she said sternly, "Mrs. Dozier will be here in a moment. Behave yourselves, Ladies!" Then she was gone.

At once the room erupted with squeals of juvenile delight. We were unsupervised! A few of the quieter girls, including me, went to our wooden "cubbies" and submissively retrieved our costumes. However, the taller and more brazen among them began to rush about the room chaotically. One of them grabbed the classroom's American flag that was attached to a dowel lodged in a metal holder next to the enormous green chalkboard. She began to circumnavigate the room while bellowing out a war cry. Several of the larger girls followed suit.

Mrs. Dozier had still not shown up. Meanwhile, the meek girls had huddled in the corner next to the cubbies to obediently put on their costumes. I was excruciatingly self-conscious about undressing in front of a whole classroom full of girls, and I was debating whether I needed to take off my underwear to put on the leotard. I finally concluded that a brief moment of exposure was better than pink ruffled panties peeking out from under my costume. Carefully surveying the surroundings, I saw that the older girls were still on their rampage, so I hid myself in a corner among the cubbies and surreptitiously began to remove my pants and underwear. When I had accomplished this, I carefully inserted my left foot into the neck of the leotard as rapidly as possible, breathing heavily from anxiety. When the war cries began to sound dangerously close, I looked up in horror to see Davida, the largest of the recalcitrant girls, rushing toward me, her brown, beaded pigtails flying. She was pointing at my bare lower body, giggling and shouting obscenities that I didn't understand at the time. I frantically struggled to cover myself with my discarded underwear, but Davida suddenly groped me between the legs, guffawing and snorting. I was too stunned to make a sound, although a tortured scream gurgled in my throat without actually voicing itself. I began to run, or attempted to, but I kept tripping over the leotard that had fallen around my ankles. Davida followed me, her long legs covering what seemed to be an enormous amount of ground with each stride. Again, and again she assailed me as I struggled to propel myself across the gray and white speckled tiles of the floor. To quell the clamor of shame reverberating in my head, I began to hum to myself the only prayer I knew, to the tune of "Twinkle, Twinkle, Little Star":

Now I lay me down to sleep;
I pray the Lord my soul to keep.
If I should die before I wake,
I pray the Lord my soul to take.

After what seemed to be an interminable length of time, a lookout, carefully positioned by the wooden door with a small hole for a window, screamed out, "Mrs. Dozier's coming!" Davida immediately forgot her prey and rushed to the farthest corner of the room to act as though she had been innocently donning her costume. The flag-waver, who had been cheering her on, quickly forced the dowel attached to the flag back in its holder and ran to another corner. Everyone was silent as Mrs. Dozier opened the door. There was no sign of the indecency that had occurred. I quickly maneuvered myself into the green leotard, and before I knew it we were all in the media center (a fancy word for "library") belting out, "I'm just a pretty autumn leaf, dancing gaily down the street." The rest of the day passed for me like a novocained blur. Davida kept trying to catch my eye and snicker, so I quickly finished my math worksheet and put my head down on my desk. My mouth felt dry, as if it were filled with cotton. After school I walked by myself down the mile-long route that led to my house. The wind was whisking dead leaves in miniature tornadoes above the asphalt. As I walked, the sound of my patent leather shoes crushing the brown leaves on the ground kept time to the jingle in my head: "I'm just an ugly rotting toad, squashed and flattened on the road." When I reached my house, a sugary odor floated through the back door when I opened it. I saw my mother, smiling rather too eagerly for my taste, standing by the kitchen table with a plate containing gingerbread men decorated with enormous grins of icing. I shuddered, remembering the story of how the gingerbread man had been chased throughout the town by people and animals who wanted to devour him. I involuntarily imagined him with arms and legs bitten off.

"Would you like a cookie?" my mother piped up brightly.

"No," I whispered.

"No THANK YOU," she corrected, followed by a brisk "How was your day?"

"Fine," I muttered.

"What did you do?"

"Nothing." Passing by my mother and the hapless gingerbread men, I shuffled to my room and closed the door. I opened my book bag, weakly pulled out the leafy skirt, and deposited it in the trash can. Then I sat at my small desk by the window and stared as the wind forcibly undressed the hapless trees. I never told anyone. But a Pandora's box had been opened, vomiting out a plethora of evils that would pursue me. One autumn years later, I would learn Robert Frost's poem "Nothing Gold Can Stay," and consider it a fitting epitaph for my innocence:

> "Nature's first green is gold,
> Her hardest hue to hold.
> Her early leaf's a flower;
> But only so an hour.
> Then leaf subsides to leaf.
> So Eden sank to grief,
> So dawn goes down to day.
> Nothing gold can stay."[27]

I carefully put away the previous memory into a dark, special box labeled "Things not to think about." I forced my traumatized mind to gravitate to thoughts of many spring and summer nights when my heart would nearly burst with the beauty of existence, and I would rush outside into the dark as if I were going to meet a secret lover:

> Away from the droning of the TV
> And my brother's moaning on the couch

---

[27] 28. Robert Frost, "Nothing Gold Can Stay," in *New Enlarged Anthology of Robert Frost's Poems* (New York: Holt, Rinehart and Winston, 1951), 227-228.

As he slept,
I crept outside into a bejeweled night,
Leaving behind the stale,
The old tale told of musty days.
No one witnessed my flight,
When I was whisked away,
A girl barely nine,
Into the fine September air.
My hair was flung down my back
In a single braid,
My knees scathed from driveway scars.
I wriggled between the parked cars
And up the hill of ivy
To a still glade
Where every blade of grass
Enclosed a secret.
I passed among trees,
Ancient and unmoving,
Like reproving prophets
Of an unknown god.
Perhaps the sod beneath my feet
Had been the bodies of kings,
Or their underlings from other worlds
Where young girls once dreamed as I did
As they slid alone into their reveries.
I felt the weight of ages,
And smelled the delicate pages of history
In its huge tome.
I sensed that I was home in the woods,
That all the world's goods
Could not compete
With one night of Beauty.
I had left behind everything—
The sureness of indoor light,
The duty of dishes,
The comforting sight of all I knew
To seek what was true.
And who was the One who saw me,

To draw me from the din
To seek a kindred Spirit?
In the quivering of the trees
I could hear it—
A message mouthing my name,
Always the same:
Forever, forever.
But what if that's too long,
And what if the Presence is too strong
For someone like me?
I gravitated toward the sky,
My face turned upward
To catch sight of the bit of moon.
But it was too soon.
The Voice would have to wait
Until another year,
When fear would drive me to hearken it.
There was, as yet, nothing to darken my way,
So I did not stay there
In the night's bright hunger,
But wandered back into the house
As if to the stroke of thunder.
I could not espouse the Giver of secrets,
So I gave myself up to the river of days,
Each one drawing me deeper into forgetfulness.
But always regret shadowed me,
Like the ghost of amber in an early autumn,
That thrust away its green—
So I had abandoned the Unseen.

The house always seemed as stifling as a cocoon, with no hope of metamorphosis, in light of the banal TV ads blaring and the superficial conversations. What did we want for dinner? When was I going to clean up my room? When was my dad going to unstop the toilet? At night, whether it was hot or cold outside, I would escape my boredom by running outside, down the driveway and up the ivy-covered bank to my forest in the suburbs—the back of our one-acre lot. I would stand there and listen, especially if there was moonlight, for some kind of ancient wisdom to be imparted to me. I felt a tremendous emptiness, but I didn't recognize it then, because it had always been there. I knew then that there was some glorious secret in the woods, and that if I stood there long enough, I would be shown the key to life. This key would unlock the box that contained the explanation of all the world's mystery. Everything would make sense then. All my hungry questions would be answered with a downdraft of manna. Sometimes, before I went out, I would change into a long red velvet gown that my mother had given me to dress up in. Avoiding my mother's questions about "what had gotten into me," I would sneak out, swathed from shoulders to toes in red, to meet destiny among the trees. I figured one should be dressed properly for such a quest. The trees seemed to quiver with a supernatural life. I felt that someone was speaking to me, but not in words, only in a whirling sea of impressions, and in the sense of a living Presence. I soaked in some kind of undefined truth that would nourish me for many days. But always, I would hear a voice from the house, surrounded in a drab halo of light. The voice would tell me that I had to pick up the Legos off the floor, the ones that I had been constructing a castle with. The voice shattered the fragile, otherworldly mirror that I had been gazing into, and the shards fell at my feet. I reluctantly moved around them with my bare feet and began the heavy trek back to the house.

I am four years old, walking home from kindergarten, my palms sweaty with guilt. There had been a birthday party that day for one of my classmates. He was turning five. There was a menagerie of animal crackers on the snack table, five cookies at each place. Miniature Dixie cups full of grape Kool-Aid accompanied them. I sat down before most of the others, eager to light into the animal crackers. Then I noticed that my place had no cup of juice. I felt a stab of disappointment. Then I looked beside me. There were balloons tied on the small wooden chair to my left. I knew that was the birthday boy's seat. I slowly turned my head and looked to my right. A little Chinese boy was sitting there, already sipping his Kool-Aid delicately, as if to make it last. I looked to the left again. The chair was empty. The smiley face on the balloon seemed to grimace. I made a decision. When I discovered no one was looking, I furtively snatched the birthday boy's cup and consumed the contents in one gulp, as if to destroy the evidence. I wiped my mouth on my sleeve and began to nibble innocently on my animal crackers. The birthday boy suddenly appeared and took his seat. His two front teeth were missing. I thought his face looked like a perfectly formed ball of pizza dough with two brown eyes pressed into it like raisins. His large body seemed to dwarf the tiny chair when he sat down. He looked around him for a few seconds. I knew he was assessing the situation. He noticed he had no cup. I carefully spied on him, wondering what he would do. He politely raised his hand.

"Yes, Eugene," said the teacher, Mrs. Banks, in a giddy soprano.
"I didn't get a cup of juice," he murmured.
"I'm so sorry, Eugene, but we don't have any more. Would you mind drinking water?"
"No, ma'am."
"Thank you, dear."
My eyes followed Mrs. Banks as she pulled a Dixie cup out of the dispenser by the water fountain and let the running water cascade into it. She let it overflow accidentally, so she had to pour some out. There were stray water droplets clinging to the outside of the cup. The cup had little red Elmos all over it. Mrs. Banks walked over to where we sat, the victim and the perpetrator, and handed the cup to the birthday boy.
"Thank you, Mrs. Banks," he said under his breath. I felt an uncomfortable twinge in my stomach.
All the way home I saw Dixie cups with Elmo on them. I stared at my feet and tried to count the cracks in the sidewalk to distract myself. When I reached my back door, I hesitated, then opened the screen door. It had a rip in it where the dog had tried to jump through. My mother was waiting for me. I felt like a hapless fly in the sticky strands of a web. Then began the familiar litany:
"How was your day?" she said.
"Fine."
"What did you do?"
"Nothing."
"You must have done something."
I felt pressure building in my chest. "We had a birthday party for Eugene."
"Oh, that's nice. Was it fun?"

I considered lying, but my conscience had begun to squeeze my body like a tube of toothpaste. I at last began to cry, pouring out the whole story to the tune of hot tears. When I finished, I looked at my mother, desperately groping for some sign of forgiveness. Her mouth opened up like a geyser: "I can't believe you did such a thing. You should be ashamed of yourself. You are so selfish. I think you need to go to your room and think about the terrible thing you did. And he was the birthday boy...."

I catapulted from the chair and ran to my room, with shame following me like a shadow. In my room I considered what I had done, deciding that my guilt could not be atoned for. I learned that day that forgiveness was a myth, that sins permeate one's soul like leprosy and make it rot. I spent the afternoon trying to pull the blue elephant appliqué off my pleated skirt. I never confessed anything to my mother again.

Thoughts of my mother made my mind wander to another image: I am sitting in her lap in a Boston rocker that creaked ominously as it moved back and forth on the dun-colored floor. I was staring at the odd arrangement of the little squares of faded shades that made up its pattern. But there was no pattern. The sheer randomness of it confounded me. I was trying to forget about my big toe that my brother had rocked on accidentally ten minutes earlier. The nail had already turned black, and I could feel the blood pulsating through my toe. Tears traced a haphazard path down my cheeks. I felt my mother's arms awkwardly clutching me, as if I didn't quite belong there. When I stopped crying, my mother silently deposited me on the couch and went into the kitchen. As I remembered this incident, I wondered for a moment why it seemed to hold such significance. It loomed large in my mind like a huge monument to something I couldn't define. Suddenly, on the hospital bed, the truth broke through and I gasped as if I had seen an apparition. I understood why the incident haunted me so. It was the only time I remembered from childhood that my mother had held me.

Cooking Lessons

You made me cut up a chicken once when I was ten.
"Cooking is an art," you said,
So I stood at the cutting board with my knife.

Confronting a greasy palette:
Yellow skin, pink tendons, lavender flesh,
The waxy white of joints.

You prepared me to sever and tear,
Handed me my tools,
Brought me the kill in Revereware.

I knew there was a time to create
And a time to destroy,
But I never could tell the difference

Or figure out why this is what women do:
Their hands wear blood at morning,
At evening perfumed lotion
To mix their strange and mandatory potion.

I stood at the cutting board with my knife.
You were painted like a priestess;
I was a pale apprentice recoiling from the altar,

A kitchen Van Gogh forced to make a crazy portrait in
the pan
With the offal of Someone else's art,
Then watch the men at dinner dismantle wings with greasy
fingers.

Though it is much harder to create than to sever,

I told you the chicken was too well put together and
wouldn't budge,
You said I'd never make a good wife.

I stood by the cutting board with my knife.

Images of my brother John began emerging like a collage of joy against
a backdrop of nothingness. I had bonded with him instead of with my
parents, and I reveled in every attention he gave me. He told me once
he had formed a "goon society," and I would be able to join, since I was
a goon. I felt honored to be included, even though I didn't quite know
what a goon was. Vague recollections of the song "Little Bunny Foo-Foo"
popped up but didn't help much. On many occasions my brother would
threaten to flush me down the toilet, and I would run screaming through
the house. I would scurry toward the safety of my bedroom, meaning
to lock the door behind me, but he would pursue me relentlessly and
force open the door before I could lock it. Then he would scoop me up
and carry me into the yellow and brown tiled bathroom, turn me upside
down and douse the ends of my long honey blonde hair in the waiting
waters of the toilet. With my hair still hanging there, he would push the
handle on the toilet, and I would watch the water swirl and contort inside
the brown bowl. Once this ritual was completed, John would place me
on my feet in the bathroom and snicker. I would always raise my fists
and pummel him in the stomach in mock anger, but this only served
to amuse him more. In addition to assailing me with toilet water, John
would always bring me little gifts of clothing, books, or toys. Once he
brought me a stuffed Pooh bear all the way from Wyoming. As he grew
older and spent less and less time at home, the gifts and attention stopped.
He spent a summer in England when I was ten, and I cried every night
until he came back. I could not understand why I had lost favor, and I
mourned deeply. I wandered around the house by myself, longing for
someone to chase me.

She cradled his picture in her pocket
In the absence of a locket,
Fingering its dog-eared edges

As she sat on the window ledge at school.
The other girls dubbed her foolish,
Laughing airily, chiming
"He's too old for you."
But she never told them
He was her brother,
And that there was no one else
To mitigate the relentless void.
She avoided the years between them,
Regarding it a petty fact
In the shadow of adoration.
He would rain down gifts on her:
White gloves that buttoned
At the wrist,
Crisp taffeta dresses
With bows at the back,
A jeweled mirror that cracked
When it fell down the stairs.
All her cares seemed
Swallowed up in him,
And the dim light of home life blazed
Into beauty when he was there.
She was amazed by his black hair
So unlike her own,
The blue eyes that hungered
Though she could not see it.
Whatever he wanted,
She struggled to be it.
But childhood always trembles on the edge of a death,
Stealing our very breath,
And hearts shatter,
Though it often matters to no one else.
He left in stealth
With a girl with copper-colored hair
Who sang like a nightingale
Escaping at last
The pale and bitter fortress of home.
And so she was alone at ten.

The gifts trickled to a thin stream,
Then ceased.
She never found her peace.
She wandered with wounds
And sorrow bloomed like an unwelcome spring.
There are some things too delicate for words—
They are broken when we mouth them,
So she never spoke of it,
But somehow continued, silent,
Her very sinews strained
With a secret anguish.
Hearts languish, and no one knows.
The agony is a noiseless snow
That settles in our wounds and stings,
Distorting our sight
Until we can no longer retort,
And we forever hunger after lost things.

I am in fifth grade. My teacher's name was Mrs. Wolf, and she always seemed to be slavering after one of us students, who were as skittish as prey. One time that morning she lost her temper and shouted, "I'm so angry I could bite you!" Staring at her quivering jowls, we almost believed she would. I had a gnawing fear of thunderstorms, and on my tenth birthday I was sitting at my wooden desk struggling with a division problem. The girl next to me, Angelica, was attempting to pass a note to her friend across the aisle. She whispered to me to take the crumpled, tightly folded paper and pass it on to the girl, who sat nonchalantly twisting one of her multiple braids. I was afraid of Angelica. She made trouble for anyone who didn't acknowledge her authority. I was about to gingerly slip the note into my hand, when out of nowhere a flash illuminated the sky outside that was contorted with dark clouds like clumps of fine steel wool. I withdrew my hand, then froze for a moment before comprehending that thunder would soon violate my ears. The crash was enormous, so overwhelming that I shuddered even though my hands were clamped firmly over my hapless ears like manhole covers. My stomach began to misbehave, gurgling and churning with anxiety.

My teacher was staring at me. I could feel the force of her eyes even though mine were tightly closed. I opened them slowly, hoping I was wrong about her eyes. I wasn't. Her gaze was fastened on me like the claws of a falcon. To my consternation, she opened her mouth, and words poured out in a characteristic drawl: "We need to stop this baby stuff. You are in fifth grade now. Take your hands off your ears."

I could feel the stares of all my classmates beaming toward me like some kind of toxic radiation. I jerked my hands down in shame and put them in my lap, as if to hide them. There were a few giggles from Angelica and her friends. Some of the boys were also laughing. I felt my face grow hot, and I knew it was turning red, as it did so often. I bowed my head over my paper as if I were intent on my math problem, and to my relief Mrs. Wolf turned her wrath toward Angelica, who was again attempting to pass her note.

I carried my humiliation with me for the rest of the day like a familiar backpack loaded with stones. I was bent under the weight of it. At recess we played kickball, and I stood in a crooked line with my classmates to be chosen for teams. I felt like a slave at a market. I expected the captain to come over and look at my teeth or something. I was chosen next-to-last. The distinction of "last" was conferred upon an overweight boy who wore suspenders to hold up his huge, baggy pants that hung around his legs like potato sacks. I was terrible at kickball. While I was waiting for my turn to kick, my "friend" Deborah (who pronounced her name DeBORah) walked over with some of her cronies. She pretended to be my friend for the purpose of making fun of me, but I was desperate. A cruel companion was better than none at all. For my Christmas gift, she had given me a hairclip that was covered in green felt to look like an alligator that could open its jaws and clamp down on one's hair. She told me she had made it, but I knew she was lying because the eyes, nose, and teeth were perfectly formed from tiny pieces of black felt, and I knew she could not be so skilled with scissors. It was obviously machine made, and rather faded and worn. I felt ashamed to have been given a cast-off, unwanted, threadbare thing that reminded me too much of myself. It made me sick to look at it, so when I went home, I slipped it inside a pottery dish that decorated our hearth. The dish was filled with gold spray-painted pinecones, which successfully hid the alligator from view. I never saw it again.

Deborah stared at me for a minute or so, as if contemplating what to do, then she tossed her blond hair coyly out of her face and spoke.

"Nancy, can you pick up that rock for me? The one that's shaped like a heart."

I bent down slowly, bending my knees and turning them awkwardly to the side, as I was in the habit of doing. I grabbed the rock and placed it in her outstretched hand. She threw it down at once and laughed.

"Did you see the way she bent down?" I heard her whisper to Jennifer, the brunette standing next to her. Jennifer nodded and giggled. I stood in front of the girls as if they were a firing squad, their rifles aimed. I thought it would be worse if I reacted or ran away, so I lingered there blushing, not saying a word. I tried to find a place to rest my gaze, but like Noah's dove, my eyes could find no dry ground. The waters continued to rise. Finally, the girls wandered off, losing interest after discovering that I was not reacting.

After a long time I heard my name called, and I ran to home base, which was marked with a dirty, canvas-covered cushion. The bases were loaded, so I knew my performance was crucial. My nerves began to cave in. As I saw the red rubber ball skidding toward me, I overheard one of my teammates, Jared Burkley, mutter like an incantation: "If she makes it, I'll kiss her." Jared Burkley hated me. He carried out his verbal vendetta with precision, always knowing exactly what barb to throw. But he loved sports and was passionate about winning. I gulped and kicked at the rubber object with all the force my skinny leg could produce. The ball catapulted over the head of the pitcher and well out into the field. I ran like a madwoman, making sure to touch all the bases, and at last I careened into home base, skinning my knee in the process. I stood up to find Jared Burkley and his friends staring at me.

"Go ahead, Jared," snickered one boy. "Kiss her."

I froze. Jared looked around nervously, as if considering what to do. I knew his honor was at stake. He would be humiliated if he didn't keep his word, and humiliated if he did. All at once I saw his eyes burn with a fierce light. I knew he had had an epiphany. Before I could move out of the way, his hand swept through the muggy air and met my cheek in a stinging blow. Tears sprang to my eyes, but I let them burn there, refusing to allow them to fall. Jared's friends chortled, apparently satisfied with the outcome. I ran away from them, but they seemed to have multiplied, and I couldn't escape. I accidently bumped into a lanky boy with freckles who snorted and pushed me aside. I kept going, stopping when I reached an enormous oak tree at the edge of the playground. I pretended to be intent on picking up acorns. My hands fluttered slightly like the two wings of a moribund moth.

That night I woke up shaking, my heart in my throat. My mind felt as if it were going to swallow me whole. My nerves flamed raw and red like the steak my dad had grilled for dinner. I lay in bed for a few minutes, debating what to do. I got up and found a piece of paper on my desk, and I wrote the words "Help me" in red crayon. I folded the paper up, tiptoed down the hall to my parents' closed bedroom door. I shoved the paper rather loudly under the door, then sat down on the parquet floor and began to sob uncontrollably. After a few minutes my dad emerged, paper in hand, his face red with frustration. This was the third time that week I had been stricken by a nameless malady. The first time it happened, my parents and I were in the mountains watching an outdoor drama, when I began to feel my chest become tight and my arms and legs grow heavy. The drama depicted a historical account about Native Americans, so there were frequent sounds of mock gunfire. Every time a shot rang out, I would jump slightly on the wooden bench beneath me. I squirmed and shifted, crossing and uncrossing my legs. Finally the weight on my chest was unbearable. I tapped my dad on the arm and whispered frantically, "I need to go to the hospital. I think I'm dying." My dad, alarmed, asked me how I felt, and I spent several minutes attempting to describe the indescribable. Visibly agitated, my parents whispered to each other for a few minutes, then my dad grabbed my hand and whisked me out of the amphitheater and into the car. The next thing I knew, we were in the emergency room where a dark-haired doctor with a slight accent was listening to my heart with a stethoscope and attempting to reassure me with a voice that reminded me vaguely of honey being poured out. After examining me, the doctor began to talk to my parents, and I quickly bored my index fingers into my ears and started humming a few tuneless notes over and over so I would not hear the dreadful tidings that I was on the brink of death.

The doctor looked me in the eye, smiling, and shouted, "Why do you have your fingers in your ears?"

I wondered how he had managed to maintain his honeyed tone, but somehow, he did.

I gingerly extracted my fingers from my ears and whispered, "Because you are going to tell me I'm dying."

The doctor looked me in the eye and gently responded, "You are going to be fine." Then he scribbled something illegible on a small notepad and handed the top sheet to my dad. There was a stony silence as we walked out of the hospital to the car. No one explained to me what had happened, and I didn't ask. I had learned to keep my questions to myself. But there I was again, a week later, my body and mind assaulted by the mysterious evil. My dad stared at me as I sat trembling in the corner of the living room.

I saw anger in his eyes, an anger spawned by helplessness. He lunged at me and I leaped to my feet and bolted down the hall. He pursued me, picking up a stray flip-flop on the way that he waved in the air. I couldn't outrun him, so in a moment I felt the sting of the rubber shoe across my bare leg. It was the only time he ever spanked me. I started crying louder, and my dad stopped short, as if he had been struck himself. I looked at his face and saw that it was contorted with grief. His deep blue eyes glistened. "I don't know how to help you," he sobbed.

These episodes continued throughout that school year, during which I had become the hapless target of the "in" crowd of my class, who labored for nine months quite efficiently and systematically to destroy my already-tenuous sense of self-worth. So, my fifth-grade year teemed with days like these, fraught with both subtle and overt playground tortures and the fever of fear by night. Sometimes I would refuse to go to school and would spend the day in my pink nightgown on the couch, wondering why the landscape had grown sickly and pale. As I considered these details in my hospital room, I noticed that other than a few of the more lurid occurrences, I could remember very little of what had happened to me at school that year. It was as though my mind had constructed an electric fence around what it considered particularly dangerous ground.

But whatever horrors I had endured that had passed into shadow, I did know that every week my mother would take me to an ominous-looking red brick building at the top of a grassy hill, and I would walk with her down the tomb-like hallway, staring down at the alternating black and white squares of tile on the floor. The heels of my shoes clicking on the floor set off what seemed to be a tsunami of echoing sound in the otherwise empty and silent hall. Finally, we would reach a door with a pane of thick, murky glass, and my mother would send me in to talk with a man whose bald head gleamed like a luminary. He cajoled and questioned me for months, but I would only answer in terrified monosyllables and focus my attention on a popgun that cleverly shot out a cork when one pulled the trigger. I attempted to shoot the bald man multiple times, but he would only warn me in an oily voice that I was only allowed to shoot the "doctor doll," which he kept in a box with an assortment of other toys. When I was especially recalcitrant, he would compel me to play a game of checkers with him, which I hated because I always lost. Once, without explanation, he removed one of my shoes and gently scraped the bottom of my foot with what looked like a nail file. I never found out why, but I had felt somehow violated. So I loathed him with a childish fierceness, refusing to speak during these weekly interrogations and begging my mother to release me from his clutches. She would tell me that he was my "happiness doctor." Then she would always add cheerfully, "Smile! God loves you!" Thus, I concluded that God, too, must force sad children to play horrible games with Him that He would always win.

My antagonism toward my psychiatrist mushroomed, yet every week I was coerced to sit on his burgundy leather couch, my breathing shallow as a cornered animal's. He frequently required me to draw pictures of my teacher, which always took the same form: a gray, crudely drawn stick figure with too much gray hair in the form of one long penciled corkscrew. But one day I concocted an ingenious plan to beat him at his own game. I decided that if I answered all his questions, he would think I was happy and release me. The scheme worked brilliantly. I began to make guarded conversation with him, and in a few weeks the hated visits ceased. At my last appointment, I heard him tell my mother in a low voice that he did not think I would have any recurrences in the future. I wondered what a "recurrence" was, but no one thought to explain it to me. I decided that it must mean that somehow, I had prevailed over the balding ogre, so I snickered in my heart in a self-congratulatory way. Only then, years later in the psychiatric ward at twenty-four, did I begin to fathom the forces that had assailed me as a child. I had received at last the awful revelation, as Gerard Manley Hopkins wrote, that "the mind, mind has mountains; cliffs of fall/ Frightful, sheer, no-man-fathomed. Hold them cheap/ May who ne'er hung there."[28] My spirit quivered, aghast at the mental peaks before me, then curled into a tight ball, waiting for the next onslaught.

One Saturday morning I awoke with plans to read all day. I had just bought *Gone with the Wind* and was eager to light into it. I grabbed it from my desk and stared at the glistening, brand-new cover. Rhett Butler was clasping Scarlett in what looked like a violent embrace. Scarlett was wearing a red velvet gown, rather low-cut, that reminded me of the one I liked to dress up in. I gazed at the book as if it were a box of chocolates that I was drooling over. I finally made my way out of the room, kicking aside the clothes, papers and bicycle helmet that littered my path. In the hall I passed my mother, who glared at me, but I kept walking silently toward the living room. I knew that look, but I wasn't going to let anything spoil my day. I quickly found the couch, which was in front of a window overlooking our backyard, which boasted a variety of hardwoods. I arranged the pillows behind my head and began to read.

I was absorbed in Scarlett's coquetry when I suddenly heard footsteps. My mother was walking across the floor, carrying a mop and bucket. She began to mop the floor, but never said a word. I had read twenty-five pages by the time she finished. She managed to glare at me again before leaving the room. At least six times that day my mother marched through the living room, laden down with various instruments of cleaning. She never spoke to me. I looked up the first few times, only to meet the angry glower. After that I quit looking up, but I could sense the look anyway.

By afternoon, my mother had ended her treks across the house. I heard her heels rapping raucously on the hardwoods in the hall. Then there was the sound of her bedroom door not quite slamming, but nevertheless reverberating loudly. I decided to take refuge in my room. As compelling as *Gone With the Wind* was, in the back of my mind I wallowed in guilt, wondering what I had done this time. I was so afraid that it never occurred to me to ask my mother. By the end of the day I had read three hundred pages. *The story was exquisite*, I thought. If only my mother's darkening eyes would leave my mind. They stuck there, disembodied, waiting to pronounce judgment on me.

---

[28] Gerard Manley Hopkins, (No Worst, there is None), in *The Poems of Gerard Manley Hopkins*, 4th edition, ed. W. H. Gardner and N. H. Mackenzie (New York: Oxford University Press, 1967), 100.

I closed my book and lay in bed as evening encroached, like a giant candle snuffer waiting to put out the sun. I didn't move for a long time, but my mind kept darting over my actions that day and the day before, desperately searching for my transgression. At last my bedroom door opened, and there stood my mother, her hair caught up in green curlers. Her face looked like the color of sand, and the light from her eyes seemed like two straight pins that punctured me somewhere near the heart. I almost felt relieved. At last she was going to speak to me.

"I am very angry with you. I told you to clean up your room yesterday, and you did not. Your room is totally unacceptable. And I cleaned house today until four o'clock and you didn't lift one finger to help me."

Before I could respond, although actually I had nothing to say, she closed my door and padded down the hallway in her pink bedroom slippers. I heard her bedroom door shut—loudly again. "Unacceptable," said the door, and all evening in my mind I heard that door thudding out that word. I did not see my mother again until morning.

Child

Small murderess with
her pensive hair
has come to unbirth me.

Her hands gleam like a midwife's.

She dawdled in my mirror today,
the ghost of her hair hanging
from a woman's head.

She thinks it's still hers.

She made me up like a story;
she mothered me, her little hands
spread across a bloated belly.

Someone let her starve.

Now she'll have me for food—
she'll gorge on my heart
like a lioness.

Memory festers in her womb.

She died in childbirth as she became me,
then crawled inside my years,
pulling the cord in after.

It wasn't my fault.

Now she is born again
to follow me
with her bare feet,
dragging her toys.

One of them is dangerous.

Every night a couple of hours after dinner, we would gather together, solemn as monks, for what was called "Bible reading time." In reality, this convocation consisted of my dad's reading from a tiny publication called *The Upper Room*. First, he would read a very brief verse from the Bible, which was printed conveniently at the top of the page. Next came some sort of anecdote which was intended to illuminate the verse. The only story I could remember was one in which the author saw a squirrel eating an acorn in full view of a large tabby cat, and the incident shed light for him on the verse "Thou preparest a table before me in the presence of my enemies."[29] After this section, my father would instruct us to bow our heads while he read the short prayer that followed. The book always left us with a "thought for the day," some pithy saying apparently designed to give us insight into God. My mind usually wandered during Bible-reading time, because I had more than likely been called in from intense play in the back yard, which had been transformed in my mind and the mind of my best friend, Emma, into another world. We peopled our world with extraterrestrials with names like "Aunt Antennae." The dry "Upper Room" could not compete with the book of my imagination, which opened to a new page every day.

I never questioned God's existence, but I was wary of Him. A god who nearly put one to sleep was to be avoided. But sometimes He was transformed into a dreadful ogre who haunted my existence like an angry Zeus ready to strike with thunderbolts. Whenever I heard about Jesus coming back to earth to judge us, I would tremble. The sound of an airplane rumbling in the distance would send me into a frenzy of fear, and I would frantically search the sky for evidence of a white-robed god being birthed in fury from the clouds. We sometimes watched Billy Graham on TV, and after he spoke on hell a few times, the very sound of his voice emanating from the black and white box would send me barreling down

---

[29] Psalm 23:5a (KJV).

the hall to my room. I would close the door, jump into bed and cover my ears with my hands while humming all the tunes I could think of until the danger had passed. I never discussed my fear with anyone. I could trust no one with the staggering secret of my guilt. So God became an enemy who could be momentarily avoided but would eventually seize me for judgment, or a being who took pleasure in boring His people to the point of exasperation with His religious clichés. Undoubtedly Billy Graham also expounded on God's extravagant love and His saving power, but I was always in bed with my hands over my ears. So I wandered alone through a maze of guilt and fear while salvation hovered over my head like a strong hand waiting to descend and embrace me, if only I would look up to see it. But I never did, until the path before and behind me crumbled, and there was nowhere to look but up, right into the face of a Lover.

With the booming funereal strains of the organ, church commenced, and I chafed beneath my starched white Sunday dress. I was absent-mindedly rubbing my black patent leather shoes together and daydreaming about the roast we were going to have for lunch. Suddenly I had a revelation, and I grabbed one of the long white cards displayed on the back of the pew in front of me. At the top, in blue ink, it read: "Piddling pad: For pee-wee Presbyterians." Although it sounded as if these cards were really for people with incontinence issues, I knew that I could pass the time writing notes to my dad. I picked up the miniature pencil from its holder beside the cards and wrote in a childish scrawl: "Dad-a roo, will you tell me a story tonight?" I furtively folded the card and poked my dad's large hand with it, careful to avoid the notice of my mother.

The organ blared on with bold and accusing flourishes. My dad opened the note, surveyed the contents and smiled. He picked up the pencil nearest him, which had several indentations in it—the telltale signs of some child's teeth—and wrote something on the card. He passed the card back to me, and I read the word "yes" in all capital letters, with an explanation point after it. Underneath this I wrote, "Be in my room at eight o'clock." He responded with a smiley face and "okay" in his characteristic, nearly illegible script.

All day long I treasured the thought of story time. It wasn't a very common occurrence, but it punctuated the tyranny of the mundane with glimpses of otherworldliness. My father, or my mother, for that matter, never discussed anything with me that I considered significant. My young mind obsessed over mysteries, like how cameras worked, or whether fairies existed. I wanted someone to tell me why I sometimes felt stabs of joy that seemed to have no explanation, when I saw the ghostly emerald-green glow of the backyard after a thunderstorm, when the water droplets hung like crystals, as if by magic, onto the verdant leaves. But no one ever shared in my secret world, which wasn't always a joyous one. Sometimes I had bizarre fears, such as the day the sun seemed to be going backwards in the sky, and I was terrified that some cosmic cataclysm was at hand. Questions nearly burned holes in my brain because they received no answers, and because I believed I was the only one in the world asking such questions.

When I grew older, I began to write feverishly each night in a notebook, recording every smoldering thought. I even personified the spirit of writing as an alter ego who could share with me in my struggles. I relied on "him" to the point of idolatry, exultant that I at last had found an antidote to my crushing loneliness. But this night I was too young to engage in such fancies, and all my thoughts revolved around the knowledge that somehow my dad and I would briefly connect in the world of imagination. His stories were always about animals, a passion we both shared. My dad taught me everything he knew about livestock. I was the only child in my school who knew what Dutch-belted cattle looked like. About 7:45, I snuggled into my bed and pulled the bedspread over me. I turned on the lamp on the table beside me. The lamp had a white lace lampshade, and the base consisted of a short brass pole topped with a globe of swirled pink and white glass. I often kept the lamp on at night for its consoling, soft halo of light, as I lay in bed, stuffed animals carefully arranged on both sides of me—warriors to defend me from the onslaught of evil.

At exactly eight o'clock my dad appeared in the doorway smiling and began to make his way across my green shag rug. He pulled up a chair beside the bed and sat down. I leaned closer in anticipation.

"How would you like to hear about Sammy Squirrel?" he said.

"Okay," I replied, wondering what adventures Sammy would meet in the tale.

"Once upon a time," my dad began, "there was a squirrel named Sammy. He lived with all his relatives in the Granger's attic." (The Grangers were our next-door neighbors. Dr. Granger was a dentist whom I disliked intensely. Once I had to knock on their door to borrow some baking powder, and he opened the door and grinned at me wickedly, or so it seemed to me. He asked me if I needed a bridge in my mouth. I spent the whole day imagining his trying to force the Golden Gate Bridge into my unwilling jaws.)

"One day," my dad continued, "Sammy, who was always getting into trouble, scampered into Dr. Granger's loft, leaped onto the ceiling fan and dropped a nut on Dr. Granger's head. The startled man jumped up so quickly his false teeth fell out, and he yelled for his wife with a mouth full of nothing but gums. 'FRANCES—THE SKY IS FALLING!'" I listened with rapt attention, giggling at the thought of Dr. Granger's empty gums. The story went on for nearly twenty minutes, and Sammy encountered a myriad of troubles, including nearly getting caught in a mousetrap that Dr. Granger had baited with a pecan. The story ended with Sammy's defeating Dr. Granger by inciting his whole squirrelly family to rip all the stuffing out of the hapless man's sofas, chairs, and bed, and replacing it with nutshells. They also left squirrel droppings inside his shoes. Dr. Granger was so disgusted that he abandoned the house and left it to the gleeful squirrels, who all lived happily ever after. Sammy Squirrel grew up to be the wise and respected mayor of all Squirreltown.

"That was great, Dad," I exclaimed as he finished.

"Now let's say our prayers," said my dad.

"Now I lay me down to sleep; I pray the Lord my soul to keep...." I tuned out the prayer, which seemed so dark and banal after the wild shenanigans of Sammy, but I dutifully closed my eyes anyway. "Goodnight," my dad said as he left the room. There was no hug or kiss, just one last smile as he disappeared into the hall.

In the darkness of my hospital room, thoughts of my dad's stories could almost make me smile despite myself. But then the apparition of my grandmother drifted into my exhausted brain, and I felt my body recoil with a very slight, involuntary movement. My parents and I would often make the five-hour trek to Anderson, South Carolina, where my mother's parents lived. My dad's father had died when he was four, and his mother had died before I was born. I would usually lie down in the back seat staring up at the sky to pass the time, dreading the approach of the large house made of white painted bricks. My grandmother was tall and large-boned, and she dwarfed my grandfather. At our arrival, no one hugged, and no one acknowledged my presence. I had become invisible, the ghost of a girl with hair like an apparition.

Days at my grandmother's house seemed to stretch on forever. We would sit in the well-furnished living room for hours, sometimes watching Jeopardy. The sing-song tune from the show would reverberate inside my head endlessly. When we weren't watching TV, we would listen to my grandmother complain: "Those good-for-nothings have stolen another one of my Hummel figurines...," she would begin, and we would be forced to listen to a bitter collection of diatribes about the supposedly kleptomaniac maids and gardeners she employed, repeated several times until it was etched in my memory. "Those good-for-nothings, those dad-gum thieves...." My mother would sit in submissive silence, nodding her head occasionally.

My dad would escape with my grandfather to the basement to play pool. My grandfather treasured his pool table and wouldn't let any of the grandchildren touch it. I would sometimes go down to the basement and run my hand surreptitiously across the green felt when no one was looking. I was fascinated by the score-keeping device that hung from the low ceiling. It consisted of a long wire stretched across the length of one wall. Strung on the wire were large bead-like circles that could be moved to indicate the score. My grandfather was a retired pharmacist who took cleanliness to an extreme. He washed his hands before doing anything and insisted that we do the same. His basement contained a large, top-opening freezer that was always stocked with multiple cartons of ice cream. He ate a huge bowl of ice cream every night of his life, saying it kept him young. There must have been some wisdom in the practice, because he lived to be ninety-three. My grandfather wanted everything ironed, including bedsheets and underwear.

I had heard rumors that my grandmother used to be humorous and fun-loving, until my grandfather's domineering ways broke her spirit. To me her spirit seemed twisted rather than broken. Gloom emanated from her like poisonous fumes. She usually looked right through me to the wall, but one day after lunch she cornered me, and to my horror, began to speak. "When we eat you need to chew quietly. You sound like a piggy at the trough." This was the only thing I could remember that she had ever said to me. She didn't wait for a reply, to my great relief, so I scurried past her looming body that was beginning to disappear through the swinging door into the dining room. I ran upstairs to the room where I was staying. It contained a cot padded with worn-out blankets, a wooden clothes-drying rack, and an ancient Singer sewing machine that ran on foot power. The wall was covered with forbidding-looking family portraits in Victorian frames. I would cower there for hours, battling with the gazes of dead relatives.

> That night I remembered how at ten
> I had poked a dressmaker's pin
> Into the cedar-paneled wall
> of my grandmother's upstairs bedroom.
> Year after year, on visits,
> I would run there like a chicken chased by a fox
> To see if someone had removed it.
> No one ever did.
> I always felt lonely then,
> As if I myself had been ignored.
> The walls of the house were dark
> with family portraits—
> Old bearded men in ornate gold frames
> And tired-eyed women whose mouths were pursed
> As if they'd eaten green persimmons.
> I wondered why they seemed to matter so much
> on this particular night—
> the straight pin, the glowering portraits?
> Why did the child inside me never leave the woman alone?
> She seemed perpetually at the moment of birth,
> Her brow pressed to her knees,
> Waiting for forever to end.

Burial

I used to creep
across the peculiar tundra of her living room;
Grandmother rocked in her metronome chair,
fierce beneath the hoarfrost of her hair.
In spring she prowled
through chosen flowers with her knife,
sorting them like sheep and goats:
Snapdragon, marigold;
violet, thorn.
How did they even grow there, in such cold?
But her arms always bloomed in the garden,
in the kitchen, where I found her
stiff in a fortress of fragrance.
Her portrait at sixteen
hung like an edict over the mantle,
her hair so long then
it swept past paint and frame to my imagination,
a Red Sea parting
to suffer the elect and swallow the damned.

Later, her legs became dangerous,
so they pruned her and arranged her in a bed,
aids and nurses forming a tidy border.
When they took the first one off,
I wondered if its soul went up to heaven
to wait for the rest.
Dizzy with the stink of flowers and alcohol,
she sprouted accusations:
"They're stealing me blind;
my crystal's gone—they've taken it all."
Her delicate champagnes were only suggestions of glass,
tentative as memory.
Later, we found them hidden everywhere—
one furtive in a box of felt hats,

wrapped in newspaper: August 2, 1949.
She died one afternoon,
an easy exchange of one silence for another.
Under the apocalyptic paintings of the funeral home,
my aunts swapped recipes,
irritated by the corpse's quiet tyranny.
Grandfather hovered over her face like a lonely god
breathing into a reluctant Eve,
stung by her insistent quiescence.
Only the lilies in her arms were moved.

She willed me a walnut metronome,
quite precise,
though she gave me no music for it to measure.
At 21 I look much like her,
and have often wanted to scratch her name off my face
so it won't seep past the skin.
Instead I will push her beneath the surface of thought
to my mind's deep loam,
where discarded things grow smaller
and wear their own dust,
or gestate like stiff bulbs in a reluctant garden,
that once buried,
sometimes flower.[30]

[30] Nancy Craig Zarzar, "Burial," in *Southern Poetry Review* (Spring 1992): 38-40. *Waiting for Pentecost* (Charlotte, NC: Main Street Rag, 2007), 16.

I was fifteen years old, sitting forlornly in my World Civilization class behind my ex- boyfriend, who had just become an "ex" the night before. He had given me my first kiss, which rather reminded me of being slobbered on by an eager dog, but it was a kiss nonetheless. He had called me on the phone to say that he thought we should just be "friends" from now on, and my emotions had wilted into a heap of nearly dead foliage. That night I tried to eat dinner—steak and salad—but the tender grilled meat had tasted like sand. It even seemed to have the texture of sand.

All my internal organs rose up in rebellion against the impossible fact that I had been rejected. The glory of having at last attracted a boyfriend, thereby becoming acceptable, had quickly dissipated like water swirling down a drain, and I was left with my familiar self without an identity, without connection to a world of people who seemed happy and perfect.

I knew that I didn't measure up, that personhood eluded me no matter what I did—until I had caught the notice of Yusef Farid. He was half Lebanese, half Scottish, which added a piquant, exotic flair to my conquest. As always, I fled for refuge into poetry, aware that pain could at least be squeezed into the form of beauty if one had the skill. That night I escaped to my room, and after sobbing into my pillow for the better part of an hour, I began to create, to seize the tangled threads of anguish and braid them, weave them into an orderly pattern:

Garden Vigil

The cruelest briar, the sharpest thorn
Is by a blushing flower worn.
And lovers lie within their clutch,
Forgetting thorns for gentle touch.
But then, alas, the gale must rise
And whirl the petals from their eyes.
Though one departs, the other must
Remain while petals turn to dust
And pine the night for fleeting morns,
Embraced by brambles, kissed by thorns,
Watching stalks among the mud
Her burning eyes await a bud.
The Lord, a seed of hope He sows
In one left waiting for a rose.

The Clock

The heart
is such
a cruel
(click)
machine
powder-white August nights
the engine
stops,
choking
(click)
the radio
in mid-explosion
asphalt and smoke and lace
(click)
the streetlight pales the stars
she says
never mind
(click)
he mumbles quietly against her hair
time falls like water
(click)
there is something I must tell you,
something I must tell—
(click)

the cuckoo crows in betrayal upon the hour

From Your Invisible Mistress

I am
A trick of light
Waiting in this room
For the rosary of your voice
Words like cool beads
On which I count the hours

With your kiss my flesh appears.
I bribe you with my body
To take my soul
And when you leave you are blind
To my face at the window
The tears seem to fall from glass
(I vanished as you shut the door)

Thus the words had become my lovers, more ardent, more faithful than any human could ever be. My soul was shattered, but I found the pieces arranged themselves in what seemed to me to be lovely mosaics, and I was enveloped in what seemed beautiful. There was no one there to tell me that my flower imagery was trite and cliched, and that the jilted lover theme was handled with a great deal of melodrama. Nevertheless, every significant experience I had, every hungry, aching need, I carried like an offering to my journal. It felt to me as if someone were dictating the words to me. They apparently flowed from an outside source that had become my intimate partner, a presence that was at once my soul mate, and someone robed in a mysterious otherness. I had found my home and my world to be populated with strangers, so I looked inside myself to find a dazzling, mysterious companion. He comforted me that night, cloaking my invisibility with a rich robe of significance. But a small chamber of my heart was still vulnerable, pumping agony to the rest of my body.

That morning in World Civilization class I was forced to once again stare at the back of Yusef's hair, which was black and shiny. I had fallen in love with his hair first, staring at it while the teacher droned on about the embalming process used by the ancient Egyptians. Now that he had rejected me, his hair glowed with a mocking aura. I felt a crushing pain in my chest, and my mind began to rebel against what had happened to me as if my heart were someone else's organ that had been transplanted into my body. *It couldn't be real,* I thought. But reality's noxious fumes filled my lungs, so denial was impossible. What could I do? Even the poetry didn't seem adequate to commemorate such an event. My mind began a frantic search, combing through possibilities like shells on a beach, intent on finding one perfectly shaped and unbroken. At last I decided on a solution. The teacher was explaining that the Egyptians pulled the dead person's brains out through his nose with a long hook. I shuddered but was undaunted. I methodically began to scrape my right thumb below the joint with the fingernail of my other thumb. At first this action left behind only white scratch marks, which then turned red, but at last I broke skin. I continued scraping through the whole class, feeling my anxiety seep out as blood finally and mercifully began to flow. Both my thumbs were streaked with blood as the bell rang. I pulled some Kleenex out of my backpack and wiped them clean. I felt empowered and vindicated. The wound healed quickly, but left a permanent scar—a small, white raised circle on my thumb.

It was Christmas. I was sixteen years old, looking forward to seeing my brothers and their wives. Since they had graduated from college my brothers had nearly disappeared into a world of real people who loved and talked and related, or so I thought. Meanwhile, I was left behind with my parents, who appeared to care only that I make good grades in school, keep my room clean, and wear a slip under my dresses. I only fulfilled the first of the three. I was methodically being raised by romance novels and reruns of *Love Boat* and *Fantasy Island*. At night, I would escape to my room and write furiously, sometimes penning letters to my brothers that I never sent. One such letter read:

Dearest John,

You do not know me, though perhaps you would not care for me if you did. For sixteen years I have wandered in this dream, and now it is murkier than ever; but yes, John, I do have a heart and it is capable of loving another human being. I am not merely a bundle of bizarre intellect and a cold mind that collects odd ideas as if they were rare breeds of birds. I have this heart and it is not made out of cement or marble or any other industrial strength material. I suppose it is made somewhat like yours, but beyond any doubt it has been maimed and broken and bruised. Right now, it is so incredibly still that I am not even certain that it is awake. But John, I love you, I love you, a hundred thousand times—I cannot say these words; I'm sure they would choke me

The letter ended there, without even a period, as if the words had broken beneath the weight of what I was attempting to say. I daydreamed about someone reading my journal because I felt that I would then be real, like the Velveteen rabbit who was transformed by fairies from an abandoned and shabby stuffed thing into a hopping, frisking creature. If only someone knew me as I really was; if only someone could look beyond the careful façade I constructed to protect myself. But that would be too dangerous. Who would approve of such a strange girl? And so, I wandered about the house that Christmas, taking in the tree decorated with an eclectic collection of ornaments. I dreamily fingered one of them—a ceramic Snoopy carrying a Christmas tree. He was hanging by a gold string beside a Victorian-looking angel. When my brothers arrived, I was delighted. They greeted my parents and me with little enthusiasm, as if they were reluctantly playing a role in a mediocre drama. At dinner everyone ate too much of the turkey my dad had grilled over charcoal, and the chocolate pie my mother always made for her bridge club. The conversation was predictable. How was work going? Fine. Busy. What ever happened to that client's dog that ate a pound of dark chocolate? He threw it up and got better. (My oldest brother was a veterinarian.) The grass surely grew fast last summer. Nearly wore out my lawnmower. Oh, really? After an hour of this I started to scream inside. *Won't someone say something meaningful? Who are all of you anyway? I don't know who you are!*

Finally, my dad announced that we were going to read the Christmas story. I listened, unmoved. I simply didn't grasp the tidings of great joy. They apparently belonged only to other people. Afterwards, we opened presents. My brother John opened one of his presents first. The promising-looking box contained only a pair of brown bedroom shoes.

"Wow. Thanks, Mother and Daddy." This scenario repeated itself about twenty-one times, until the neatly arranged packages had been transformed into piles of crumpled gilt paper, reused boxes from last Christmas, and the plethora of items that had been concealed inside them. I felt a familiar pang of emptiness and regret, as if someone had walked across my yard after the first snowfall and left ugly, muddy footprints behind. The packages had promised everything, as usual, but did not deliver. Nothing had changed. I was now the proud owner of a powder-blue sweater, a butter knife in my silver pattern, and three leather-bound books, but the "great joy" simply didn't materialize. For a while we all milled around in the living room, where hung a large, decorative ball made of huge quantities of plastic wrap in tufts. Glued to the bottom of the ball was a sprig of plastic mistletoe, complete with red berries. No one kissed under it. The dull repartee resumed, until finally my brothers and their wives made their escape, pleading responsibilities at home. I knew I would not see them again for at least six months. I watched out the living room window as their cars backed down the long driveway. It was a difficult driveway to maneuver unless you were used to it, so my brothers left a few tire marks on the grass. My parents and I were left with the disheartening task of cleaning up the remains of dinner and gift opening. I felt like an undertaker shoveling soil on top of a casket. Although there had not been much life in the gathering, it had at least been an out-of-the-ordinary kind of nothingness, a break from the routine. My mother told me to pick up all the wrapping paper and try to smooth some of it out to use for next year. I was to save all the bows for the same purpose.

When the house had been restored to an insipid order, my dad turned off the Christmas tree, and we all went to bed. After the holidays were over, for my creative writing class I wrote a fictionalized account of my family's Christmas gathering. I called it "The Strangers."

I was lying on a bottom bunk in a rustic cabin at a Presbyterian camp an hour away from Raleigh. I was staring at the underside of the bed above me. It reads: "Dirk was here. Life sucks. Maureen is hot." I stopped reading and began to listen to the conversations around me. All the girls from my Sunday school class were unpacking their gear and chattering. We were on a weekend retreat that my parents had forced me to attend. I had told them that the other high-school kids were mean, but they insisted that I go anyway. They informed me I would benefit from the spiritual instruction. The girls suddenly started giggling, and I wondered what was causing the stir. I looked toward the floor, where Melissa was opening her suitcase and pulling out a small, amber-colored flask.

"It's whiskey," she whispered. "I stole it from my dad's liquor cabinet. You guys want some?"

Everyone eagerly crowded around for a swig, and I continued to lie on my bed, feeling suddenly righteous. I know that the boys had taken advantage of the cover of darkness and were sitting in a circle in the woods, smoking marijuana. The trees were hovering around them like dark sentinels. Earlier I had overhead Elizabeth and her boyfriend discussing contraceptives. Elizabeth was Catholic, the girlfriend of one of my Sunday school classmates. Suddenly the giggles erupted again, and I returned my gaze to the floor, where the girls were gathered. Melissa had accidentally spilled the whiskey into her suitcase and was trying to wipe it up with her towel.

"Uh-oh. It got all over my Bible." This remark was greeted by a paroxysm of more giggles. I was beginning to muse over the spiritual instruction I was receiving, when a heretofore silent observer spoke from directly above me. I recognized the masculine-sounding voice as belonging to Pat Baker, a girl with a box-like face and cropped hair. She apparently did not know I was in the room.

"Have you seen that stuck-up little scumbag, Nancy Craig?" said the voice in a raucous tone. I felt my stomach sinking. I saw that the other girls had gone pale and silent. Several of them were gesturing violently toward my bunk.

"Oh," said Pat. Everyone was quiet for a moment, then Pat burst out loudly.

"I don't care if she hears me. She is a stuck-up little scumbag." The others began to chortle. I felt the heat rising in my face, so I slipped out of my bunk, out the door and into the waiting night. I wondered if I were going to be sick. The woods no longer seemed lovely or deep, but treacherous. In the distance I could see the orange glow of the boys' joints like misplaced stars.

Later that night we all gathered to sing hymns and play games. The youth minister was in charge. All the students secretly despised him and looked for opportunities to make fun of him behind his back. Melissa suggested we play the "chicken game," which no one had heard of.

"It's easy," she says. This is all you do. You squat down, flap your arms like wings and say, 'And the chickens get down and lay them eggs.' Then you cackle."

The youth minister, attempting to be polite, agreed to the game, although no one knew its object. The boy next to Melissa, Parker, squatted down, flapped his arms, and made the required speech. Then he cackled. In horror, I was counting how many students there were between me and Parker. Several more students performed the ritual. Next in the circle was the youth minister. He squatted, flapped, and cackled with fervor. Unbeknownst to him, Melissa slipped out of her chair and scurried behind the youth minister to lay a small object on his chair. As he was beginning to sit down, an egg rolled off his chair and onto the floor, where it cracked, spewing out its yellow and white liquid. Laughter erupted. The youth minister opened his mouth to speak, then closed it. His pock-marked face began to bloom with embarrassment. Finally, he laughed tentatively.

"Well," he said, "let's sing some more hymns. How about 'Amazing Grace?'" The group settled down, someone pulled a guitar out of a case, and we began to sing.

"Amazing grace/ How sweet the sound/ That saved a wretch like me...."

Scumbag like me, I thought.

The next day, someone snitched on the perpetrators, and all the liquor and marijuana were confiscated. The youth minister led a devotion that night, and afterwards addressed what had occurred.

"Some of you didn't participate in what went on last night. You're thinking, 'I don't smoke. I don't drink. I don't sleep around or hang around with those who do.'" There was a slight pause that hovered over us with a pregnant silence. "You're probably thinking you're better than everyone else because you don't do those things. But you're not."

His lecture ended there. I was appalled. *Surely I deserved some kind of consolation prize for being the shy, righteous victim of insult who had never touched a drop of alcohol? Where was the justice in the minister's strange speech? What kind of God did he believe in anyway?* As I continued my puzzled musings, everyone began to scatter. I went over to the snack table, where a girl stood with her back turned. I didn't recognize her as Pat, because she wasn't wearing the chains around her waist. She turned around and faced me, to my horror, and moved slightly forward. She held a Styrofoam cup in her hand, which she pushed toward me. "Want some hot chocolate?" she muttered sheepishly. I took the cup from her hand and felt its warmth spreading to my trembling fingers. I wondered what had happened, and if I were still a stuck-up little scumbag. I had no idea that I had just witnessed grace. Even in the present, on my hospital bed, I saw only an innocent victim—me—and a culpable perpetrator. How many ravaging years were left to stumble through before granting and receiving forgiveness would even occur to me!

I was in high school, and dancing in the high school cafeteria with Fred, a classmate who worked part-time programming computers for a clothing store for plus-size women. His hair was white-blonde and puffed up on top of his head. It was a Sadie Hawkins dance, but he had invited me to go. It was our first date. The mirror ball spinning above us was peppering my two-piece, lime-green sweater dress with squares of light. The sweater had no buttons. The two flaps were held together by a tie around the waist. My mother had bought the dress for me half-price at an outlet store. Fred's arms were clutching me possessively, and his head was on my shoulder. He was not really my type. I remembered my journals, beginning as early as the summer after fifth grade, in which night after night I would write: "How I wish I had someone to hold me, to put his arms around me…." At last it had happened. I tried to decide if the embrace met expectations. It didn't, but it was better than nothing. It had been a year since the World Civilization class, and I had survived, even after overhearing Yusef refer to me as "that ugly slut I used to date."

The song changed from Abba's "Dancing Queen" to a Bee-Gees tune. Everyone began to gyrate wildly to the music, but Fred kept me in his arms, swaying to some slow, unheard melody in his head. After the dance, Fred took me in his ancient, enormous truck that backfired frequently to the parking lot behind McDonald's. His car didn't have power steering, so at every turn he would muster all the force of his thin arms and violently assail the steering wheel. We sat in the car for a while discussing the dance, then suddenly Fred slipped across the seat and kissed me hungrily. He told me earlier he had had a root canal that day. I wondered how it felt to kiss after having had a root canal. I figured he must be on some heavy-duty drugs. The kiss went on for some time when I felt Fred's hands fumbling with the tie around my waist. He managed to undo the knot, and the sweater opened slightly. I felt his hands move underneath it. I froze for a moment, then relaxed as I felt the curious sensation. "I love you," Fred muttered several times, and I felt my heart begin to pound. No one had ever addressed those words to me before, so they rang with a monumental sound. I was sixteen years old. Fred continued his caresses until somewhere deep inside me a voice spoke, dredging up from my innermost being the shred of dignity and self-respect that I still owned. I pulled away from his embrace, rearranged my sweater and retied the belt.

"That's enough," I said firmly.

"Okay," Fred replied.

"I need to be getting home now." Fred obediently started up the truck, gunning the engine, and began the laborious task of turning the car around. I was silent all the way home.

So, this is love… repeated like an insistent refrain in my mind. I felt mildly confused. Fred kissed me again before I got out and told me he loved me. I walked up the driveway to my back door, the floodlights illuminating the yard like police searchlights. I opened the screen door, letting it slam behind me. As I went inside I noticed a gaping hole in the mesh, where the dog had tried to jump through several years ago. In the kitchen, the clock hands pointed to midnight. My parents were waiting for me at the kitchen table.

"How was your date?" they asked me.

"Fine," I replied. I kept walking, through the den and down the dark hallway to my bedroom. "I love you, love you, love you," tapped my heels on the hardwood. A fly was buzzing around my head. I swatted at it, then opened my bedroom door. I felt enlightened.

It was the summer of my 18th year, and I was with my parents on a three-week tour of ten European countries. Our tour group consisted mainly of women over seventy who were hoping to grasp longevity by becoming quietly drunk and giggling at every restaurant that we patronized. Three in particular—Dot, Violet, and Ada—had taken me under their wing to shield me from the ever-vigilant supervision of my mother, so that I could sip French and Italian wine unhindered. There were two other young girls on the trip who had captured the imagination of the elderly trio, and we formed a tight-knit group of six, determined to bring down the Eiffel Tower and the Vatican with our inebriated carousing. I was also in a secret but unconscious tournament with the other two girls—Chris and River—over who was the most beautiful and could attract the most European men. We all shamelessly flirted with our non-English-speaking Italian bus driver, Claudio, who much to my chagrin seemed to have placed his affections on River. But I was confident that there were other masculine prey to pursue.

One night in Rome our tour group was scheduled to have dinner at an Italian hotel, and all the older women were fussing and clucking in dissimulating fear because they had heard that Italian men loved to pinch American women on the buttocks. Fear or not, I noticed that Dot, Violet, and Ada's cheeks were blushing with rouge, and their bluish hair looked as though they had slept in tightly rolled curlers. Spirits were high among the young girls as well. I chose my clothing carefully—a close-fitting red jumpsuit that I thought perfectly accentuated my slim figure. When the much-anticipated night arrived, we boarded the bus, and Claudio cranked it up and whisked us rather treacherously through the streets of Rome to the hotel where we were to eat. We were somewhat abruptly ushered into a room furnished with a very long table and decorated with garish, gold and naked cherubs. As we filed into the room, I desperately tried to discreetly part company from my parents, but my mother was behind me holding onto me by my belt, as if daring any young Italian to touch her daughter. Years later, as a grown woman, I learned to appreciate her motherly instincts and wisdom, but at the moment she seemed a monumental obstacle to my fervid quest for titillation. I tried to seat myself next to my elderly compatriots, but my mother dragged me by my belt to a seat between her and my father, who was engaged in a one-sided conversation with a rather annoyed-looking Italian. My father, good-natured and somewhat naïve, could and would talk to anything that breathed, for as long as possible.

During the meal I kept trying to make eye-contact with any waiter I could capture in my crosshairs. I ignored my food, which consisted of a bony, overcooked pork chop and a generous helping of gelatinous green peas. An entire crew of waiters was constantly circling our table, to whisk away empty plates and fill up wine glasses (except, of course, mine—my mother had made a point of turning all three of our goblets upside down). Just as I was beginning to give up on excitement for the evening, I heard loud big band music blaring from the overhead speakers, and the waiters rushed around the table in a line, like kindergartners playing duck-duck-goose.

Suddenly I heard an elderly woman squeal, and I looked up just in time to see Violet blushing to the roots of her hair and exclaiming, "Oh my stars and little fishes! He pinched me on the butt!" Then the proverbial all-hell broke loose. Waiters poured into the room from every door and began to thus pinch all the women, setting off a cacophony of gleeful squeals. My mother's face practically erupted into her most censorious frown, which remained until she, too, became a target. She gave an involuntary screech, then frantically tried to push away the waiter, whom she saw in horror had moved on to greener pastures—me. I felt the squeeze on my posterior, and was mulling over whether I liked it or not, when suddenly the waiter bent down and assailed me with a rough French kiss. Then he handed me a rose, which I placed in the empty wine bottle in front of me—after I had regained my composure, of course.

My mother looked stricken for a moment, then turned to my dad and howled, "Dad-gummit, did you see that, Brad?" But she didn't wait for an answer. She grabbed me by the arm and dragged me out of the dining room and into the hotel lobby, where she sat beside me for the rest of the evening—a righteously-indignant sentinel. I begged to return to the dinner, but she just kept mumbling something about a "den of iniquity" and kept her hand clamped onto my arm.

After what seemed an interminable stint in the purgatorial shadow of my mother's frown, Claudio emerged from the dining room to tell us that the bus was getting ready to leave for our hotel. My dad came out also, his face beaming with a characteristic grin. He was a good-natured man anyway, but I wondered if he had made good use of his time without my mother's oversight. As I got into bed that night, I swore to myself that tomorrow I would keep the sun from setting until I had run headlong into an adventure. I could feel the adrenaline surging through me as I lay in bed, kept awake by the stertorous duet of my parents' snoring. I remembered what my childhood heroine Scarlett O'Hara told herself in difficulties: "After all, tomorrow is another day."

The next morning we woke up early to catch the tour bus to the Colosseum and then on to the Vatican. I had little respect for anything Catholic—what good could come from a bunch of celibate men in dresses? And I knew they had a penchant for the overly ornate—"tacky" in my mother's vocabulary. But I knew there were bound to be attractive Italian men there.... On the bus ride on the way to the Colosseum, since we were going to have our tour group picture there, I took out a pair of toenail clippers, peered into the reflective metal to monitor the state of my hair and face. I preferred a dimly reflective, narrow surface that would show me only parts of my physiognomy, which I unconsciously considered unattractive. (Because of this strange habit, my mother had taken me to the eye-doctor, thinking I had some strange optic sensitivity.)

"She won't even look in the mirror without squinting!" she had told him.

He had looked at me approvingly and told my mother, "She's not seeing bad."

She had responded with a frustrated "humph." Nevertheless, I was hoping for the best in regard to the photograph. When we arrived at the Colosseum, the photographer shooed us out of the bus and onto the grassy area in front of the tallest remaining section of the structure. Then she lined us up in four neat rows, told us to smile, and moved away to snap the picture. For a moment I thought it incongruous that we should create smiling memorabilia where thousands of people had once been violently killed, but the thought quickly vanished as I decided to make one last modification to my hair. I froze my face into a smile and held it that way until the photo session ended. Years later, looking at my pert face and stylish clothes in the souvenir picture, I felt a keen sense of astonishment and guilt that I could have been so oblivious to the weightiness of such a place. Surely the ground was so ponderous with the voices of oblations that we all should have hidden our faces. And why could I not hear the ever-living murmur of inculpable blood from beneath the ground? But I just walked nonchalantly back to the bus in anticipation of visiting St. Peter's Basilica, and before I knew it we had abandoned the Colosseum and its ponderous memories.

As we walked through the ninety-foot columns at the entrance to St. Peter's, I forgot my aversion for churches and became duly impressed with the complex beauty of the place. I had just entered the largest church in the world, I mused, and it was superbly ornate. Everywhere I wandered in the vast expanse was decorated with mosaics and statues. Crowds crushed against me, muttering in a cacophony of tongues I could not understand. Suddenly, in the midst of the garish pulchritude, I noticed an alcove containing the likeness in marble of a seated woman with a nearly naked full-grown man draped limply across her lap. I walked forward to the glass that kept the crowds at a distance from the sculpture, and I stared. It occurred to me this was the only statue of a woman I had seen in St. Peter's—the plethora of others were replicas of men. Being largely ignorant in regard to art, I had never seen a pietà before, but I vaguely recognized the woman as Mary, holding the dead body of her son. Suddenly, I gasped audibly, as if something ancient and sharp had pierced my lungs. The exquisite marble image of the Dead was so, inexplicably, alive. The mother held a burden that no one could hold—the corpse of God—yet she was strong. Everything about the sculpture suggested weight; the folds of Mary's garment rippled with it. The dead son's body seemed to overwhelm the small feminine hand with splayed fingers. She stared down at the impossible, the unforgivable, the irreversible. But, oh God, her face… Why did I look at her face and see a heavy peace, a serenity I myself had never known? What did she know that I did not? I had never wanted to touch anything so desperately as I did that hand of

Christ that even in death seemed to clutch at Mary's garment. I put my hand on the glass barrier, willing in my soul that I should distill from this woman her strange tranquility, that I should bear the dead body of my own desires with such equanimity, that I should be, like her, forever transfixed upon the only sight that mattered. But the gossamer thread that held me to desire broke suddenly as I heard my mother screeching across the basilica—"Naaaaaaancy. We're going to miss the bus!"

That night I couldn't sleep. Amid the whooshing and rattling of the ancient air conditioner, I lay awake trying to understand the peculiarity of the woman's face, and the allure of a dead Man. I got up very quietly and crept into the bathroom with a pencil, desperate for something to write on. I frantically unwrapped the paper cover from a roll of toilet tissue, smoothed it out on the bathroom floor, and began to write on it:

Pieta[31]

I shaped Him from soft clay
In the strange, ocher light of winter.

His thighs were like doves
Cupped in my hands—
Trembling;

His mouth,
Two ibis in mirrored flight
Parting beneath my fingers.

I breathed myself into Him
And now He is draped
Like a soft, heavy bird
In my arms.

He is made of words.

In my loneliness
I wait for Him to speak.

---

[31] Nancy Zarzar, "Pieta," in *Waiting for Pentecost,* (Charlotte, NC: Main Street Rag, 2007), 41.

The next morning, I got up as if nothing had happened, as if I had not been stunned by the cunning blow of God. I labored over my makeup, wound my long hair into a piquant bun on the top of my head, and hid all my angst under a hot pink blouse and miniskirt. But somehow, unaccountably, a die had been cast.

A mist was rising in my mind, a thick and terrible darkness such as fell on Abraham when God passed through the rent animal pieces. Yet this time it was no god passing through, and the rent pieces came from my own soul. A memory arrived, raven-like, to peck at me without mercy. I was nineteen years old, dancing with Apollos Godfree in a bar near my college. The strobe lights, in tandem with the thunderous beat of the music, pierced my body with strange exhilaration. The two contraband beers I had drunk had made me slightly giddy. I was unaware that a shadow had fallen over me that year, drawing me imperceptibly to the edge of a chasm. I was pursued by an unnamed darkness, a carrion-eater, that waited for me to step into death. His hunger breathed into my face, but I was only aware of the incongruous mixture of alcohol and the heady, exotic-scented cologne that Apollos always wore. For some reason it reminded me of pine trees, a dense forest where I could possibly be swallowed up, and I was longing to be consumed by something, heedless of the distinction between being consumed and being destroyed. Apollos had a girlfriend back home, but he had dated me without qualms all year. I knew he longed to add me to the list of his sexual exploits, but I doggedly hung on to what I believed was my virtue. I could not give myself away completely, although I toyed with destructive intimacy until there was very little of myself left. Apollos was older than I was, and tall, with curly blond hair and dark green eyes that belied the danger lurking inside. I thought he resembled a Greek statue, cast in flesh instead of marble. Apollos had quickly assessed my weaknesses and had begun at once to prey on them.

One evening we were lying in his bed and he began to gently caress my face with his fingers. I was surprised by this uncharacteristic tenderness, and my heart began to throb with an infatuation that I did nothing to check. I was overcome with elation until Warren, Apollos's roommate, came in and stared at me strangely.

"Nancy," he finally said, "what's that black stuff on your face?" My hands instinctively moved toward my cheeks, as if to ward off a blow. I slowly edged toward the mirror, squinting as I always did so I would not have to bear the full effect of my face. Impossibly, I saw random black streaks like gashes across my forehead, cheeks, and chin. For a moment I was confused, wondering what poison had sprung from my skin to discolor it, until I turned around and noticed the bicycle next to the bed, complete with its greasy chain. I took one look at Apollos's face, with its air of amused triumph, and scurried out of the room like a hunted thing, rubbing my face furiously as I ran down the hall. The next night we went out again, as if nothing had happened. I was willing to sacrifice nearly anything because of my fascination for Apollos. I had dated Fred until the end of high school, unmoved by him, yet clinging to him out of a need for security. He was in love with me, but I casually broke off the relationship without a qualm as soon as college began. But Apollos had bewitched me by some unknown enchantment that devoured me, and strangely, made me long to be devoured.

That next night we were alone in his room, and Apollos began to whisper in a lilting voice: "I could lure you into the woods and no one would know. I could rape you, and no one would hear you scream. I could even kill you and get away with it. Everyone would think you committed suicide because they know you've been depressed lately." His words penetrated me like a charm, and I stared at him, fascinated, as if at the face of Death himself. He was right about the depression. As my relationship with Apollos became more intense, the world around me had become distorted and strange. I felt as if I had gone back to my home one day and found that someone had rearranged all the furniture in a bizarre pattern, without explanation, and when I attempted to move it back, it wouldn't budge. I had become obsessed with the musical theme from *The Exorcist*, a song like the pealing of hundreds of mad bells, and one night when I was with Apollos on the sidewalk outside my dorm, I heard its mesmerizing sound seeping through a window on the third floor. I stopped, transfixed, the music etching itself on my soul like a prophecy of doom. Apollos stared at me, aware that I was being transported into otherworldliness.

He loved to analyze me and seemed to thrive on my vulnerability. "I don't know what it is about you," he told me one day, "but you're so much fun to hurt." He also told me that he was drawn by my innocent, child-like qualities. All the other women he had dated had been experienced and easily conquered, but I remained in some ways aloof and pristine, untouched by his persistent hands. I knew things about him that I considered unspeakable, so I constantly struggled with a horrified uneasiness and disgust. But the person of Apollos himself kept drawing me back, as if I were swimming furiously toward a shore of safety, but always pulled out to sea again by an unforgiving tide. Thus I clung to my infatuation almost to the point of madness.

Apollos had even coaxed me into visiting an adult bookstore. I was deliberately dressed in a girlish-looking pink wool sweater with pearl buttons, and white silk pants. I carried a white wool coat that had been made in Czechoslovakia. As we walked into the store, I held my head up as if someone righteous had at last graced the doors of the place. As I stared at the paraphernalia, I told myself that I didn't belong there like Apollos did. I was only visiting, observing without taking part. In the back were a dozen small cubicles with doors where one could watch pornographic movies. We watched several, but I remained detached, again telling myself that I was somehow different from others who went there. After all, I believed in God and went to church! Thus I elevated my whitewashed hypocrisy over his honest depravity. After we got bored with the movies, we drove home in Apollos's bright red Mustang. And there I was, once again in a "den of iniquity," as my dad would say. I was in Apollos's arms, entranced, barely moving as Prince's "Purple Rain" blared from the multiple speakers.

> I never meant 2 cause u any sorrow
> never meant 2 cause u any pain
> I only wanted 2 one time see u laughing
> I only wanted 2 see u laughing in the purple rain
>
> Purple rain purple rain
> Purple rain purple rain
> Purple rain purple rain
> I only wanted 2 see u bathing in the purple rain
>
> I never wanted 2 be your weekend lover
> I only wanted 2 be some kind of friend
> Baby I could never steal u from another

Its such a shame our friendship had 2 end
Purple rain purple rain
Purple rain purple rain
Purple rain purple rain

I only wanted 2 see u underneath the purple rain[32]

I could almost feel the purple rain enveloping me in a mixture of fascination, disgust, and an incomprehensible proclivity for destruction. Apollos tightened his embrace and spoke softly, although the noise was overwhelming. I heard him anyway, as if my ears were tuned only to the sound of his voice, to the exclusion of all others. "You know, Nancy, that in my own way, I love you." I was startled, elated, and horrified all at once. I began to see love as a killer who gorged on blood. I began to believe that this was the love I was destined for, and the knowledge left me weak and shaken. As we walked out onto the patio of the bar together, I noticed an incongruous object in the corner: an upside down, abandoned toilet. I knew it was a sign, but I took no heed. We left the bar and walked back to campus, the night sky drizzling me with a soft rain that could bring no redemption.

On my hospital bed I began to shudder in both body and mind as this last and most distressing snapshot appeared to my mental eyes. I remembered how the relationship with Apollos had intensified until I had almost reached a point of no return. My schoolwork began to suffer slightly. One night I even took out an X-Acto knife and cut a tiny incision on my left wrist. I emitted vague distress calls to my parents, who were concerned, but all I remembered my mother saying was, "You're not going to make any B's, are you?" Yet in her letters, which she wrote to me faithfully, she unveiled a side of herself I had never seen before. She tried to encourage me to rely on God in the face of my difficulties, and she seemed to have keen insight into the spiritual tug-of-war going on within me. She told me that she and Edith (her African-American housecleaner and close

---

[32] Prince and the Revolution, "Purple Rain," from the album *Purple Rain*, released June 25, 1984, by Warner Bros. Records.

friend, despite the fact that they both distrusted people of the "other race") would scrub floors together and pray for me.

Once I described to her a dream I had that appeared to continue even after I was awake. In my sleep, a gray mist-like presence emerged from my head and swirled around it violently, leaving me with the distinct impression of captivity. I struggled to escape the presence, but it continued to hover around my head. When I opened my eyes, I saw the gray cloud rushing away from my head toward the open window, through which it disappeared. When she heard the dream, her only comment was, "I've thought for a long time that Satan was after you." Around that time, I began to hear that same message from a source that I readily identified as God, although I had long since given up praying. A few times I had made some feeble attempts to tell Apollos that he needed God, but I still had no idea that my own soul was equally dark.

However, halfway through the fall semester of my sophomore year, I began to sense that I was in danger. Although I did not understand the idea of original sin, I knew that my relationship with Apollos had been like a key that opened up an abyss in my soul, and when I peered into it I saw the face of demons like gargoyles that had come to life within me. I knew that despite what Apollos said, he did not love me, though I had no well-defined concept of love. Yet somewhere deep inside, a Voice told me that love was an exquisite, holy thing that bore no resemblance to the sexual and emotional manipulation game that Apollos played with me. It was as if I heard inside me the voice of prophecy:

Fallen! Fallen is Babylon the Great!
She has become a dwelling for demons
and a haunt for every impure spirit,
a haunt for every unclean bird,
a haunt for every unclean and detestable animal.
For all the nations have drunk
the maddening wine of her adulteries....
Come out of her, my people,
so that you will not share in her sins,
so that you will not receive any of her plagues....[33]

---

[33] Revelation 18:2-3; 4b (NIV).

I suspected then that, through no goodness of my own, I did not truly belong on that campus, which was a pit of illicit sexuality and other evils, that my destiny, whatever it was, lay beyond the reach of this man who delighted in destroying me. Spurred on by the clear warning to flee, I made plans to transfer to Davidson College, where I had wanted to go in the first place but didn't apply to because I thought I wasn't intelligent enough to be accepted there. And so I left Babylon behind, with a vague and disturbing knowledge of my own depravity, yet no real sense of how to be redeemed. I would wander in the dark for several more years before the darkness itself would overtake me and forcibly catapult me into the waiting Light.

As I reviewed my life that night, each memory reopened a small section of the ravaging wound in my soul until despair came pouring out, unstaunched. My anger had quelled, but settled quietly in a corner, waiting for an opportune time to erupt again. In my musings I had seen the gaping blankness of my beginnings, and how I had struggled to write in blood some form of meaning there. But could the ordinary struggles of a typically dysfunctional family and schoolyard bullying explain the severe break with reality that I had experienced? Somehow, I didn't think it could. I also recognized that my own foolish choices had contributed to the disaster, but even those could not fully account for my fragmented state. As I considered this, I remembered Hopkins' "mind-mountains;" my memories stretched formidably before me fiercer and more unforgiving than the Alps, and I hung there, unable to scale them anymore. I was reminded of lines from another of Hopkins' untitled sonnets:

> Not, I'll not, carrion comfort, Despair, not feast on thee;
> Not untwist, slack they may be—these last strands of man
> In me, or, most weary, cry I can no more. I can;
> Can something hope, wish day come, not choose not to be.[34]

---

[34] Gerard Manley Hopkins, ("Carrion Comfort"), in *The Poems of Gerard Manley Hopkins*, 4th edition, ed. W. H. Gardner and N. H. Mackenzie (New York: Oxford University Press, 1967), 99.

I took comfort in the familiar thoughts of a man from another era that resonated with my own. Though we were separated in time and space, this Jesuit priest and I, we had become one in experience. So I curled up tightly on my bed, as if to brace for impact, and wished for day to come, choosing once again to be.

5

You Can Check Out Any Time You Like

*T*HE DAYS BEGAN to take on a strange rhythm. I was entering my fourth week in the hospital, and I almost started to forget my former life and become someone else, someone who belonged behind locked doors, someone whose life reeked of brokenness. I had seen my depravity before, like a psychological shadow that looked and talked like me but came out only in the night of my soul, leaving behind evil and destruction. I had accepted darkness as part of my birthright, as something that must be flooded with divine light to be incapacitated, and I knew that it never would be in this life. But I had not anticipated gazing within myself and seeing gaping holes with ragged edges. They had formed surreptitiously, with few symptoms, until at last my moth-eaten emotional framework had given way. I didn't know what to make of myself anymore.

I felt the strangeness most often on "field trips," when a few lucky patients boarded a van (one that, fortunately, I thought, did not read "Ivy Hill Hospital" on the side) and went somewhere "normal." One night the patients were taken to see the movie "Sea of Love," which I had heard was about a psychopathic serial killer. I wondered at the wisdom of such a choice, but I kept my mouth shut and waited for a more innocuous occasion. I soon found myself with Chase, Roland, and Patrick (a middle-aged lawyer), and a handful of other patients in the van with two nurses, on the way to the art museum. When we piled out into the parking lot of the museum, I felt the alien-ness creep over me. I had been to the museum probably a dozen times, but never with a guard. I was someone else now. I wondered if my skin were going to turn slightly green, or if I were going to sprout antennae. I speculated about what people thought when they saw us—the normal people, that is. We looked like everyone else, but I could feel some kind of force field around us, as if we had just popped in from a parallel universe. We were walking freely about, in a free country, but we were prisoners. Apparently "Hotel California" wasn't a place at all—it was an identity. Roland followed behind me like an oblivious puppy and didn't look at any of the paintings. Chase looked but scowled at all of them. The only one he seemed drawn to was a huge white canvas that was bare except for a rather small black circle in the center, or was it slightly off-center? He stared at it so long the nurse had to prompt him to keep up with the group.

My thought processes had normalized to a certain extent since I'd been on the medication, but still some of the paintings disturbed me. I was horrified by a painting of a man in old-fashioned pilot's attire running through a barren field. The field and the man shared the same dull ocher color. The painting haunted me for some reason. When we reached the gift shop, I saw the scene reproduced on a postcard, so I bought it. I don't think I ever looked at it again, but I thought of it often as somehow representative of my mind. Some of the paintings gave me an irrepressible urge to jump inside them and become paint on a canvas myself. The museum had a Monet in its collection, and when I saw it, at once I longed to be painted in the scene as an indistinguishable smudge of watercolor. Perhaps if I were two-dimensional, all my hidden strangeness would disappear. If I only had no depth, there would be no place for the emptiness....

Patrick was giving Chase and Roland a lecture on painting techniques, it seemed. Even Roland looked bored, if that were possible. Patrick pretended to know a lot about everything. He even offered to critique my poetry for me, and I took him up on the offer, without knowing why. He obviously knew nothing about poetry. He wrote little comments like "nice" and "interesting" all over the page, and at the end wrote a brief exhortation to "revise." His status as a know-it-all would not have been so ridiculous if we (Chase and I) had not passed his room one night and seen right through his open door, into his bathroom where he sat on the toilet, with his bare knees visible, as well as his dark polyester pants bunched up around his ankles. We were speechless for a moment, but after we had walked safely down the hall a few yards and recovered from our shock, we burst into helpless laughter. What could have possessed the man to leave BOTH doors open?

"He's really a mental case," I remarked ironically to Chase, whom I had never seen laugh before. I was oblivious to the fact that I was desperately attempting to whitewash the darkness and absurdity of my own inner world by highlighting the weaknesses of other people. I also did not see that cruelty possesses an awful fecundity that drives it to reproduce itself: that slap across the face that I had suffered at the hands of Jared Burkley, I was now inflicting unawares on Patrick. I only knew that I felt an uncontrollable desire to laugh at the ludicrous atrocities that I saw around me, that threatened to engulf me like the pseudopods of a giant amoeba. Like all of us, Patrick was always struggling to retain the shards of his dignity in a most undignified situation. He enjoyed playing the part of the therapist in our group therapy sessions, throwing out remarks like "How did that make you feel, Naomi?" or "Can you tell us more about that?" He never revealed anything about himself, as if he were playing a carefully scripted role intended to cover all signs of mental illness. But Chase and I knew better. The bathroom scenario gave him away. This was the first time we had seen him on a field trip. He was attempting to act as guide: "And over here we have some exquisite Egyptian artifacts…"

After we had exhausted the museum, we scuttled in a kind of self-conscious clump back to the van. It was warm for October. I was fanning myself with the haunting postcard. The van inevitably propelled us back to the hospital, where we belonged. I was teetering on the edge of anxiety. It was time for my afternoon medication. The field trip had only succeeded in pointing out my peculiarities. Perhaps I was better off sequestered, with no hazardous objects or substances, like makeup, which they still kept up at the desk for me. I tried to imagine someone eating it, since it must be poisonous. It annoyed me to have to waltz all the way down the hall, hiding my bare face behind my wet hair, to retrieve my cosmetics. It seemed an insufferable indignity. I shuddered at the memory, fresh from that morning.

After receiving my medication, a bland-looking, smooth gray pill, I was told the doctor wanted to see me. I found my way to the coffin-like room again, willing myself to look undepressed. My doctor looked rather disheveled, as always, as if he had been up all night delivering babies or something, which of course, he had not.

"You're doing much better," he announced, without asking for my opinion. "You're going to be discharged tomorrow."

117

Discharged. Wasn't that for people leaving the military? I wondered if it would be an honorable discharge.

"You look better, too," he added. "You were pretty depressed when you came in here."

I wondered if I were really "well," or if my insurance had just run out. We patients always joked that people became mysteriously better when their insurance ran out.

"However," began the doctor, and I winced. There was a "however."

"However, you are not well enough to begin normal activities yet. I want you to attend day hospital for two weeks as a transition time. You will spend part of your day here, and then you will have evenings at home." Home meant my parents' house, since my roommate had decided to get an apartment by herself for a while before she got married. I had a sudden flashback to the perfect, blonde-colored hardwoods in my bedroom. There had been blood there. "What's done cannot be undone."[35] Perhaps, like Lady MacBeth, I would continue to see the blood, though no doubt the floor had been carefully purged.

I nodded submissively at the doctor, then he dismissed me. I ambled down the hall with little enthusiasm, knowing that in some sense, I could never go home. A line from T.S. Eliot fluttered to my memory: "After such knowledge, what forgiveness?"[36] I unzipped my red bag and started retrieving my belongings from the dresser drawers, soon realizing it wouldn't hold everything. After nearly four weeks in the hospital, I had collected a lot of stuff. I would have to resort to filling up the paper grocery bags that my parents had used to bring me goodies and various other paraphernalia that I requested. I called my parents and told them the good news, asking them to pick me up tomorrow. I was embarrassed by the excitement in their voices. I slept restlessly that night, uneasy about leaving the chrysalis I had been encased in for so long. What would I do? I couldn't go back to work and face fifty curious faces, so I determined, half in my sleep, that I would quit. Before I could come up with an alternative to work, I began dreaming of an Egyptian sarcophagus that began to open ominously, and out popped Patrick the lawyer, with his

---

[35] William Shakespeare, *MacBeth,* in *The Norton Shakespeare,* 2nd edition, ed. Stephen Greenblatt (New York: W. W. Norton and Company), 1398.

[36] T. S. Eliot, "Gerontin," in *T.S. Eliot: The Complete Poems and Plays* (San Diego: Harcourt Brace Jovanovich, Publishers), 22.

hair looking, as usual, like a toupee. He stared at me for a moment, then started lecturing me on how I could improve my iambic pentameter. I woke up for a moment, startled, then slept until morning.

The next day I moved about uneasily, feeling as if I were already gone, and not sure if I should tell everyone goodbye or not. What would Emily Post say about such an occasion? I finally decided to tell Roland and Chase good-bye, as well as my roommate, and let all the others figure out for themselves that I had gone. It turned out that Roland was being discharged, too, and would be attending day hospital. Great. My parents arrived around noon, and I loaded them down immediately with bags before they could say anything. The nurse came in to have me sign some paperwork, then we moved like a caravan of camels across the desert of the hallway. They were watching me from the front desk, their eyes like hidden cameras, perhaps recording also. Another nurse pushed a button behind the desk, and I heard the door in front of me unlock. Magic. As I opened the door I tried to suppress the voice that droned in my head: "Relax," said the night man, "we are programmed to receive. You can check out any time you like, but you can never leave."[37]

As we drove home, my mother chatted about her bridge club party that she was planning to attend now that I was home and everything was okay, as if three and a half weeks and a few pills could undo such carnage. Her bridge partner had just had a hysterectomy, but she thought she could come anyway if they rolled her in, in a wheelchair. She always got such bad cards, though, Martha did, not like that Louise. Why, it was disgusting how she was always dealt a perfect hand....I tuned out the rest, in favor of speculating about whether my dog would remember me. She did. Her stubby tail went into overdrive as she jumped all over me, pausing only to lick my sweaty palms. The dog followed me down the hallway, into the room with the blood. My bedroom. I stared at the floor. It looked pristine, of course, but in my mind, I saw ghostly red smudges there. I could hear the monk's lilting voice, crooning about mystical union with God. I shook my head rather violently, as if to dislodge the memory. I laid my bag down on the braided rug, then sat down on the bed, unsure of what to do. What should one do after leaving a mental hospital? I got up, walked over to the antique walnut bookcase, nearly

---

[37] Eagles, "Hotel California," written by Don Henley and Glenn Frey, from the album *Hotel California,* released December 8, 1976.

tripping over my bag, and grabbed a copy of *Wuthering Heights*. When in doubt, read. I began reading, leaping into the book, leaving my body behind on the bed, an empty shell. I spent the afternoon there, a prose being, present in spirit as a silent observer of the story's events. I felt at home there. Weren't Cathy and Heathcliff as wildly erratic as I was?

My parents left me alone, except for an occasional surreptitious opening of my door every hour or so, with an apprehensive face peeking in. I was trouble, I decided. I could only guess at how mortified they were by my initiation into weirdness, courtesy of my hospital stay. I was sure they had kept it carefully under wraps, my mother perhaps telling only Edith. My mother often confided in her about problems, even embarrassing ones. I was still not able to comprehend the revelation that my childhood had been dysfunctional. The anger had imploded and was smoldering like Vesuvius somewhere in my psyche. I wasn't aware of it anymore. My mind had apparently ignored pain for most of my life so that it hadn't even registered, so it was easy for me to submerge this new unpleasant information. I knew I would continue to relate to my parents in the bland, superficial way I always had. It was somehow like eating boiled potatoes every day, without butter or chives, of course. It was sufficient as famine food.

The next day I drove to the hospital, dressing stylishly, all in pink, in an attempt to look cheerful. I wasn't. Roland accosted me first thing, looking overly eager.

"I've got a new poem!" he enthused. Without asking if I wanted to hear it, he launched right in: "Once upon a time, I made up this rhyme."

"Sounds great, Roland. Keep up the good work," I offered magnanimously.

I brushed by him, heading for the plaid overstuffed chairs in the day hospital room. Suddenly I remembered that I needed water to soothe my mouth, constantly left too dry from the medication. I saw a foam pitcher of water and some cups on a nearby table, so I poured myself some, sticking a bendable straw in it. I sat back down, sipping petulantly on my drink. A staff worker breezed into the room, looking rather too much like a kindergarten teacher.

"Good morning, everyone," she flounced. "We're going to start the day with some relaxation therapy, so everybody find a spot to lie down on the floor."

I groaned inwardly. Kindergarten again. Naptime. I found an unobtrusive area in the corner of the room, close to the table, so no one, namely Roland, could park it next to me. I didn't relish the idea of being juxtaposed in a horizontal position with him.

The staff worker dimmed the lights, then gushed, "Is everyone ready?"

I assumed that was a rhetorical question. She pushed a button on a tape player, and a man's soothing voice intoned "We are going to begin a progressive relaxation exercise. Make yourself as comfortable as possible."

Right. We're lying on the floor with a bunch of strangers, except for Roland, of course.

The disembodied voice continued: "Begin by tensing up the muscles in your forehead for five seconds. That's right." How did he know if we were doing it right?

"Now, relax your forehead. Very good. Next, open your mouth as widely as you can, tensing your jaw and chin." I was glad the lights were dim. Undoubtedly, this wasn't a very attractive posture.

"Now, let go. Good." The voice proceeded to cover every muscle from head to toe, until I felt rather limp and slightly sleepy. *Not bad,* I thought. After the muscle relaxation, the voice moved to guided imagery.

"Imagine you are lying on the warm sand on a deserted beach. The sun is pouring its rays on you, and you feel completely warm and relaxed all over. A slight breeze is blowing...." As the voice continued to describe the idyllic scenario, I found myself at Oak Island with my dog lying beside me in the sand. I felt as if my body were wax, melting slowing like the wings of Icarus. Everything was superb until a crab scuttled over and bit my toe. Whoops. That wasn't supposed to happen. I was quickly transported back to the darkened room. So much for relaxation. I decided to covertly observe the other patients. Roland was asleep. I noticed the gleam of drool on his chin. Suddenly, the voice ended, and the staff worker announced, "Now we're going to listen to some soothing music with sounds of nature in the background." That sounded promising. No crabs. I settled down to listen. Pachelbel's Canon emerged from the archaic tape player, sounding rather one-dimensional, but still beautiful. It was accompanied by the patter of rain, which gradually increased in intensity. Suddenly a mild rumble of thunder erupted from the tape player, and I was on my feet, trying unsuccessfully to navigate through the clumps of people on the floor. I accidentally stepped on Roland's hand.

"Hey!" he yelped.

"Sorry," I mumbled, and kept going until I reached the door, where the staff worker was standing. "I can't stay here," I said, trying not to gasp.

"Why not, dear?" she said condescendingly.

"I, uh...have a phobia of thunder." The words sounded absurd to me.

"Oh, I'm sorry. Why don't you wait in the hall, honey. I'll call you when we're finished."

"Thanks." I cautiously opened the door and slipped out into the carpeted hall. I took a deep breath. I recalled the many times when my parents had found me huddled in the bathroom with a blanket and my dog, waiting out an encroaching thunderstorm. It was not really the thunder that frightened me, but the possibility of a tornado forming from the storm. But even the sight of cumulonimbus clouds in the sky could send me into panic. Doctors and other passersby gave me fleeting glances as I stood in the hall, feeling foolish. I stared at the carpet, which sported a rather erratic geometrical design. I searched for a pattern to pass the time. Finally, the staff worker opened the door.

"It's safe to come in now, sweetheart." I wondered how many terms of endearment she could wield from her arsenal. I reentered the room to find everyone standing up, looking bleary-eyed and disheveled. One girl's green eyeliner was running. "Okay, folks, you are free to go to your next activity: crafts. The craft room is down the hall." I obediently followed the herd to said room, where I found rows of tables covered with small wicker baskets and a variety of plastic flowers. A young girl, whose tag read "volunteer" above her name, was ushering us in and began to direct us toward the tables.

"Today we're going to decorate baskets." Uh-oh. We had regressed from kindergarten to preschool. "It's very simple. Just pick out the flowers you like, and I'll come around and glue them to the basket for you." Okay, she was lying about the "we." SHE was going to decorate baskets. Of course patients weren't allowed to use a glue gun. I decided to play along, so I sifted through the plastic flowers until I found a few that were less tacky than the others. The volunteer, whose nametag read "Sunny," asked me if I were ready to have the flowers glued.

"Yes, please," I murmured politely.

"Okay, you tell me where you want them to go."

"How about putting that one on the side?" I offered.

"Oh, that will look fabulous," exclaimed Sunny, a little too eagerly. Then she pressed on the handle of the glue gun and squeezed the glue onto the basket. "Let's get it on there before the glue dries." Then she deftly pushed the flower into the glue and held it for a few seconds.

"Okay, great. Where do you want the next one?" We repeated the process until the basket was covered with pink and purple blooms.

"All done," Sunny finally announced. "You did a wonderful job. Let's put your name on a piece of masking tape and stick it to the bottom of the basket so you'll know which one is yours at the end of day." After this task was accomplished, I decided to wander around and look at everyone else's baskets. Chase had showed up for the craft. *I guess he's been discharged, too,* I thought. His basket was bare. I noticed a flower with all the petals torn off sitting next to it. I supposed he wasn't any better. His right leg was twitching nervously.

"Hey, you wanna come to Scrabble club at my house next week?" he asked.

"Sure, I guess." I liked Chase, and I figured it might make Issa jealous.

I continued to roam around the room. Roland had stuck yellow daisies all over his basket. There was no wicker showing. He had even glued (or Sunny had) flowers on the handle on top, but he had left the stems attached and they were sticking out at odd angles.

"How do you like it, Nancy?" said Roland, pride oozing from his voice.

"Way to go, Roland," I evaded. I gave him a high five.

Finally everyone finished the basket-making efforts, and we dispersed to go to various activities. I was told to go see Rick for biofeedback, so I trekked upstairs to the appropriate room. After greeting me, Rick indicated for me to sit in the brown lazy boy chair in the dimly lit room. Then he wiped off my forehead with an alcohol pad and proceeded to attach some electrodes to my head. The alien image resurfaced.

"Okay," he said. "Let's get started." I had done this before, so I knew I was supposed to try to will myself to relax, and if I were successful, the colorful image on the screen would start to disappear. The intent was to teach me how to relax. I mulled over the word "relax" several times. The image got larger. Okay, try again. This time I let go of the muscles in my forehead. The image shrank a little. I moved in my mind back to the sunny beach, minus the crab, and felt the warmth creeping over me. After a minute or so, I opened my eyes. The image had disappeared. Suddenly the room began to look odd. Everything in it seemed covered in a gray mist. I felt as if I were in a trance. I panicked. Was it possible to get too relaxed? Could one relax to death? The image blared across the screen again, screaming anxiety in yellow and orange.

"You were doing pretty well there for a while. What happened?" said Rick.

"I started to feel strange."

"Let's try one of the dots," suggested Rick.

The dots were small pieces of plastic that worked like mood rings. They responded to body temperature. If one were anxious, they stayed black. They changed color from dark blue to green, depending on one's state of relaxation, with green being the most relaxed. Rick handed me a dot, and I placed the sticky side on my finger. I waited a few seconds. The dot stayed black.

"Well, maybe we've had enough for today. I'm going to give you some dots to use at home. You can use them to measure your relaxation, and you can stick them in strategic places around the house to remind you to use your relaxation techniques throughout the day."

"Okay," I murmured compliantly.

"I guess you're about done for the day. You're free to go home."

I grabbed my pink purse, which I had brought with me, and shuffled through it to find my car keys, preparing early for the unlocking process. *That's odd,* I thought. *Why do I do that?* But I had come to believe that nearly everything about me was odd. I belonged to the ranks of those who had spent time in a mental hospital and nothing would erase that mark against me. It was literally tattooed on my wrist like a concentration camp number. As I walked down the hall, I fingered the raised lips of the wound there. The bandage was long gone. My secret was shouting from that mouth for the whole world to hear. Even when it healed, I knew it would leave a wicked scar. I drove home without turning on the radio. Silence seemed more appropriate, somehow. My mother was waiting in the kitchen.

"How was your day?" she inquired cheerfully. I guessed that going to day hospital was a bit more respectable in her eyes than being an inpatient.

"Fine," I replied—my standard response. It did the trick for school or work, but I wasn't sure about an asylum. But perhaps the question was inappropriate, anyway.

"What did you do?"

"Oh, the usual." I had always been skilled at evasion. I never stopped to wonder why I guarded myself like Fort Knox around my parents, as if revealing the least bit of information would somehow leave me naked. I kept on walking, all the way down the hall to *Wuthering Heights*. There the moor took me in, where plastic flowers and black plastic dots couldn't touch me. I read until bedtime, then fell into a fitful sleep.

Each day of outpatient care was identical to the first. At least the crafts changed. By the end of the two weeks I was the proud owner of a plethora of trinkets, all carefully glue-gunned by someone else. The bead necklace, at least, I had done myself. I guessed no one could try to purposely choke on a bead. I stuffed the crafts into a box of miscellaneous items in the back of my closet where I didn't have to look at them. And what else had I gained during my five-week experience at Ivy Hill? My psychiatrist gave me a slip of paper before I left. At the top, the logo read: "Ivy Hill Hospital—Helping People Heal." Underneath was a doctor's name and phone number.

"Who's Dr. St. Clair?" I inquired.

"He's a psychologist," came the reply, as if I should have known. I walked down the corridor for the last time, clutching the slip of paper a little too tightly. I thought they could have at least given me a diploma. Hadn't I graduated from something? I remembered the metaphor Sylvia Plath used for depression in her novel *The Bell Jar*. "To the person in the bell jar," she wrote, "blank and stopped as a dead baby, the world itself is the bad dream."[38] I reflected on the isolation, the suffocation of being in the bell jar. After her recovery, the main character of the novel, based on Sylvia herself, wonders, "How did I know that someday—at college, in Europe, somewhere, anywhere—the bell jar, with its stifling distortions, wouldn't descend again?" How did I know, either? The inexorable desire for blood—my own—had abated, leaving behind a tenuous sanity. But in the mirror, I could still see the mark of Cain on my forehead, dooming me forever to be a restless wanderer on the earth. From then on, I would define my life in terms of the hospital—before and after. Experience had

---

[38]   Sylvia Plath, *The Bell Jar* (New York: Harper and Row, 1971), 156.

laid down for me a barbed wire fence so I could never again cross over into innocence. It was somehow like losing one's virginity. I felt used, like a thing fit to be sold at Goodwill.

When I reached the house, I didn't know what to do with myself. I suddenly remembered the plastic dots and fished them out of my bag. I began methodically sticking them to non-porous surfaces in my bedroom and bathroom. When I ran out of dots, I surveyed my handiwork. The dots turned into malevolent black eyes, staring at me, accusing me. You can check out any time you like. Slowly, mechanically, I tore off all the dots and threw them in the wicker trash can, where they still watched me, smoldering with condemnation.

Panic Attack

Suddenly I see that we are all glued
To a rabid orbiting rock hung by nothing,
Flung to god knows where
And I flame up in fear.
I swallow the universe and all its empty worlds
And it tastes like perpetual winter,
Gargantuan gall.
Other people become trees held by a skeletal spell,
Limbs stark and violently still.
They are mute medicine without effect.
I am nowhere.
The signature on my fingertips vanishes—
I leave behind faceless prints.
My cells become prisons for fire that can't escape
And my breath is rationed.
I stutter a prayer,
And, like Moses,
I see God's back.
But He walks away
Without telling me His
Name.

In Memory of a Good Day

I remember
Kissing Your wrists
Where the cobalt-colored veins gather
Like the stems of a wild bouquet
Tight in the hand of a girl in green.
I lingered over Your scars
That are like towers to a sky
I cannot see.
"Take me there," I murmur,
And you do.
I am dizzy with hunger
And brittle with kaleidoscope joy
As a fecund shadow
Leaves behind the scent
Of Your almost voice
Butterflying in my head.
Forgetfulness will be a rabid dog tomorrow
Foaming lies
And I will feed it gobbets of my flesh
In an unholy Eucharist.
Drown me then, my Love,
In the merlot of memory
And let my mind devour the wafer
Of Your fingers braiding into my hair
And Your voice tattooing my bare skin.

6

The Rains are Over and Gone, Temporarily

ONCE I HEARD a preacher tell a story about a little girl who made a beautiful creation in art class; perhaps it was made of wood or clay, I don't remember which. But the child was desperately proud of her artwork, and she lovingly carried it home to her mother. However, as she was skipping across the kitchen floor, carrying the precious thing, she tripped, and it shattered into fragments when it hit the stone tiles. The girl's grief could not be consoled, until her mother picked up what was left of the creation, looked her straight in the eye, and said, "Let's see what we can make with the pieces." Thus, I served my sentence at day hospital and wandered aimlessly back into what others would call "normal life," wondering if I could do anything with the fragments of myself that were left. They were dark, sharp pieces of glass that threatened to wound me if I weren't careful, and yet surely something of beauty could be fashioned from them. I was profoundly aware that I had lost something immeasurable: innocence, perhaps. From then on my life would suffer from a stark line of demarcation: before the hospital, and after the hospital. I felt that Satan had posted "Wanted: Nancy Craig, Dead or Alive" all over the universe, and that I must flee his pursuit for the rest of my life. I was haunted by feelings of loss. One night I wrote the following in my journal:

> Our need for a Redeemer becomes clearer every day, though we live a life of ease upheld by technology. The secure, peaceful façade of our lovely neighborhood cannot

disguise that death and sorrow are the unwelcome tenants of our lives. At our very core we know that we are helpless and pitiful, like some blind and hairless newborn animal. In someone's driveway I saw a very small dead creature, possibly a squirrel, lying on the rain-darkened cement. He was about two inches long, with pink skin and tiny yet perfectly formed paws. His stillness tore out my heart, because he represented yet another being carefully made by God, intricate in design and lovely, yet found and ravaged by our Enemy. We are grieved by such sights not so much because of the loss of this insignificant scrap of life, but by the abomination at its root. Loss in itself is unbearable, whether it be loss of two hundred passengers on an airliner, or the loss of a sparrow newly hatched, or the loss of sanity…We groan under the weight of our losses, which begin at birth and thread their way through the tapestry of our lives like dark and unwelcome threads. Our hearts break. They are born to break, and nothing created by our wealth or our leisure can overcome the raw, intolerable reality of our grief. We mourn for Eden. By the rivers of Babylon we hang up our harps, weary of singing, knowing we live in a hostile and foreign land. The cherub with the flaming sword turns us away at the entrance of the place we remember, though we have never been there. There the children put their hands into the hole of the cobra, and they laugh. Their laughter reaches through to this world, falling like an unexpected and ethereal snow into our day. We stop our cooking, or cleaning, or fierce running of errands, and we weep. They are tears for our Redeemer.

So, I crawled like a helpless, hairless rodent back into life, unable to face that shattering of my soul that had occurred. I yearned for a savior. Having cut my teeth on romance novels, I felt that this was the time for the tall, dark stranger to sweep into my life and rescue me from the villain. Surely romantic love would put me back together again, hapless Humpty-Dumpty that I was. So, I set my hopes on the logical source for salvation: the compassionate, sensitive Issa. My hospitalization had directly resulted from my sense that he was pulling away from me emotionally. I had unleashed all my feminine charms on him, but to no avail. The rejection opened up the place in my soul where all previous rejections still festered, unrelenting. Like a room full of mirrors, the pain reflected on itself to infinity. After my release from the hospital, however, I somehow mustered up the self-respect to tell Issa that I could not bear the emotional roller-coaster anymore. I told him I wanted to stop dating him. So the prince in the fairy tale became disappointing, and the heroine is left on the side of the road hitchhiking. He bore the news good-naturedly, much to my chagrin, leaving me with one request, that he wanted me to write him letters. I muddled through my days afterwards, reeling from the fallout of a broken relationship.

I had quit my job, realizing that I couldn't stand one more day as a technical writer. My last project had been to edit a voluminous dissertation analyzing the advantages and disadvantages of eating pork. I had nightmares about pork. I couldn't look a ham in the face. Perhaps I had also been afraid to show my face at work again, since they had all no doubt heard of my great transgression of having been committed to a mental institution. Perhaps they would be able to see the mark of the beast on my forehead, or on my wrist. My wrist. I had previously heard co-workers muttering about the cuts they had noticed.... I tried to fasten my watchband over them, but sometimes my watch slipped, revealing too much. So, I was unemployed and unattached, living in my parents' house.

I immediately tried to remedy the unattached part. I was determined to find my savior. I decided to take Jesus literally, and become a fisher of men. I started attending SOLO, which stood for "Singles Offering Life to Others." It was a Christian organization emphasizing service, but everyone knew it was for singles on the prowl. I was immediately asked out by Mark, a good-looking man with curly black hair. He worked for a software company and he took me to the lake by his office, where we ate a picnic lunch, topped off with huge chocolate chip cookies. I tried my best to be charming, fluttering my eyelashes at all the right times, putting on my best damsel-in-distress act. I must have failed miserably because Mark went by the wayside after one date. Then there was Olaf, a tall, lanky Swede who worked for a wastewater treatment plant. I gave him my phone number out of desperation (he smelled faintly of sewage), but I had my dad get rid of him when he called. Always the gentleman, my dad chatted with him for fifteen minutes about the weather before releasing the heartbreaking news that I was permanently unavailable.

"Nice talking with you…" I heard my dad intone pleasantly as I hid in the other room eavesdropping. I made a vow after that. No more sewage.

I went to a few Scrabble club meetings with Chase, but he told me I was too old for him, and that one of the nurses had advised him against hospital romances. I finally settled on Frank, a pasty-faced boy who drove an MG and was enamored with a missionary kid nicknamed Pumpkin whose parents lived in Venezuela. She wouldn't give him the time of day. So, we stuck to each other like the two halves of a bivalve, both of us pining after someone else. Frank told everyone he met about how he had joined a "ROCK" group, which stood for "Reaching Out to Christ's Kingdom." He had attended one service project in which he helped roof some old lady's house, and he managed to weave allusions to this event into nearly all his conversations. I was secretly amused, but Frank was male, and perhaps he would make Issa jealous….I was thrilled when Issa showed up to SOLO one night. I quickly introduced him to Frank, who immediately said," Guess what, I've joined a ROCK group. You know what that stands for?" I blushed to the roots of my hair and smiled weakly at Issa.

As he requested, I had been sending him letters, pouring out my heart to him as I never did when we were dating. Much later, he told me he fell in love with me through my letters, because they revealed the emotionally-charged landscape of my heart that my conversation belied. I had been reading *Wuthering Heights* again and when I finished it, I watched the movie. By the end I was sobbing with a deep, gut-wrenching longing. I pulled out the book and read the passage in which Catherine speaks to Nelly:

> "My great miseries in this world have been Heathcliff's miseries and I watched and felt each from the beginning: my great thought in living is himself. If all else perished, and he remained, I should still continue to be; and if all else remained, and he were annihilated, the universe would turn to a mighty stranger: I should not seem a part of it. My love for Linton is like the foliage in the woods: time will change it, I'm well aware, as winter changes the trees. My love for Heathcliff resembles the eternal rocks beneath: a source of little visible delight, but necessary. Nelly, I am Heathcliff! He's always, always in mind: not as a pleasure,

any more than I am always a pleasure to myself, but as my own being. So, don't talk of our separation again...."[39]

My tears fell on the page and stained them like blood. Heathcliff and Cathy's relationship had exacerbated a seeping wound, a world-wound that loomed like a yawning chasm inside me, yet I had not been aware of it. I wept myself into oblivion, then made my decision. I would write to Issa and tell him about *Wuthering Heights*. "Dear Issa," I began, then paused, unsure if I dared to reveal myself. I swallowed hard, then continued. I had nothing left to lose. "You wanted me to write you, but you probably didn't know that I would vomit all my emotions onto paper with abandon. I don't know if you can understand any of this. I don't even know if I understand it, but somehow, I have to tell another human being that I have a black hole inside me that threatens to suck me in with its gravity. When I was a child, I was terrified of black holes from the time I heard about them. I just knew the earth was going to be vacuumed up inside one at any moment. Little did I know I harbored a black hole in my soul. I want to be loved. I want someone to love me desperately, the way Heathcliff loves Cathy. I want the whole universe to be contained in my love for someone. Maybe it's a sin to want this, but I can't deny it. As Cathy says 'I am Heathcliff,' I want to say 'I am...someone.' At eleven and twelve years old I kept a journal, and nearly every entry contained a plea for someone, anyone to hold me. Perhaps because my parents never held me, I hungered to be touched. I wanted a Prince Charming to sweep into my life and fill all its empty spaces. I am still twelve years old inside, and I am longing for someone to hold me. I long for the adventure of love, for a passion that stops the world's rotation, that can be seen in the stars. I wept when I saw *Wuthering Heights*, because I want a raw, wild, exotic love like theirs. I want a love that reaches beyond the grave, as theirs did. Perhaps I am overly romantic, but I can't shake the idea that life is all about love, that it is healing and glorious and redemptive. Please don't think I'm trying to come on to you. I simply needed to voice my feelings to a real person. When I pray, I often feel like I'm talking to empty air, or to the ceiling. I hope you understand."

---

[39] The Project Gutenberg. 1996. Emily Bronte, *Wuthering Heights*. Accessed August 7, 2020. https://www.ucm.es/data/cont/docs/119-2014-04-09-wuthering%20heights.pdf.

I didn't know how to close the letter. "Love, Nancy" seemed too intimate. "Sincerely" was too formal. I finally settled on the very spiritual sounding "Blessings." "Blessings, Nancy." I didn't stop to think how incongruous this was, considering the content of the letter. I put it in an envelope, sealed it, and licked the stamp, which was decorated with hearts and the word "love." I drove across town to find a mailbox that had a pickup late in the day. A few days later I received a phone call from Issa.

"Would you like to go for a drive?" he asked.

Against my better judgment, I agreed. My vows to keep my distance dissipated. I still felt the raw wound from *Wuthering Heights*. We drove for miles, not really paying attention to where we were going.

Issa told me he had been fasting, waiting to hear from the Lord.

"What about?" I asked, curious.

"You," he answered.

"What about me?"

"Whether I should marry you."

"Oh." I gasped. But my mind whispered to me: *Heathcliff.*

There was an awkward silence, then I snapped it like a brittle twig.

"What did God say?"

"He said I should."

I had never heard anyone say that God spoke to him, so I didn't know enough to question his response. Then he told me that he had fallen in love with me through my letters (I had written him several more after the "Heathcliff" confession).

"I knew you were the one for me when I found out you were born on Christmas Eve in Bethlehem, and your name means 'Jesus.'" I replied, unaware of how absurd that statement sounded. Another awkward silence.

Finally, Issa said, "You know that passage in Acts when Philip preaches to the Ethiopian eunuch, and the eunuch says 'Here is water. Why shouldn't I be baptized?'?"

"Yes." I wasn't following him.

"Well, why shouldn't we be married?" That was a line if I ever heard one, but my whole being welled up in ridiculous joy. Prince Charming reappears. Heroine lives happily ever after.

"OK."

We drove to a nearby college campus where there was a picturesque lake with ducks. We lay down in the grass. The rolling hills could almost have been Cathy and Heathcliff's English countryside...."You haven't proposed to me yet," I reminded him.

"Nancy, will you marry me?" he said.

I couldn't think of anything witty to say, so I just said "Yes."

Issa took a blade of grass and formed it into a ring, placing it on my left hand. I remembered a song from one of my favorite movies, *Brother Sun, Sister Moon*, which features the story of St. Francis:

> "Oh, green are the leaves
> On the old apple tree
> Those sweet perfumed blossoms of spring
> Entwined in your hair
> A smile in your eyes
> A soft blade of grass for a ring." [40]

After a few moments he said, "I guess you want a diamond, don't you?"

"Heck, yeah," I answered. I thought of all those nights as a child when I had read Song of Solomon, relishing the romantic love poetry. My memory went back through the years and seized a passage:

> "My beloved spoke and said to me,
> 'Arise, my darling,
> my beautiful one, come with me.
> See! The winter is past;
> the rains are over and gone.
> Flowers appear on the earth;
> the season of singing has come,
> the cooing of doves is heard in our land.
> The fig tree forms its early fruit;
> the blossoming vines spread their fragrance.
> Arise, come, my darling;
> my beautiful one, come with me.'" [41]

---

[40] Donovan Leitch, "A Soldier's Dream," from *Brother Sun, Sister Moon*, produced by Franco Zeffirelli.

[41] Song of Songs 2:10-13 (NIV).

And so, the winter passed, and the rains vanished. Our engagement ushered in a period of unprecedented peace and happiness in my life. I felt as if the culmination of my whole existence were about to occur. I seemed no longer fragmented. I had found the other part of myself, the missing puzzle piece that would make me complete. My panic attacks subsided; the depression lifted. I decided to go back to school to pursue a Master's degree in English. The only knot in the perfect silk thread that my life had become took the form of my mother's continual attempt to rein in my unconventional ideas about the wedding. I wanted red roses, since we were getting married at Christmas; she said white was a sign of purity. I decided not to tell her I was not exactly the epitome of purity. However, Issa managed to smooth her ruffled feathers with sweet talk. I got my red roses.

But as the wedding date drew nearer, I became afraid. *I'm a poet,* I thought. *I'm marrying an engineer!* My misgivings culminated in a revival of the panic attacks. I assured myself that I loved Issa, that everything would be wonderful. The night before our wedding, I spent panicking. I took Xanax that night. I took Xanax before I walked down the aisle. I took Xanax before I got on the plane to go on our honeymoon. I spent most nights during our honeymoon in a warm bath, drinking hot tea, trying to calm my racing heart. I wondered if Issa regretted what he had done, now that he was forced to live night and day with my neurosis. But he never complained as he sat night after night by the bathtub, holding my hand.

We spent Christmas Eve and Christmas day in Las Vegas. We walked through the casino to get to our hotel room and saw a teeming horde of gamblers transfixed by the slot machines, silently pulling the handles over and over as if they were waiting for living water to pour out. The next morning as we left to go home, we saw the same people still standing there as if they had sprouted roots that reached down below the floor, trapping them there. I could relate to the empty look in their eyes, the vacuum-for-eyes. They looked hungry, as if all the power, money, food, and sex in the world could never fill the cavern of their hearts. I felt a frightening oneness with the gamblers. Here I was, in love with the tall, dark stranger, even married to him, but the ghost of emptiness still haunted me. I was reminded of the U2 song, "I still haven't found what I'm looking for."[42]

---

[42] Bono, "I still haven't found what I'm looking for," from the album *The Joshua Tree,* 1987.

I realized I was still somehow shattered inside. My worldview couldn't hold water. I had no idea how to love another human being, and I was scared to death. On the plane from Las Vegas to Dallas I was panicking. I felt like I was thirty thousand feet up in a floating tin can. In the Dallas airport I burst into tears and refused to get on the plane to Raleigh. Issa tried to soothe me, but I continued in my tantrum. He finally offered to buy me a stuffed animal from the gift shop if I would get on the plane. I agreed, and he bought me a stuffed monkey with silky gray fur. I named him Saguaro, after the cactuses we saw in Arizona. We brought some saguaro seeds home with us and tried to grow them in a tiny clay pot covered with plastic wrap. The seeds sprouted, then died. On the plane to Raleigh, I read my journal entries that I had written before our marriage. On the day of our engagement, my entry read:

> My Heathcliff has come to me, and my wasteland has flowered. Can he really love me, the one with the mark of Cain? And yet he says that I have stolen his heart. Could it be that instead I have stolen fire from the gods? Can I live with such joy, or will it consume me? I have heard my beloved speak, and he has allured me into a world of beauty, a world where trees bear twelve crops of fruit and their leaves are for healing. Perhaps his love has erased the mark of Cain. Perhaps emptiness and darkness will no longer be my bedfellows. We will be led by a cloud by day, and a pillar of fire by night....

As I read, betraying tears began to run down my face. I quickly wiped away one that hung suspended on the end of my nose. Issa was reading a magazine, so he didn't notice. Where was the pillar of fire? Where was the cloud? I realized that I carried a desert in my soul and that no man could irrigate it. Everywhere I looked there was sand. My mind was a Sahara. But I got off the plane in Raleigh and I continued walking beside my husband, whom I could barely see in the midst of a sandstorm. Yet I always felt his hand clamped tightly around mine. But I still limped through life, and several years later I was yet the chosen prey of a hungry Darkness. Issa had believed that once I got used to being married, the security would cure me of all my ills. But my journal entries spoke otherwise:

I have not written since I got married, and I wonder why, but even more I wonder why I should bother now. What can be said that will make a difference? Yet there might be a hope in it. I used to think years later these books would be treasures, but they are not. Does anyone care, including myself, about the strange revelations of a teenager, or a psychotic young woman in her twenties? I must sound hopeless, though I am not. It is just that sometimes hope itself seems as unexplained and useless as everything else. And could it all be brain chemicals gone wild—too many or too few? That would be a joke, and yet strangely comforting. What is it that tears at me, reduces all things to nothing in one instant, with one small yet sickening flutter in my stomach? They would all mouth their platitudes at me, tell me to have faith and the whole thing will fizzle out. Are they right? But what is the thing that makes faith seem like a weak glimmer in a field of endless shadow? I am afraid—deeply, inexplicably afraid, and there is no one here but religious people and blasé psychiatrists. Yet there is so much beauty here, beauty that is painful and must have a source. It is laughable, but my parakeets give me a kind of belief that few things can. They are so delicate, so perfect, and were made by someone without the least ulterior motive. They are useless and beautiful, and the Creator of such things I must love. Their voices speak more of God than any sermon I have ever heard; a God who would take such absurd care with these birds that can only make me laugh with a deep, reverential laughter. The Awful Thing has not overcome creation. It tries to tell me that parakeets and aardvarks and otters are blank and meaningless, but I cannot believe it. They give me hope by their very existence. They seem to speak lovingly, undeniably of redemption. My theology is no doubt heretical, but when has theology ever stood in the face of the Awful Thing? The God who would love a bird into being must surely love us, love me, and surely will not let the Black Thing press me to the ground. Oh God, I feel now that all I have is the "barely prayable prayer," as T. S. Eliot wrote in his poem "The Dry Salvages."[43] I can hardly say the words to you, and I cannot explain, or lift my voice above the dark, consuming, weakening force. Even now my words seem to mock me, seem to speak of emptiness more absurdly than any silence, but if He hears all prayers, He must hear this one that cannot be voiced surely, He will hear this one that can barely be said. God, don't let it take me. I don't understand what's happening, but I cannot, must not be taken to that place. Although I am only one insignificant person, it seems that all things will die if that darkness is allowed to encroach on me. It has no power over the beautiful, delicate birds, but it would kill me with my own complexity. I cannot write. I cannot think. I cannot.

And so, I drifted through the years like a castaway floating with only a life preserver in an ocean of disappointment. Prince Charming, though kind and adoring, turns out to have foot fungus. Heroine pines away for perfection. I spent my days teaching English at N.C. State University, riding the bus back and forth with my leather briefcase. There was inevitably someone beside me with body odor or dirty fingernails. I stared straight ahead, careful not to make eye contact with any of my fellow castaways.

I was reminded of a short movie I had watched called *The Music Box*, which tells the story of a hapless man who lives in a town infused with deadness. Everything in the movie seemed to happen in slow motion. His plain wife serves him a tasteless breakfast. He ventures from his gray apartment onto a gray bus with gray, nearly comatose people. He works in a gray factory where he very slowly puts tops on soda bottles. One night he is in his bedroom and a group of angels appears to him, singing joyously. He is overwhelmed with delight for the first time in his mundane life. He begins to smile with evident joy. After the angels disappear, he notices that they have left behind a small, ornate box. He opens it, and more angelic music pours out. He closes the box quickly, and the music ceases. He opens it again, and the music resumes. The man's

---

[43] T. S. Eliot, "Four Quartets: The Dry Salvages," in *T. S. Eliot: The Complete Plays and Poems* (San Diego: Harcourt Brace Jovanovich, Publishers, 1950), 132.

life is transformed. His movements become swift and energetic. Every time he is alone, he opens the box and rejoices to the music. Finally, the angels return to him and tell him that his secret is meant to be shared, so he begins to open the box for the shattered people on the bus and in the factory. They are all transformed, too. The gray pallor over the city lifts, and it becomes a place of rejoicing.

When I observed the people on the bus, I felt as if we were all living in the town of the movie, where men spend their lives putting tops on soda bottles, and a non-descript fog envelops everything. Secretly I was waiting for an angelic visitation, but it never came. I would step off the bus, trudge into our house, and lie on the bed for hours, staring at the ceiling. When I wasn't staring at the ceiling, I was obsessed with crocheting doilies. Somehow seeing patterns and shapes emerging from a formless ball of thread soothed me. It gave me purpose. Like Theseus, I was guided out of the labyrinth by a thread, but the Minotaur still lived; I could feel his breath on my neck. But one day I reread the following verses from the Song of Solomon:

"My beloved is radiant and ruddy,
Outstanding among ten thousand.
His head is purest gold;
His hair is wavy
And black as a raven.
His eyes are like doves
by the water streams,
Washed in milk,
Mounted like jewels.
His cheeks are like beds of spice
Yielding perfume.
His lips are like lilies
Dripping with myrrh.
His arms are rods of gold
Set with topaz.
His body is like polished ivory
Decorated with lapis lazuli.
His legs are pillars of marble
Set on bases of pure gold.
His appearance is like Lebanon,

Choice as its cedars.
His mouth is sweetness itself;
He is altogether lovely.
This is my lover, this my friend,
O daughters of Jerusalem."[44]

A seed was planted in my mind that bore no fruit at first. I began to suspect that the Prince may have been waiting for me from everlasting. For all eternity he had been clutching my other glass slipper, waiting for me to notice that I had lost it. It was not an angelic visitation, but it was a supernatural insemination of a gossamer hope in my disillusioned heart. I also stumbled upon the book entitled *The Sacred Romance*, by Brent Curtis and John Eldredge, and I started to see that Jesus is the ultimate lover, the true Prince, complete with white horse. They wrote:

> "Romance is the deepest thing in life; it is deeper even than reality. Our heart is made for a great drama, because it is a reflection of the Author of that story, the grand heart behind all things. We've seen how we lose heart when we lose the eternal Romance, which reminds us that God sought to bring us into his sacred circle from all eternity, and that despite our rejection of him, he pursues us still.... Our Lover has come to rescue us in the person of Jesus; he has set our heart free to follow him up and into the celebration that begins the adventures...."[45]

But the idea of Jesus as the Hero of my heretofore dismal drama, my Prince, was only the ghost of a thought at that time. In the years to come God would flesh out its gossamer beginnings and allure me with a cruciform love that I could only tenuously grasp. I would discover that, like a mother obsessed with her red, squawking newborn, God kept a running tally of each hair that erupted from my ruddy scalp, or that fell otherwise unmourned to litter the ground. I eyed this obsession cautiously, finding it too absurd to accept as yet. But in the meantime, I found that

---

[44] Song of Songs 5:10-16 (NIV).

[45] Brent Curtis and John Eldredge, *The Sacred Romance* (Nashville: Thomas Nelson Publishers, 1997), 196.

the rains had begun again, relentlessly. On my honeymoon I had seen a tear—my own—fall into my cupped hand resting in my lap. Slowly, insidiously, the storm mushroomed and exploded upon me, and I fell to my quivering knees in despondency before an altar of despair. But as the debris cascaded down, I could almost hear a voice lilting a strange yet beautiful descant that spoke of redemption.

A Love Song for Jesus

Come out of the bookcase,
Slip out and bring
Your body Your Word
Into the morning.

You will smile at me softly—
I'll boil water for tea
And tear loaves of bread
While the sun opens dimly.

My hand on Your hand
Will brush soft as a leaf
Let go from a seedling
Swept down a backstreet.

Or I'll become words—
So my lips may in prose
Touch the wounds that are blooming
On the feet of my Rose.

Taste and See

You are light
and I am shadow
and when You pass through me
my body becomes seismic.
But I am the Lady of Shallot,
grown half sick of shadows,
and I will die
if You do not flame into flesh for me.
The heat will exorcise my heart and lungs
until they are swallowed by the sky
and trapped within a rainbow
like an iridescent thoracic cage,
if You will, just once,
baptize my mouth
with Your sweet searing breath
and allow me at last
to taste the orchard of Your lips.

7

Angel Visitation

*I*T WAS A STORY about an angel visitation. "Besides," it read, "the few miracles attributed to the angel showed a certain mental disorder, like the blind man who didn't recover his sight but grew three new teeth, or the paralytic who didn't get to walk but almost won the lottery, and the leper whose sores sprouted sunflowers."[46]

The tale was a haunting one called "A Very Old Man with Enormous Wings," and it recounted the adventure of a family who suddenly finds an ancient, bedraggled man with wings inhabiting their chicken coop. They call him an angel, but there remains an air of mystery about the man throughout the story. His feathers harbor lice, and he eats only eggplant mush. He develops a case of chicken pox, and the doctor who listens to his heart finds "so much whistling in the heart and so many sounds in his kidneys that it seemed impossible for his to be alive."[47]

The old man draws a crowd of onlookers who treat him like a circus animal, and some even throw stones at him. The family becomes rich from the proceeds from pilgrims who come to visit the man, and they are able to build a lavish new house, with the angel still living in the chicken coop. One day the man's bedraggled feathers begin to grow back, and soon afterward he flies away "with the risky flapping of a senile vulture."[48]

---

[46] Gabriel Garcia Marquez, "A Very Old Man with Enormous Wings," trans. Gregory Rabassa, in *Literature: Reading Fiction, Poetry, Drama and the Essay,* 2nd ed., ed. Robert DiYanni (New York: McGraw-Hill Publishing Company, 1990), 365.

[49] Ibid., 366.

The story resonated with me because I so longed for the supernatural in my life, yet I seemed earthbound, and the only angels that visited me looked like senile vultures. When I looked for healing, my sores merely sprouted sunflowers. The story captured the pathos and sickly otherworldliness of my life, where miracles fell flat and angels contracted lice. I stood that day in front of a room full of college freshmen, attempting to lead a discussion on the story. I wore a tailored gray suit with black high heels, attempting to look older than my twenty-six years. My long blond hair cascaded nearly to my waist. I had struggled through half the class to engage the students, but the blank faces staring back at me indicated that I was failing.

How had I ended up here anyway? Rather haphazardly, the way I did most things. I had never returned to editing papers on ham and other administrative delicacies, so with all the forethought of a ten-year-old, I decided to go to graduate school to study English. I was always up for more learning, so I figured it couldn't hurt. The doctors told me I shouldn't do it, but I flounced my way into my first class with characteristic stubbornness, and I had stumbled along until graduation. I lost a few limbs on the trek in the form of dropped classes and late papers, but lizard-like, I always managed to grow them back in some form or another. I had even swallowed my gargantuan fear and taken a job as a teaching assistant for two years, which turned into a lecturing position after graduation. Something to keep me from staring at the ceiling. As my reverie about how I had gotten there ended, I redoubled my efforts to extract intelligence from my students.

"So," I finally asked, "what strikes you about this story?" That question set them off.

"I think it's dumb," said a football player in the front row.

I brushed aside his comment. After all, he was barely scraping by with a D average.

"Yeah, this doesn't make any sense," said another. "Why are we reading this junk?"

"Angels don't have lice."

"This is stupid." I caught the eye of one of the students in the back row. He could barely put two words together in an essay, but when he had turned in a paper late, he had provided an eloquent two-page explanation of why his paper had been AWOL, citing a "raging tooth" as the culprit. He had spent the day at the oral surgeon's office. I saw in his eyes, or so I thought, a vacuous preoccupation with girls and beer, and a total disregard for the finer points of good literature. Suddenly I felt publicly humiliated by my failure to control the class discussion, and the physiognomy of every male in the room transformed into the leering visage of Jared Burkley. My fear rose up in the form of a nauseatingly elitist and self-righteous venom, and I fell into my own raging.

"Stupid?" I said. "I'll tell you what's stupid. It's a class full of ignorant freshmen who can't tell excellent literature from a nursery rhyme. You all should be ashamed of yourselves. Don't you even think? I've had it. I'm not wasting my time trying to lead discussion with a bunch of juvenile delinquents. This class is over."

I tried to storm out dramatically, but I ruined the effect when I tripped over my briefcase and lost my shoe. In exasperation, I pulled off the other one and stomped out barefoot, carrying my shoes. Thus fell the first domino in a series, setting off a chain reaction that would bring about irrevocable change in my life. I had suffered disillusion with my marriage, and now teaching had begun to sour. I knew I wasn't cut out for teaching large groups anyway. I was so terrified the first time I stood in front of a class that my voice failed me. The words turned to sand in my mouth. I had to ask my psychiatrist for a special beta-blocker that eased the symptoms of stage fright. I was already on four other medications. My hands would still sweat profusely, leaving a faint damp tinge on their papers when I passed them out.

As I stumbled back to my office that day, ranting in my mind, a bizarre logic began to form in my brain. *If I had a child,* I reasoned, *she would be raised on Shakespeare.* (My mind would not allow the possibility that I could give birth to a boy.) *I shouldn't be wasting my time teaching unresponsive, literature-hating adolescents. I should be at home raising my own children to be intelligent and deep.*

Domino number two fell a few days later, when we got together with Issa's sister and brother-in-law for a Labor Day cookout. Their three-month-old son, Thomas, was gurgling and cooing in his car seat. I did not like babies. I had never liked babies. But Thomas had a head full of curly black hair, and I suddenly saw his hair with new eyes. I thought it was the most beautiful hair I had ever seen, framing his face like an unconventional halo. It was an angel visitation. I was smitten.

All at once I wanted, more than anything else, to have a baby with beautiful black curly hair. Never mind my shattered psyche, my gargantuan fears, my woeful ignorance—the list went on and on. I didn't mention my idea to Issa. It percolated in my brain for a week or two, finally coming to a head one night when I was overcome with depression. I was in the shower crying. I cried often in the shower, because the pouring water seemed to augment my tears and release more of my emotion. I got out of the shower without drying off.

While a puddle was forming on the floor, I retrieved my single-edged razor blade from its hiding place behind the molding surrounding the bathroom door. I slowly drew lines of blood on my wrist. As I felt the familiar release of tension, my mind began to toy with two different options, deliberating which would be best. Option one: commit suicide. Option two: have a baby. I felt as if I were the nation of Israel before Moses, who told them: "This day I call the heavens and the earth as witnesses against you that I have set before you life and death, blessings and curses. Now choose life, so that you and your children may live..."[49] Heaven and earth were poised and waiting to see what I would do. The voices in my head were spinning: "life," "death," "live," "die." I could almost see the bright apparitions of angels in the room, and more ominously, the dark visages of demons. I had the razor blade in my hand. I could feel the water still dripping off my naked body. I began to contemplate death, the final cessation of all my struggles. I saw the boatman come for me to ferry me across the river. Yet the dominant voice, strong and luminous in the darkness was "choose life."

I let the razor blade fall to the floor. I heard its tinny retort as it hit the tiles. I methodically dried myself off, put on a bathrobe, and walked into the bedroom where Issa was taking a nap, unaware that a cosmic drama had been unfolding in the next room. I shook his arm violently, still feeling the demons rearranging my hair. He woke up and stared at me with groggy eyes.

"What's wrong?" he said.

"I want to have a baby."

He pulled me into bed beside him. "It's about time," he murmured.

---

[49] Deuteronomy 30:19 (NIV).

The next day I stopped taking all four medications I was on. After a few days I began to feel as if I had the flu. I was aching all over and felt strange whooshing noises when I turned my head. I was plagued with dizziness. Monday came around, and I was unable to teach class because of the withdrawal symptoms. But I was able to endure them because I was excited about the possibility of having a baby. It had not yet occurred to me that I was in no shape to become a mother, that I could barely take care of myself, much less someone else. All I could think about were Thomas's curls….In retrospect, I can only see that a steel bubble of grace had been surrounding me, despite my twisted psyche, my sinful attitudes and woeful immaturity. I should have been divorced. When I became a mother, I should have been unable to care for my children. I should never have had the wherewithal to homeschool them for fourteen years. How could I, foolish wretch that I was, have fallen into pit after pit and found those shadowy abysses overflowing with favor? But that is to run ahead of the story….

After a few weeks I began to suspect that I was pregnant, so I proudly purchased a pregnancy test, holding it prominently in front of me so that everyone in the store would be sure to see it. I read the directions with care, produced the appropriate body fluid in a cup, and dipped the applicator tip into it. I carefully placed the pregnancy test on the counter and set my egg timer for two minutes. I stared at the clear window as the yellow fluid seeped past it. As I stared, a faint yet unmistakable line began to appear. The line was pink. I wondered if that meant the baby would be a girl. My heart began to beat wildly. I marveled at how easy this pregnancy thing seemed.

But soon enough, of course, I began to unravel, physically and emotionally. I was plagued with constant nausea, always on the edge of running to the bathroom. We went to a football game with friends, and I found myself in the woods on the border of the stadium, throwing up violently. I found that the nausea grated on me. My stomach seemed to take over my mind and body until even my thoughts were nauseous. I sunk into an abyss of depression, without the benefit of medication, and I knew that I had many months before me before I could be medicated again. My doctor suggested hospitalization, but I recoiled from the idea of being trapped again in that box of sorrows.

My thoughts moved from excitement and elation from the novelty of pregnancy, to a strange mixture of fear and uncertainty. I began to sense that another creature was living inside me, although I had not yet felt it move. Its presence seemed alien, as if it had green skin and multiple eyes. Or perhaps it was a parasite, funneling life from me into its own greedy body. I felt sure that I was the only woman ever to experience such a bizarre reaction, and I was plagued with guilt. God had given me a child, and I responded to it as an alien presence. This did not surprise me, however. I knew that my mind was not like other people's minds. It was always bent on destroying me or those I loved. It stalked me, pursued me, breathed down my neck like a rapist.

I also started to fear that I would never be a good mother, that I could not love this child the way it deserved. My parents had never learned to show love; what if I couldn't either? I was so distressed that I considered counseling, if only to have someone to talk to. Counseling was a bad word in my book. I had already met with several counselors, to no avail. The first was a handsome man in his forties that I had seen when I was still single. I felt an immediate bond with him. He, of course, attributed this to the fact that we had nearly the same Myers-Briggs score. I was an INFP, and he was an ENFP. He was a guru of Eastern religions, and he recommended a book called *Healing into Life and Death*, which had chapters such as "Meditation of the Womb." My mother found the book and warned me against it. She was afraid I was into transcendental meditation, so she wrote me a note that said, "I hope when you repeat words over and over that you repeat that name of God." Every once in a while, my mother exuded some type of uncanny wisdom. But at the time this counselor fascinated me, and I was too young a Christian to recognize the danger. He spoke of how he had glimpsed eternity once through hallucinogenic mushrooms. Glimpsing eternity sounded promising. Once when I entered his office, he walked over to me and embraced me tightly for what seemed an infinity. When he released me, he looked me straight in the eye and said, "I just wanted to see how deeply you had repressed your feelings." I continued to see this counselor until I was hospitalized, but afterwards I had the nagging feeling that he was somehow dangerous, so I never went back.

My next counselor I saw after my hospitalization. He told me to bring pictures of myself when I was a little girl, and I found one of me holding hands with my brothers at the beach. I was about four years old. This picture tore open a sore in my heart for some reason, and I wept in the shower that night for an hour, the water pelting my body and reverberating with my tears. When I described for him my reserved parents, he exclaimed, "My God, doesn't anyone in your family fart?" I would often tell him about my dates with Issa, and how I was attracted to him. He spent half our sessions telling me that I better have some condoms on hand, as if we were animals for which a sexual encounter were a matter of instinct and not choice. I told him we had no intention of sleeping together, but he would not believe me. I never felt he reached the heart of my suffering, so I quit seeing him also.

My last encounter with counseling had been with a woman who lived in a nearby town in a double-wide trailer. She called herself a "Holy Spirit counselor," and she claimed that God showed her what was in my heart. She often prayed against the "death wish" that she believed I harbored, and I sensed that she was right. I might have stayed with her if she hadn't claimed that God told her that I had been sexually abused as a child, in addition to the incident in elementary school. She told me that it happened in the spring, because I told her that spring was the most difficult season for me. When the flowers began to appear and I could hear children's voices ringing in the air, something in me mourned. I was reminded of Eliot's assertion that "April is the cruelest month, breeding lilacs out of the dead land."[50] The lilacs that grew out of my heart cracked it with their roots, and the scent of the blooms mocked me. So, this counselor told me that in the spring a specific person had abused me, and she went into graphic detail about what had allegedly happened. She finally told Issa that she couldn't help me anymore until I came to terms with my "abuse." Unfortunately, God neglected to tell me anything about this incident, so my soul was fraught with confusion. She also told Issa that she thought I was schizophrenic.

---

[50] T. S. Eliot ,"The Waste Land," in *T. S. Eliot: The Complete Poems and Plays*, (San Diego: Harcourt Brace Jovanovich, Publishers), 37.

Thus, even though my previous counseling experience had ended somewhat precariously, during my pregnancy I was desperate for someone to talk to, so I began having weekly sessions with a rather bland Christian counselor. I unloaded my strange musings to her, telling her what I dared tell no one else, that I felt I should give my baby up for adoption because I didn't think I could love her properly. My counselor humored me by agreeing that that was an option, if necessary. I was so afraid of scarring my child irrevocably that I thought someone else could raise her more successfully. Issa humored me also, although he told me later that he, of course, had no intentions of giving up the baby.

And so I stumbled through my pregnancy, suppressing my unnatural ravings, waiting for the moment of relief when the other soul that had invaded my body would be expelled. I survived until the last trimester of pregnancy, and then the doctor believed that I could safely take an anti-depressant. Relieved, I began taking a new drug, and slowly my mood improved. My feelings toward the baby evolved into love, and I enjoyed shopping for tiny clothing and various other baby paraphernalia. But I was haunted by an overwhelming fear of childbirth. I hated pain, but I was comforted by the fact that a wide variety of drugs was waiting for me, to deaden any discomfort I might feel. I dutifully attended childbirth classes, and practiced all the "hee hee, hoo hoo" breathing exercises while lying on the floor, feeling like an idiot.

One night about eight days before my due date, we went out for Mexican food. I ordered the spiciest dish on the menu, a jalapeno quesadilla with guacamole and salsa. I devoured it with relish, then decided that we should take our usual two-mile walk. We stopped every few feet, because I had been experiencing what I assumed to be false labor. The childbirth instructor had drilled into our heads that with our first baby we would probably go to the hospital, only to be sent home because it was a false alarm, or because I would not be dilated far enough. So I just kept walking, becoming more and more uncomfortable. We got home, and I went to bed. Around midnight I felt some kind of "snap" in my abdomen, and I wondered if something had happened to the baby. I woke up Issa, who called the doctor. She told us to come in. I had not packed yet, so I tried to rush to throw my personal items together, pausing every few minutes for the contractions. I threw my underwear in a bag, then stood in the bedroom for a few seconds while my lower abdomen crunched into a ball. Next, I packed the most necessary item: makeup. Of course one must look beautiful while having a baby. I paused a few more seconds, then packed my magazine, and so on.

Finally, we were ready to leave. The trip in the car was agonizing. I was beginning to feel intense pain, and fear was creeping into my heart. When I got to the hospital, I was bleeding. The nurse scolded me for getting blood on the floor. I began to cry for someone to help me.

"Is this your first baby?" snapped the nurse.

I nodded, unable to speak.

"Okay, I suppose I can check you." I climbed onto the table, and the nurse felt for the dilation. All at once I saw alarm register on her face.

"I can feel the head," she screamed. "Call the doctor!"

Suddenly I was whisked onto a table with wheels and rolled down the hall into another room. There was no time for drugs or an IV. I was terrified and began screaming, "Somebody help me. Give me a C-section." Issa remained by my side, looking dazed in his Tasmanian devil t-shirt. The Tasmanian devil grinned wickedly in typical devil fashion and was spouting off some expletive represented by @#$%. Once in the delivery room, I realized that all the techniques I had learned in childbirth class were of no use. I tried for a moment to "hee hee, hoo hoo," but the pain would choke me in the middle of the breath. The instructor had told us to try to focus our sight on a particular object, so I picked the Tasmanian devil. I wondered if the baby's face would come out with a devilish grimace.

The focal point didn't work either. I felt as if my lower body were being turned inside out. I tried pushing, and the foreign doctor muttered with a thick accent, "She's not doing it right. She's not trying." I wondered if I were supposed to know how to do it. I saw the doctor pick up a pair of scissors and bring them toward me. She began to cut near the baby's head, and I remembered that I had had no anesthesia. I nearly fainted, but decided that wouldn't be a good idea. After two more pushes, I felt the baby emerge, and at once I was blissfully aware that the pain had ceased. I was suddenly afraid because I didn't hear the baby crying. "Is she okay?" I shouted. I was relieved to find that she was, indeed, a girl, and that the ultrasound had not lied. I didn't like boys. Because of my experiences in elementary school, I thought little boys must have been created by the devil to inflict evil on mankind.

The nurse assured me that she was fine, that she just needed the fluid suctioned out of her throat. They laid the baby on my chest. The first thing I noticed was the ugly purple cord that had connected her to me. I thought it was hideous. Perhaps she was an alien, after all. Then all at once, I saw her face. A song went through my mind: "Then I saw her face; now I'm a believer." I became a believer immediately, a believer in an impossibly storybook-style love at first sight. Her face was incredibly beautiful, like a cherub painted by one of the great masters. A visitation. A holy light seemed to flood the room. I forgot that there was a suspicious yellow stain on the floor, and that she was connected to an ugly purple cord stained with an even purpler dye. I stared, transfixed.

Her eyes were huge, brown, and luminous. Her skin was a flawless olive tone totally unlike my own pink-and-ivory, yet her lips were a repeat of mine: a full lower lip, with a slightly thinner top lip. Her lips reminded me of a ripe cherry. I ran my finger across them, fascinated. At once she began to cry, and I was enchanted. Her cry was not like all those obnoxious squawks I had heard from all other babies. It sounded, impossibly, like music. "She's singing," I gasped. I had no way of knowing that this child would become incredibly musical and would songbird her way to adulthood. All I knew was that celestial strains were emanating from the perfect, tiny body that was my daughter. "Eva Elise," I murmured to her. I had picked the name "Eva" for her because it meant "life," and because of her I had chosen life over death. Her name was a resplendent monument to the grace of God, to the eternal "Yes" at the center of the universe.

As I lay there staring at my daughter, I suddenly thought, *I recognize her. I have seen her before!* Lines from the "Sleeping Beauty" theme popped into my head: "I know you, I've walked with you once upon a dream; I know you, the gleam in your eyes is so familiar a gleam." *Oh dear,* I thought. *I'm hearing Disney. I've really lost it.* The next day I wrote in my journal:

> "Before Eva was born, I was often unnerved by the presence of another being living inside me, a being whose face I could not see. An intruder. As the pregnancy progressed, I began to have feelings of love, but still there was the uncertainty of who this creature was. Yesterday, when she was born, I remember thinking, oddly, that I recognized her.

I know you! I thought to myself. *I have seen your face in my heart. All along that was you, and I thought the stirring, unseen one was a stranger.* I think it will be so when I see the face of God. At times I feel afraid or uncertain of who He is. I sometimes wonder if He is friend or foe. I feel the stirrings but do not really know the Being who is their author. When I see Your face, Lord, I will cry out 'I know You! I have seen Your face in my heart. All along that was You, and I thought the stirring, unseen one was a stranger.' It is You who burgeons inside me like the secret fluttering of an unborn child. I will welcome Your movements within me. You are not the Unknown One, but the Beloved One."

The days after I brought Eva home from the hospital passed in a blur of happiness. I was occupied with the daunting but lovely task of raising a child. I felt that at last I had found the secret to life, that my salvation had come in the form of a six-pound, four-ounce baby. I dressed her all in pink, boasted about her incredible precocity, and basked in the beauty of her musical cries. My mother saw me sitting in the rocking chair feeding Eva and said, "You look like a Madonna with your long hair, holding that baby." I felt warmth creep over my heart at those words. I felt like a Madonna, the eternal Mother, the Mother of all the living. Eve. I had also named my daughter Eva because I wanted her to celebrate being a woman, to rejoice in her femininity, as I was doing. I felt powerful, as if I had dynamite inside me that could explode and change the shape of the world, that could amend that orbiting path of the planets. I enjoyed every moment with my daughter and could hardly fathom how women were dying to go back to work after the birth of their babies.

Issa and I had had a heated argument over work and children some time before we had Eva. I told him I wanted to continue to work if we had children, and he insisted that we would not have children unless I stayed home with them. "No daycare is going to raise our children," he said. I had chafed at that. I couldn't see myself spending my days changing diapers and cleaning spit-up off onesies. I enjoyed teaching for the prestige it gave me, even if it failed to deliver in other ways. At least I could always say, "I teach Freshman English at N.C. State," and my identity would be established in all of its glory. But if I quit working, what would I call myself? Mother? Housewife? Homemaker? Domestic Engineer? All those titles fell flat, suggesting a woman with pink curlers in her hair watching reruns of "Days of Our Lives." The world seemed to promise that I could have everything: a prestigious career, and cherubic, well-adjusted children who would adore me. But over time, as my frustration with my students grew, I started to believe I could change the world through motherhood, and I viewed my then-imaginary children as projects that I could form, as if out of play dough, to make beautiful human beings. Thus, now that I had a real, live baby, I rushed into mothering, dripping with idealism.

However, my dreams of grandeur did not sustain me for long. As with any idol, the excitement waned. I could see Mick Jaggar with his debauched face moaning, "I can't get no, sa-tis-fac-tion. And I try and try and I try. But I can't get no satisfaction."[51] The ever-present darkness crept into my heart, or rather it emerged from its hiding place, having never left, like a rattlesnake that has lain crouched behind a stone, waiting for the opportune time to strike. I felt as if my personal black cloud had returned. I thought, incongruously, of Winnie-the-Pooh, singing "I'm just a little black rain cloud, hovering over the honey tree." My days at home felt like years in purgatory, with blankness nipping at my heels. One day I wrote the following poem on a scrap of napkin, because I couldn't find any paper in our perennially messy house:

---

[51] 51. The Rolling Stones, "(I Can't Get No) Satisfaction," from the album *Out of our Heads*, released June 5, 1965.

Jonah

While my small child sleeps, I watch
Cars go elsewhere and come back from there,
Unaware that toys float here like shipwreck debris
And the house digests me like a giant fish.

It seems I have become a prophetess
Swallowed by childbirth to watch my daughter breathe
As I drown between the great ribs of the living room
That heave in and out.

I have not run from the Lord.

I would gladly go to Nineveh
And cradle her beneath a gourd,
But my city is this:
To love her in the belly of a fish.

One year the house will cough her up
To rise from foam and go elsewhere.
I will call to her through these bones,
And watch the seaweed loosen from her hair.

Cars outside will go elsewhere and come back from there,
Unaware that now all I can do
Is rearrange the furniture of my fish
Or make a tasty dish from what remains.

Birth pains all over again—
To glimpse her on the shore
While I am still here,
Bleached with gastric juices,
A prophetess left polishing the bones.

I gave to her alone all my Words,
Sure to come true after 40 days,
And now she is born in a blaze of beauty
On the beach.

It doesn't matter that in my heart a worm
Has chewed my vine
And I await a scorching east wind.

I would do it all again.

And I did do it again, and again. If one baby were not enough, then perhaps two or three would do. After a year or so I began yearning for another child, so I stopped my medicines and waited for them to leave my system. I had been taking Xanax for sleep and without it I spent my nights staring at the darkness above me like an unwanted lover. Exhaustion overtook me. I would put Eva in her playpen for hours and lie on the rose-colored nursery rug staring at the yellow Beatrix Potter wall hanging. The cheerful, whimsical figures seemed to mock me. Issa would come home and find me still lying there, crying. But I wanted another baby so badly that I dragged myself through every day like a lame grasshopper. Meanwhile, Eva had grown into a beautiful, intelligent toddler with, ironically, a head of very curly dark hair like Thomas's.

Finally, almost exactly two years after Eva's birth, I became a mother again with the birth of Abigail Maryam. She had her father's large, dark eyes, and her intense stares seemed to drill openings in our hearts. I often wondered what profound thoughts could produce such gazes, and only later would I learn that she had indeed taken on the weight of the universe on her tiny shoulders, like Atlas, and was trying to unravel life's mysteries. She became an affectionate child, who called everybody "sweetheart." By the age of three she was reading short words and would go on to become an avid reader. So, I was now the mother of two beautiful girls, but they could not eclipse the dark hunger that stalked me. I loved them desperately, but many days the only reason I got out of bed was their relentless need. I was responsible for them, so I couldn't spend my days staring at the ceiling and crocheting doilies.

Looking back, I realize that motherhood pulled me out of myself in a miraculous way. I could no longer nurse depression at my breast as my unwanted, but needy child. Love for my children compelled me to fight for life in a way I had never done before, to refuse to let death be my paramour. So, I would arise every morning, or at least most mornings, and read Shakespeare and *Goodnight Moon* to them, then make pink Playdough spaghetti and meatballs. I learned what I had never known before, with all my idealistic notions of motherhood, that love is about sacrifice, about laying down all that one has for the good of someone else.

But the girls were tender teachers. I lost my life, but I found it in the end, as the Bible promises, in the angelic tingle of their laughter.

I still felt the raw, aching hunger that was nearly insatiable, and depression would continue to haunt me during the years to come; yet the very molecular structure of my heart had changed forever. My daughters had marked me with the sign of love, and the mark of Cain turned into a faint, formless smudge, then nearly disappeared. I had carried life inside me, and death had been swallowed up forever. "O Death, where is your sting?"[52] I was reminded of Dylan Thomas's poem, "And Death shall have no more dominion," or John Donne's poem that begins "Death be not proud, though some have called thee mighty and terrible," and ends with the stirring words "Death, thou shall die."[53]

So, Eva's name became a prophecy. She, along with Abigail, became the "Mother of all living"[54] in me, birthing me into a person who had learned to give of myself, and yet found that every time I emptied myself I would be miraculously refilled, as in the Bible story of the widow whose jar of oil never ran out. Thus, when Abigail was a little over a year old, I became pregnant with my third child.

One day in my first trimester, the doctor called, and I was alarmed that he had called. He told me that I had a one in seventy chance of having a baby with Down's Syndrome, according to a routine blood test that the doctor had done. "You need to have further testing done as soon as possible, in case you want to terminate the pregnancy." My heart began to stutter in my chest. I knew that further testing meant amniocentesis, which could cause miscarriage. We decided not to do the amnio but found ourselves on the way to the hospital to do a level two ultrasound, which might reveal any problems.

We were shocked on the day of the test to find that the doctors were pushing the amniocentesis, even though we had told them we did not want it. Suddenly the idea of knowing for sure if the baby was healthy or not seemed incredibly comforting. I was already anxious and depressed, and the thought of five more months of uncertainly was unnerving. I

---

[52] 1 Corinthians 15:55b (ESV).

[53] John Donne, "Holy Sonnet 10," in *The Norton Anthology of English Literature,* vol. 1, 4th ed., ed. M. H. Abrams (New York: W. W. Norton and Company, 1979), 1101.

[54] Genesis 3:20b (ESV).

began to waver in my resolve. As I considered this, we were ushered into an exam room. Our doctor was a woman who was in the last stages of pregnancy. I was immediately comforted. Surely, she would understand our predicament. I lay on the table and the doctor began to show us the baby on the screen, examining each part carefully. We both felt as if she were cradling the baby's head, arms, and legs in her hands as she slowly scrutinized them, describing to us in a gentle voice what she was doing.

Suddenly the room seemed to fill with light, even though the lights were dimmed so we could see the screen. We felt the presence of God descend, and a voice whispered in our hearts, "Do not lay a hand on the child." We were assured then that the baby was healthy, a conviction which was strengthened by the doctor's examination, although she told us we couldn't be completely sure everything was okay. However, we had a word from God that we should not do the amniocentesis. The Lord's word to us had echoed what He said to Abraham as he was about to sacrifice Isaac: "Do not lay a hand on the boy."[55] Thus we decided to name the child "Moriah," because that was the mountain where Abraham had offered up Isaac. I looked the name up in my baby name book and found it meant "The Lord is my teacher." We knew that God was teaching us to trust, to offer up this child and her health to the Lord, and to release our hold on her. Her middle name was to be "Hope," because I wrote down on flowered stationery every verse I could find about hope in the Bible. Every day I read over the verses, and reminded myself that this child's hope, and mine as well, both originated and culminated in Jesus. And so, we gave her up to the Lord, and the Lord gave her back to us. On June 5, 1998, I gave birth to a perfect baby girl, completely healthy.

Thus I had been visited by a trinity of angels: three, the number of God. And so I awakened from my dark slumber, partially at least, to learn at the hands of children the heart of the gospel: we can only truly live when we "die" for the sake of loving another.

---

[55] Genesis 22:12a (NIV).

Birth

We have all borne You,
Like Mary,
Like Eve,
When God had something
Up His sleeve,
A secret that would tarry
Until it was time.
Our names spelled out
An ancient rhyme
In a book before the beginning
When the spinning stars
Were flung like embers
Across the sky.
We panted in childbirth
On that silver night,
Afraid to die,
Caught between terror and delight.
We, too, carried God in our recesses
And at last
We covered the infant with caresses.
Through the cross we became Your mother,
Sister, lover.
You bought us a burgeoning womb
Where You yourself dwell.
You are caught up in our flesh
So that nothing can quell
Your quivering heart.
It nestles there
Like a dove brooding
As our souls wrestle with the God within,
Excluding all other opponents.
Each moment we beget
Something of You,
An infant design perhaps not yet seen,

A sign of the grace interred inside,
A whisper that is a Word
A Word that died
And lifted the yoke of death
From our shoulders.
And now life smolders in You,
In us, in our shared fire.
What is this leaven of loveliness
That inspires our hearts to swell,
This canticle intoning like a bell,
Announcing we are made one.
And though we cannot pronounce Your Name,
We have invoked Your flame
And borne in darkness and danger
The babe that will rest in our manger.

Birth Announcement

(for Eva Elise Zarzar)

All my youth is in you, little girl.
I had grown tired of what seemed new
And now my brain's gone gray.
But you sprang forth,
A tiny wisdom in soft array,
Oh, like a delicate thought
From a carapaced old mind.

I find that from the forge
Of forsaken hope
Where flames gorged on my heart
Like mad ravens,
Your name was graven on my palms
And my raging sea of self was calmed.

Though birth is an ending,
A rending of the flesh,
Since yours was so enmeshed in mine,
Yet I am still entwined with your being
And seeing you is like a glimpse of grace.

Some day you may deny me to my face
And turn into a laurel as you flee,
But now you are the mother of all living in me.

I thought I'd never find again
A nursery inside,
A place where anything could grow,
Since hope had died,
But by your cradle I am

Thousands of years ago awakening

Between where the Tigris and Euphrates
Heave with waters.
I warm you at my wonderful wounded side
And call you "Eve."

Nativity Scene

Someday I must tell you, daughter
How much birth is like death,
How we begin and end with weeping.
Birth comes dressed for reaping
With knife in hand
And the womb is bright with rage.
You tore my flesh like prey
As I forced you headlong into day.
With such beginnings, no wonder
Your cries could not be slaked
And my body quaked as though
Birth were Armageddon.

And so the Christ-child beckons
From the womb,
From the tomb,
With swaddling, with grave clothes.
Are we born?
Or is He born in our death?
Before our first breath
We wrestle like twins, He and I
In the fluid light.
Oh, Holy Son, touch my thigh and overcome.
Whisper in my ear that you have won.
Where is the gentle Jesus shepherds adored?
You are born into my life by the sword.

8

That Way Madness Lies

*I*T WAS A TYPICAL Saturday afternoon. Four women came over to my house to cast a demon out of me. They rang my doorbell and I let them in reluctantly. They clucked over me like mother hens, hugging me warmly and commenting on my "lovely" sweater. I had had trouble that morning deciding what to wear. What does one wear to an exorcism, after all? I finally decided on a pair of gray jeans and a burgundy velour sweater. Nothing too showy. Maybe demons were like bulls and got enraged by bright colors. I took one look at the women who were smiling a little too exuberantly, and perhaps, I thought, condescendingly, and began to wonder if I were doing the right thing.

My anxiety increased when one of the women thrust a huge bundle of cloth at me and began to gush, "The Lord has revealed to Mary Lou that you will be healed over a period of fifteen days, and you are to sleep with these fifteen bed sheets on you the first night. The next night, take one off, and so on, until you have removed all of them. After that, you will be well." I wasn't sure how to respond to that, so I just nodded and put the bed sheets on a chair.

How did it ever come to this? I wondered. The answer was simple. I had been depressed for thirteen years and had prayed for healing and been prayed for innumerable times. I desperately wanted a way out, and Mary Lou told me she had a deliverance ministry. She said everyone she had ever prayed for was healed. She was a chubby, motherly woman with curly red hair and powdery skin. I had approached Mary Lou and asked her to pray for me for deliverance, because the episodes of depression were not abating. I had written in my journal a few days earlier:

"This sadness is someone else's sadness. It belongs to a time long ago. It smells like another house, like someone else's clothing, like someone else's emptiness. This sadness is faded in color, like a photograph long hidden in the bottom of a drawer. I want to discard it like something that belonged to a long dead relative that I never liked. It is fit for the trash pile, fit to be burned. And yet it burns me, and keeps showing up in my kitchen, in my garden, in my mirror...."

I had struggled for years over why I was mentally ill. Was it my upbringing, my brain chemistry, a curse in my family line? Or was it demonic in nature? Because I had cut myself so many times, I often thought of the demon-possessed man in the gospels who lived among the tombs and cut himself with stones. I had surely lived among the tombs myself, and my behavior was self-destructive, so I wondered if some evil spirit inhabited my body, controlling my thoughts and bringing darkness upon me. Fortunately, I had stopped cutting myself several years earlier, but my black moods were unrelenting.

I had tried to read Christian books on the subject of depression, but they either had titles like *Happiness is a Choice*, which was an obvious indictment on those of us who had "chosen" misery, or they categorized depression as a form of self-pity. One such book stated something like this: "Whenever I inform people that depression is self-pity, inevitably some sad-eyed soul will come up to me afterwards and say, 'Aren't there any exceptions?' And I have to say 'no.'" The only book I found comfort in was one written by a non-Christian, William Styron, who had experienced depression himself. In *Darkness Visible*, he writes:

"What I had begun to discover is that, mysteriously and in ways that are totally remote from normal experience, the gray drizzle of horror induced by depression takes on the quality of physical pain. But it is not an immediately identifiable pain, like that of a broken limb. It may be more accurate to say that despair, owing to some evil trick played upon the sick brain by the inhabiting psyche, comes to resemble the diabolical discomfort of being imprisoned in a fiercely overheated room. And because no breeze stirs this caldron, because there is no escape from this smothering confinement, it is entirely natural that the victim begins to think ceaselessly of oblivion."[56]

Thus I clung to another "soulmate's" words, another of countless unsuspecting humans who had been kidnapped by an unknown masked Intruder, who tormented them with carefully twisted and absurd chiaroscuros from their own minds. But I still found no Christian kindred spirits. Christian speakers were as condemning as the authors. I once went to church to hear a well-known prophet speak, hoping desperately that he would call me out of the congregation and prophesy something over me, anything, a prophetic crumb from the children's table that would give me hope.

I sat listening eagerly as he began to speak: "Do you know that there are people going to the hospital thinking they are having a heart attack? And it's just plain old sinful anxiety! Can you believe that??? All those people out there who are depressed or have panic attacks just need to REPENT!" I felt my soul slipping away into a black slime of shame, blocking out all sound except the explosive, corrosive voice of the woman behind me shouting, "AMEN!"

I had wrestled with God over why He hadn't released me from this "smothering confinement," as Styron so aptly characterized depression, a confinement that attracted only shame and condemnation from the church like magnets that stuck to me indelibly. I was sure that I had many sins to repent of, but I did not believe that a malfunctioning brain and a scarred psyche were among them. Some days I concluded that God had visited this scourge on me for my own good, to build my character, because "suffering produces perseverance."[57] He merely wanted me to develop dependence on him, which I had, in great measure.

I was haunted by the passage of scripture that spoke of Paul's "thorn in the flesh,"[58] and how it was given to him to keep him from becoming conceited. The Bible goes so far as to call this thorn a "messenger of

---

[56] William Styron, *Darkness Visible: A Memoir of Madness* (New York: Vintage Books, 1990), 50.

[57] Romans 5:3b (NIV).

[58] 2 Corinthians 12:7b (NIV).

169

Satan" sent to "torment" him.[59] I wondered if God were harrowing me for my spiritual well-being. But my agony seemed to be more than a thorn; it seemed to be a whole thorn tree, a black locust, perhaps, that had taken root and twisted in my soul continuously like barbed wire. It was a crown of thorns to mock me.

Mentally healthy people believe that they are in control of their minds, and they take sanity for granted. I knew that I wasn't in control of mine, that every sane thought and mood I had were gifts of God. Normal people don't realize how delicate the brain is, how their mental health rests over an abyss of madness that they could easily be plunged into. I was deeply grateful for every good mood I experienced; I exulted in them. I sometimes thought of depression as a kind of mental fast in which nothing gives pleasure and one must live completely by faith, bereft of the Lord's blessings, a kind of "dark night of the soul," as St. John of the Cross called it. He believed in a spiritual purgation by which the soul is made ready for union with God. He writes:

> "The first and chief benefit this dry and dark night of contemplation causes is the knowledge of self and of one's own misery. Besides the fact that all the favors God imparts to the soul are ordinarily wrapped in this knowledge, the aridities and voids of the faculties in relation to the abundance previously experienced and the difficulty encountered in the practice of virtue make the soul recognize its own lowliness and misery, which was not apparent in the time of its prosperity....As a result the soul recognizes the truth about its misery, of which it was formerly ignorant. When it was walking in festivity, gratification, consolation, and support in God, it was more content, believing that it was serving God in some way.... Now that the soul is clothed in these other garments of labor, dryness, and desolation, and its former lights have been darkened, it possesses more authentic lights in this

---

[59] 2 Corinthians 12:7b (NIV).

most excellent and necessary virtue of self-knowledge. It considers itself to be nothing and finds no satisfaction in self because it is aware that of itself it neither does nor can do anything."[60]

Thomas Merton also writes of finding life when one reaches the end of oneself:

"Hope then is a gift. Like life, it is a gift from God, total, unexpected, incomprehensible, undeserved. It springs out of nothingness, completely free. But to meet it, we have to descend into nothingness. And there we meet hope most perfectly, when we are stripped of our own confidence, our own strength, when we almost no longer exist. 'A hope that is seen,' says St. Paul, 'is no hope.' No hope. Therefore despair. To see your hope is to abandon hope. The Christian hope that is 'not seen' is a communion in the agony of Christ, it is the identification of our own agonia with the agonia of the God Who has emptied Himself and become obedient unto death. It is the acceptance of life in the midst of death, not because we have courage, or light, or wisdom to accept, but because by some miracle the God of Life Himself accepts to live, in us, at the very moment when we descend into death."[61]

I reasoned that I must be sharing somehow in the sufferings of Christ in Gethsemane and on the cross, sharing in the despair and utter sense of abandonment that the Savior felt in the moment of apparent separation from His Father. Somehow, I had kept vigil with Him during His long hours of agony and had achieved some kind of mystical union with Him in the process. By being depressed one learns to give up the idol of pleasure and seek only the Lord. But just when I was tempted to think that I was blessed by mental illness, because God had chosen the weak

---

[60] Saint John of the Cross, *The Collected Works of Saint John of the Cross*, revised edition, trans. Kieran Kavanaugh and Otilio Rodriguez (Washington, D.C.: Institute of Carmelite Studies, 1991), 386.

[61] Thomas Merton, *The New Man* (New York: The Noonday Press, 1961), 4-5.

and foolish things of the world to shame the wise, I would seesaw the other way and blame it all on Satan, because only a sadist of a god would torture his creatures to foster dependency on him.

And so I cried out to God for answers, and was met with a roaring silence. God did not even appear out of the whirlwind and tell me to brace myself like a man and answer Him. I hid my affliction from Christians, because they usually met my confessions with silence, never bringing up the subject, never asking me how I was doing. Or worse, they would give me articles about people who were taking psychiatric medications "even though they knew they shouldn't" and finally decided to trust God and threw all the medication down the toilet. Of course, these people never felt depressed again. I had been on so many medications that I lost count. Years earlier, I had reached thirty. One well-meaning friend commented on how these "besetting sins" are hard to get rid of. My only allies were my husband, who believed my illness was not my fault, and my ob-gyn, who called me a "hero" for putting up with such suffering. She was not a Christian, obviously. I also found solace in my faithful psychiatrist, who assured me that I was not to blame for my illness and that it was not a sign that I was somehow spiritually lacking. Although most of my days met with struggle during this time, a strange new element began to creep into my life.

Inexplicably, incongruously, episodes of joy emerged. I began to sense the presence of a holy God in a way I never had before. Sometimes I was so overcome with the presence of God that I would lie prostrate on the floor for an hour, sucking in my breath from the ponderous glory. When I was prayed for, I would often feel myself melting inwardly, and fall backwards as if into the arms of God. I remembered the first time I had been "slain in the Spirit," years ago at a Bible study conducted by a friend of Issa's. We were not yet married, and he was attempting to introduce me to his Pentecostal culture. That night they were praying for a woman named Yolanda. As they began to pray, Yolanda began to sob, until finally she produced some high-pitched sounds that could only be described as howls. I grew more and more uncomfortable. One of the men praying for her suddenly yelled "now," and Yolanda fell backwards into the arms of another man. He laid her gently on the floor, where she stayed for the duration of the meeting. The man praying for her said he had felt a rush of heat flow through his hand before she fell. I swiftly concluded that Yolanda had gotten overly emotional and had hyperventilated. Until they prayed for me. I stood there calmly, unsuspecting as the men laid hands on me and began to pray. Suddenly I felt as if my insides were turning to jelly. I started to sway. Warmth spread through me, and at last I fell back into Issa's waiting arms. I quickly changed my mind about Yolanda.

In addition to being "slain in the Spirit," I began to experience another supernatural occurrence. Once when I was overcome by the Holy Spirit, I sensed incomprehensible words pouring out of my soul, words that were not quite words and could not be expressed aloud. I wondered if this were speaking in tongues gone bad. I had never heard of anyone "thinking in tongues." But I experienced this over and over: a rush of feeling, as if the wind of the Holy Spirit had come over me, and the ecstatic utterances in my spirit. That spring I had felt the new life burgeoning within me, but very gently, tentatively—just punctuation marks of beauty in a long text of blankness. Most of the time, depression tended to turn me into that piece of Styrofoam. But as the trees began to bud one spring, I wrote in my journal:

> "As many springs as I have seen, the joy and excitement of new life has not lessened in my adulthood. Though other joys have grown cold or lost their freshness, to spring I always come as a child, amazed again by the renewed earth as though it were happening for the first time. Seasons are, I believe, another way that God reminds us in a physical way who He is. Although anyone, even a non-Christian, would say that spring represents new life, do any of us fully grasp the weight of what happens before our very eyes? All winter we feel the force of the cold, the bone-chilling heartless terror of frost. And though many say that ice is beautiful, it is not a beauty that comforts but one that kills. We shiver in the face of an awful Beauty, and if we did not know the love of the Creator, we would believe the beauty mocked us. Is it not more cruel to be tortured by a thing of beauty than by ugliness? Doesn't the stinging beauty mock us as we die? Yet this is not the case, because

we know that at the center of the universe is the Person of Divine Love, where beauty does not mock, even when it kills. Yet each winter seems the last, the final gasp of a world gone mad with ugliness. We are humbled by our shivering. We run for comfort from the sharp swords of ice. Sometimes the bleakness seeps into our very souls. But all this sets the stage for our total astonishment at the spring. I know without a doubt that those trees that lined the gray, forsaken streets were DEAD. They were sticks, skeletons—bare, nightmarish ghouls. Yet I am astounded to find that again, buds and blossoms creep out of these brown and bony tombs. The whole creation is crying out "Redemption!" in every blooming, building, birdsonging thing. How can we miss it?

What is this "spring fever" that people scorn, but a response to creation's utter desire to LIVE! A response to our Creator's utter desire that we should LIVE! "LIVE!" he cries over this squirming, bloody, infant world, as Yahweh declares over the infant Israel in Ezekiel 16. Spring is not here merely to please our aesthetic sense. This fragrance is not merely sweet. If we receive it, the spring is urging us away from Death. God makes a beautiful appeal, but underlying its delicacy is a profound urgency. For if we do not heed His call to live, where else can we go but back inside the spectral, bony branches? Back inside that suffocating soil that in its very nature desired to be rid of us, to push us upward toward our true destination. As we rise beneath the soil, no one, not even we ourselves, can see the mysterious upward surge of the green in us. On the surface, we may look as dead as ever. Yet the green points are guided upward by the hand of God until, one day, unexpectedly we are astonished to find that death, again, has flowered. I have felt the deadness in my soul giving way, imperceptibly, to the "force that through the green fuse drives the flower,"[62] as Dylan Thomas wrote.

---

[62] Dylan Thomas, "The Force that through the Green Fuse Drives the Flower," in *The Poems of Dylan Thomas*, ed. Daniel Jones (New York: New Directions Publishing Company, 1971), 77.

But life hurts. Deadness is easy. To embrace the spring takes courage. Am I up to the task? Will I let winter be my lover, like Persephone, the bride of Hades, or will I emerge from the Underworld like Venus born from the foam of the sea?"

With my partial spiritual awakening, I felt a desire to be baptized again. I had been baptized as a baby, but suddenly wanted to experience it as an adult, to publicly proclaim my allegiance to Christ. So, I dressed in black shorts and a t-shirt decorated with cats and headed to Falls Lake with the pastor of our church and a handful of attenders. I felt the water rush over me, and I immediately felt joyful and new, as if I had indeed been buried with and raised with Christ. My children were waiting on the shore, cheering as I came up out of the water, although they were too young to really understand what was happening.

Our church life had changed drastically, also. We had stopped attending our traditional, non-denominational church and had joined a start-up church that met in downtown Raleigh in a park frequented by homeless people. We met on Saturday nights, and sometimes the worship would last for hours. Once in a while we would just start running around the park shouting while the worship team played, as if we were defying the powers of darkness. Often, we danced, with flags and tambourines. I enjoyed the worship immensely. One night, after a particularly meaningful worship service, I wrote:

"All the rivers of our longing seek you, O Divine Ocean whose breakers make us weep with joy. We have prayed until our bodies become prayer, under the cupped hand of the night, whirling with prayer like dancers with our hands full of jewels that we fling into the darkness, words we do not understand, longings that will tear us. The sky stretches like black paper over our heads, but the sound of our rejoicing rises like unhindered flame to consume the canopy of emptiness and despair. On such nights we can see the stars, set like jewels in the endless ornament of sky. The shuffling passersby are startled for a moment, as if in the corner of their eyes they glimpsed a chariot of fire in the sky over this place of sorrow and refuse...."

We even had church outside when it stormed. One night we danced in the rain, keeping time to the music with primitive instruments made of gutters and scraps of sheet metal that we beat with sticks. There seemed to be something primeval in our worship, as if we had thrown off all the trappings of traditional church and reached the very bones of worship, the heart of communion with a holy God. Yet I felt that sometimes we reached the point of absurdity, such as when someone had the idea that we should buy one hundred helium balloons and anoint them with oil, then release them over the city. One woman prayed that if anyone who wanted to curse the effort attempted to put his hand in the oil, that it would burn him like acid. I was highly skeptical, but I went along anyway, and the oil, fortunately, didn't burn me. I vaguely wondered if we were littering. The balloons were supposed to release an anointing of revival over the city. On another occasion we were told to form a square, and people on each side of the square were to exchange places with those opposite them. We spent the evening doing this because the Lord had given someone the following scripture from Ezekiel:

> "When the people of the land come before the Lord at the appointed times, whoever enters by the north gate to worship is to go out the south gate; and whoever enters by the south gate is to go out the north gate. No one is to return through the gate by which he entered, but each is to go out the opposite gate. The prince is to be among them, going in when they go in and going out when they go out."[63]

I felt as if I were back in kindergarten, playing "Red Rover" or musical chairs, or as if I had stepped into a Flannery O'Connor novel. I should have taken these oddities as a warning not to trust everything people claimed to be an oracle of God, but I was so desperate for healing that I had still found myself in my living room, staring at a pile of bed sheets, about to have an exorcism performed on me. The Lord had told Mary Lou that the demons would not manifest themselves in any way as they came out, so I had nothing to worry about. She told me that demons, like

---

[63] Ezekiel 46:9 (CEV).

other things, can enter through the pores of our skin, a kind of demon osmosis. I listened to her every word, sure that freedom was on its way.

The deliverance lasted about an hour. Mary Lou cast out every demon imaginable, down to the demon of the kitchen sink. She targeted demons of infirmity, insomnia, depression, and a deaf and mute spirit, which she said was making me shy. I felt nothing as she prayed, but hope swelled within me that soon I would be able to get off my medicine. Mary Lou finished praying, and I couldn't keep a ridiculous grin off my face, partly from hope, and partly from my amusement at the pile of fifteen bed sheets. But, hey, I figured, God had certainly performed stranger actions.

"Look at the change in her!" remarked one of the women.

"Oh, yes, what a difference!"

The women hugged and fussed over me for a while, telling me that they were to me like the four men who had lowered the paralytic man through the roof to get to Jesus. After they left, I stared at the pile of sheets and absently began to look through them. Hmmm, a paisley print, two twin sheets with lambs on them. Oh, here was one with a Beauty and the Beast theme. That night I stopped my medication, and dutifully but skeptically piled the fifteen sheets on top of me before I went to bed. Without the meds, of course I couldn't sleep, so for many nights after that I endured insomnia. I did not really feel depressed, but I still felt anxious frequently. However, I was determined to stick to my "cure," so the only medicine I took was a tranquilizer at night to help me sleep. I was relieved to get off the drug I was taking, because it made me horribly irritable. When I was teaching Eva to read, every time she would stumble on a word, my irritation would explode such that I had to suppress an urge to shake her.

For six months I hung onto my hope that I had been delivered, until finally it became excruciatingly obvious that I was still, in fact, seriously ill. We were in the mountains on vacation, driving to take the girls to Tweetsie Railroad. Suddenly, out of nowhere, terrifying thoughts invaded my mind. I began to believe that I was not saved and that I was going to hell. These thoughts were unlike any I had ever had before, not in content, but in character. Ever since that sermon I had heard years ago, I had struggled with the idea of predestination. I saw that there was some evidence for it in the Bible, and yet I could not reconcile the five-point Calvinist position with the idea of a loving God who "desires all men to be saved."

I pondered the horror of being a reprobate, the one that God has rejected. I pored over books on the subject, trying to come to some resolution, yet I never reached a satisfactory conclusion. And so the haunting refrain played over and over in my mind, *I'm not chosen. I'm not chosen.* The thoughts were repetitive, as if a tape recorder inside me were droning the fatal words, over and over. They were also all consuming. I did not think the thoughts; they thought me. Fear gnawed at me relentlessly. I saw the door to madness open, and I watched my bare foot step through it. I decided to take Xanax, and after a while the thoughts subsided, but I remained overly sensitive all that day. As I watched the people spinning and squealing on the teacup ride at Tweetsie railroad, I was overcome by emotion. I wondered how many in this press of humanity were going to hell.

By the end of the week, the thoughts took over my mind completely, with no relief. I was so anxious that I felt as if someone had kicked me in the stomach, and I experienced waves of heat and cold that swept over my body. I attempted to fight the thoughts, for as King Lear declared as he wandered out in the storm, "That way madness lies."[64] I tried rebuking Satan out loud, but the thoughts continued to bore holes in me. I would lie awake at night in torment, repeating a verse from Psalms over and over in my head: "He ransoms me unharmed from the battle waged against me." I found that my mind had incapacitated my body: all I could do was lie on the couch in agony. Because my children obviously needed care, my parents faithfully came over every day to attend to them.

I made an appointment with my doctor and two days later walked into his office and blurted out unceremoniously, "WHAT happened to me?"

"Your brain went haywire," he told me, and handed me a prescription for an anti- psychotic medication. It didn't work. I felt as if I had fallen in an abyss that was deeper than any I had ever known. My mind no longer belonged to me. I had become someone else. I began to have suicidal thoughts but was afraid of going to hell if I killed myself. My doctor told my husband to send me to the hospital, or else have someone watch me

---

64 William Shakespeare, *King Lear*, in *The Riverside Shakespeare*, ed. G. Blakemore Evans (Boston: Houghton Mifflin Company, 1974), 1276.

all the time. Either my parents or my mother-in-law came over every day while I drowned in thoughts. *My God,* I thought, *I'm being crucified.*

Desperate, I called a woman from our church who was a self-proclaimed prophet.

"Do you have any idea what is happening to me?" I begged.

She was silent for a moment, then said, "The only word that comes to mind is 'pharmacopeia.' I think you have a spirit of mind-altering drugs. What would happen if you got off all your medication?"

I shuddered. I had just started on a new anti-psychotic and was praying it would work soon. So, I had a drug demon. But I was terrified to stop the medicine. I would just have to coexist with the drug demon.

After a few weeks, I felt somewhat relieved. The thoughts were still there, but they had lost some of their venom. I began to reduce my medication because the doctor believed the anti-depressant would begin to alleviate the thoughts after a couple of weeks. I even felt well enough to go out to Starbucks with Amanda, a woman from church. She was tall and thin, with long light brown hair and black-rimmed glasses. She loved to dance at our worship services by swaying back and forth and waving her arms sinuously in air. At Starbucks I ordered a venti Earl Grey tea, and she ordered a mocha latte. We sat down, and she asked me how I was.

"I've had a rough time lately," I admitted. "You know I struggle with depression, but lately I've had these frightening thoughts that I'm not saved and I'm going to hell."

Amanda was silent for a moment, then she replied, "Nancy, have you ever thought there might be a reason for your anxiety? Can you tell me for sure when you began trusting in Christ and stopped trusting in yourself for salvation?"

I started to shake visibly. The Earl Grey tea spilled on my hands, burning them. My fingers turned red. So, it was true. Even other people believed that I wasn't saved.

"I have to go," I muttered quickly and ran out of Starbucks, leaving behind my spilled tea. I rushed to my car, fumbling with my keys and dropping them in a mud puddle. I drove ten miles over the speed limit.

Issa took one look at my face when I got home and exclaimed, "What happened?"

"Amanda questioned my salvation." I saw a look of horror pass over Issa's face. Then his expression became angry. He saw that I was hysterical, so he suggested I take some medicine. I went back up on my dose that night and was not able to reduce it for five years.

Over the years my fearful thoughts subsided to periodic episodes, alternating with seasons of returning joy followed by bouts of crippling depression. Finally, one day, the thoughts ceased altogether. I was walking on the treadmill in my bathroom, reading the book of Philippians. I came across the following passage, as if for the first time:

> ...[H]ave the same mindset as Christ Jesus:
> Who, being in very nature God,
> did not consider equality with God something to be used to
> his own advantage;
> rather, he made himself nothing
> by taking the very nature of a servant,
> being made in human likeness.
> And being found in appearance as a man,
> he humbled himself
> and became obedient to death—
> even death on a cross![65]

I had an epiphany, and the power of the word of God seared my mind. I was not making myself nothing. I was obsessed with myself and my own salvation, when I should be emptying myself, as our Lord did. My thoughts about going to hell ceased abruptly, but new obsessions took their place. I began to think, *What if God doesn't exist, and I'm believing in a lie?* Then I would wallow in guilt for having betrayed Christ.

One day when I was lying in bed, my mind writhing in angst, sure that I had lost my faith forever, my mother-in-law came to try to comfort me. When I laid eyes on her, all I could do was moan over and over, "I've lost my faith!"

"Don't worry about your faith, honey," she reassured me. "The Lord is holding it for you." I could picture Jesus' open hands, cupped around the poor, trembling, featherless sparrow that was my faith. Her words consoled me.

Over the years, my obsessions grew less and less frequent, but I was unable to get off my medicine, which caused me to gain weight, so that

---

[65] Philippians 2:5-8 (NIV).

I eventually weighed 225 pounds. I had always been rather vain about my willowy figure, so now my self-image began to plummet. I was too depressed to diet. Food was one of the only sources of pleasure I had. I tried a new medicine to replace the old one that my mother, rather unhelpfully, always called "that medicine that makes you fat." The new drug did not cause weight gain, but frequently I would feel a strange anxiety, as if all my cells were vibrating and my body were turning inside out. I would pace the floor, unable to sit or lie down until the episode passed. Then I found myself on two anti-psychotic drugs, unable to reduce either one.

During this time, I attempted to make sense of what had happened to me, to heal from the wounds of lost hope. We began going to a church where no one claimed to have the gift of prophecy, and where no one ever said, "The Lord told me…." I often thought of Mary Lou's revelation that I would be healed over fifteen days, via the sheets and the deliverance prayer. I concluded that I was like the man in Jesus' parable who had a demon cast out of him and seven others invaded, more wicked than the first, when they found the house in order and swept clean. I later thought that perhaps because the wounds in my heart had not been healed, that demonic oppression had continued, and had even gotten worse.

At that time, I was just deeply confused, wondering how God could have let me go through such torment. Yet even when I was in the throes of anguish, there was always a tiny, nearly imperceptible voice in my head that told me I belonged to God and that He was holding me. Always, always, throughout my years of depression, the Spirit of God rallied in me and provided me with the ghost of a hope that God would deliver me. This voice sustained me, though it was a spider's web of a thought, a gossamer thread. But every once in a while, I wondered what waited at the center of the web: a loving God, or a villainous spider? As a result of my sufferings, God grew strange to me, in a way, as if He were the tall, dark hero in those romance novels who always acts so mysteriously that the heroine wonders if he is friend or foe. I tried to come to terms with this in my journal:

"I have considered the Christian life from every angle, and I have not yet been able to deny the presence of an awful, bloody, tormenting cross. Though I have known many blessings and felt at times the irrepressible stab of joy, though I have felt peace settle on me as an inscrutable dove, I cannot explain away the fierce, relentless pursuit of my soul by Satan, or the fact that he sometimes seems to win. I have stared him in his dreadful contorted face as I was swallowed up by panic or despair. I have felt his breath on my neck. I cannot help but ask myself what kind of God would allow His children to become the plaything of a sadist. Where is the promised peace, at such times, when the heart pounds, when one's whole body is on fire with fear? Where is God when His Silence screams alongside the taunts of the enemy? Where is the Shepherd when the green pastures are scorched, and the still waters become tsunamis?"

This is the Cross, I decided. This is Gethsemane. Jesus asked that the cup be taken from Him, and we, too, rebel against the pain with our whole beings. Why does Paul say he delights in hardships when all I felt was a sickening, deadly fear of what trial I may have to face next? I had suffered beyond the limits of what I could bear. I had longed to die. I had, indeed, felt the sentence of death, as Paul did, and despaired of life. But what amazed me was the incredible resilience of my spirit, the way I rose from my own ashes like a phoenix to a place of triumph. Even though God seemed to abandon me again and again, I still worshipped Him, followed Him, called out to Him. I said with Peter, over and over, "To whom shall we go, Lord?"

There is nowhere else except the dark, despairing shadow of a cross on the Place of the Skull. Some of Jesus' disciples left Him when He told them they had to eat His flesh and drink His blood. This is the call of the gospel: to enter into something that seems abhorrent, contrary to nature, where we must rejoice in trials, where we are blessed because we mourn, where troubles achieve glory for us. God claims only to be close to the broken-hearted, to those who mourn, to those poor in spirit—and in my case He had seemed to make it inevitable that I would fall into those categories. What is it about suffering that is so necessary, that even

Jesus Himself had to experience it to become "perfect"? Why must we be trampled by the enemy to become holy?

And yet God the Father answered Jesus' prayer with an unequivocal "No." He said it was not possible to avoid the cross. If suffering entailed mere circumstances or even physical ailments, these could be borne, because the Bible says that a man's spirit sustains him in sickness. But it goes on to say, "a crushed spirit who can bear?"[66] Why does God strip us of peace and joy and leave us absolutely without consolation at times? Why is our very sanity threatened? Why does the mind become a monster that ravages the soul without mercy? And God sits by, watching. But deep down I believe He enters into our distress, as Isaiah states, "In all their distress he too was distressed."[67] Someday He will punish Satan for having tormented His saints. Surely, He is boiling with rage over all the enemy does to taunt His precious people. But isn't it easy to have faith, Satan would say, when the believer is filled with peace and joy? Take these away, says the accuser, and the saint will curse God to His face.

And what if she perseveres, in spite of the loss of everything that brings her comfort and joy? Is not Satan defeated, and God vindicated? What a price to pay to win a cosmic battle. But is it not worth it in the end, to see Satan flee, having fallen into his own pit? During the trial, I would rather forgo holiness than suffer another moment of anguish. But afterward, when my spirit rises above its turmoil, I feel awed and thankful that I have not lost my faith when everything in me was screaming that God could not be a God of love. Yet He is—HE IS!—and it is only this belief that propels me, that keeps me from taking to my bed in despair. This is the Gospel, that we can be, as Paul puts it, "hard-pressed on every side, but not crushed."[68] In truth, we are beaten to a pulp, stoned and left for dead, and yet something illuminates our nearly lifeless bodies and sets them back on their feet only to face a new cross, a new shadow, a Gethsemane where sweat becomes blood and prayers are not answered. I can say, borrowing the eloquent words of Gerard Manley Hopkins:

> Thou art indeed just, Lord, if I contend
> With thee; but, sir, so what I plead is just.
> Why do sinners' ways prosper? And why must

---

[66] Proverbs 18:14 (ESV).

[67] Isaiah 63:9a (NIV).

[68] 2 Corinthians 4:8 (NIV).

Disappointment all I endeavor end?
Wert thou my enemy, O thou my friend,
How wouldst thou worse, I wonder, than thou dost
Defeat, thwart me? Oh, the sots and thralls of lust
Do in spare hours more thrive than I that spend,
Sir, life upon thy cause. See, banks and brakes
Now, leaved how thick! Laced they are again
With fretty chervil, look, and fresh wind shakes
Then; birds build—but not I build; no, but strain
Time's eunuch, and not breed one work that wakes.
Mine, O thou lord of life, send my roots rain.[69]

And what if I should grow tired of being tossed to and fro, and decide to desert my God? But how can I desert my very soul, the one who is united with me in spirit? If Cathy can say "I am Heathcliff," then I can say "I am Christ," in the sense that I have died and He has been born in me. As Athanasius wrote in "On the Incarnation," "God became man that man might become God."[70] And what if He has asked me, as Abraham, to slaughter what is dearest to me on the altar of holiness? I will bind it and take the knife in my quivering hand. Poe wrote of his lover, 'Nothing can ever dissever my soul from the soul of my beautiful Annabel Lee." Likewise, "nothing can ever dissever my soul from the soul"[71] of God, my exquisite Spouse." What else can I say? To leave is folly. "That way madness lies."[72]

[69] Gerard Manley Hopkins, ("Thou Art Indeed Just, Lord"), in *The Poems of Gerard Manley Hopkins*, 4th edition, ed. W. H. Gardner and N. H. Mackenzie (London: Oxford University Press, 1967), 100.

[70] Athanasius, *On the Incarnation*, in *Christology of the Later Fathers*, ed. Edward R. Hardy (Louisville, KY: The Westminster Press, 1954), 107.

[71] Edgar Allen Poe, "Annabel Lee," in *The Norton Anthology of American Literature,* volume B, ed. Nina Baym (New York: W. W. Norton & Company, Inc., 2012), 644.

[72] William Shakespeare, *King Lear*, in *The Riverside Shakespeare*, ed. G. Blakemore Evans (Houghton Mifflin Company, Boston, 1974), p. 1276.

Psalm 151

Dear God,
Have You noticed
That my tears are like acid
That weeps flame
And my mouth has melted
From Fahrenheit prayers
That skirt the bullseye
Of Your heart
And burst like shrapnel
Back on my head?
And have You seen
How my fingernails
Have tormented the sky
Like a turquoise chalkboard
Just so I can maybe
Paint them with Your Presence?
Is this because I have swallowed a gnat,
Or a camel, or a gin-and-tonic
At a bar You don't happen to frequent?
If I don't see a few of Your ready-to-eat Words
Dangling from tiny red parachutes
Scuttling through the empyrean
Into my backyard
I will set up shop in Sheol
And sell cups of gall.

9

The Heavy Art of Joy

"I have heard the mermaids singing, each to each.
I do not think that they will sing to me.
I have seen them riding seaward on the waves
Combing the white hair of the waves blown back
When the wind blows the water white and black.
We have lingered in the chambers of the sea
By sea-girls wreathed with seaweed red and brown
Till human voices wake us, and we drown."[73]

*T*HUS LAMENTS J. Alfred Prufrock, the disillusioned, middle-aged anti-hero of T.S. Eliot's poem, "The Love Song of J. Alfred Prufrock." The summer I turned forty years old, the mermaids began to sing to me—to me, one of the "weak and foolish things," one of the "despised things," one of the "things that are not."[74] At first it was a faint hum, then it broke out into a symphony. And I did not drown there, lingering in the chambers of the sea. I had heard this voice before, in the last five years, on occasions, but seemingly overnight the music became a daily occurrence. Perhaps they were not sea-girls at all that sang, but angels, as joy inexplicably broke into my life. I was still on medication and attempts to stop it were unsuccessful, but in the past I had been on as many as five medications at once, and still felt depressed. I believed

---

[73] T. S. Eliot, "The Love Song of J. Alfred Prufrock," in *T. S. Eliot: The Complete Poems and Plays* (San Diego: Harcourt Brace Jovanovich, 1967), 7.

[74] 1 Corinthians 1:27-28 (NIV).

that at last, the Lord was shining his favor on me. I hardly knew what to do with my new-found joy and peace. I saw each day as an exquisite gift from God and I squeezed every drop of pleasure from it, wondering if, as Sylvia Plath put it, the "bell jar" would descend again.

I had begun homeschooling my daughters some years before, even in the throes of depression, against the advice of my relatives. Homeschooling gave me the motivation to get out of bed every morning when everything in me screamed for inactivity. Many days I struggled through worksheets, math activities, and read-alouds, draining my short supply of mental energy to meet my children's needs. But suddenly homeschooling them was glorious, and each day spent with my children was like a jewel appearing in my mailbox where before there had only been flyers for Merry Maids or for products designed to eliminate unwanted body hair. I began wearing lipstick and earrings again, and my wardrobe sported pink and purple again instead of blacks and tans. My whole being seemed to come to life, and at last I understood what Jesus meant when He said He came that we might have life "to the full." What was the secret? Can I now write a book called "Overcoming Depression for Christian Dummies"? I have no idea. The Spirit is like the wind—it blows as it pleases, and we don't perceive where it comes from or where it's going.[75] All I know is that I somehow had become a beleaguered princess in a cosmic spiritual drama, and the elusive Prince had begun to allure me in the desert. One day I wrote in my journal:

> I am longing for the Wedding Night with God, and I no longer care how shocking that is. If there is to be any sort of wedding, or any sort of bride and groom, then must there not be a wedding night, a consummation? And what will that entail, actually? Surely something wholly other—not like a mere sexual encounter here on earth. Something impossibly wild and unearthly. Will I be burned at the ever-present heresy stake for asking such a question? But if the shadow of our relationship with Christ—marriage—is so intense, then how can one conceive of its true archetype?

---

[75] John 3:8.

I must confess that I crave the exquisite, nearly unbearable romance of God. I live in the hope that one day I will press my lips to the wounded feet of Christ, and He will never again say *"noli me tangere."* He will take my hand, drawing me toward Him, and whisper my new and virginal name against my hair.... And then my fragile imagination falters and returns to the ground from which it came. But I know that we will share at last the true and holy Eucharist—I will taste the living bread of His flesh and quench my unbearable thirst with the blood of His innocence.

And then I draw back from the vision, as if I have toyed with blasphemy, but the piercing longing drapes my face like a widow's veil. Without this—the perpetual hope of the *Parousia*—how could I possibly rise up every morning and face my own likeness in the shards of the broken mirror that I have been given? But I have read my Bible, birthed prayers in agony, memorized part of Song of Solomon, and tried to run away from myself into worship. And yet I feel deeply unsatisfied, like the Lady of Shallot who moaned, "I am half-sick of shadows."[76] The more I call across the chasm to God, the more I simply find some rude, bloody beams and a handful of spikes. The more I reach out my arms for an embrace, the more empty they become.

Not that I haven't felt satisfaction. Not that I haven't at times fallen deep into God's Presence. But ultimately, what I know best is what I do not have. How does one walk down the aisle with an apophatic Lover? I am longing for a kind of kiss that I have never known—a kiss so real that it is not. It seems almost cruel that God should leave us here with such desires, staring upward like the disciples after Jesus's ascension. And then we hear the angels all around saying, "Men and women of Galilee, why do you stand here looking into the sky?"[77] But what is the purpose of all this painful waiting? Why the intense longing, and only shadows to satiate it? It is painful to want God on this earth. I want him so badly that I am ashamed of my desire; I try to suppress it, yet there it is, swelling inside me like a supernatural fetus. I find myself wondering if Jesus finds me beautiful, so I dress nicely and put on makeup and perfume as if He were an ordinary lover. It is strange, being a mortal in love with the Divine.

---

[76] Alfred Tennyson, "The Lady of Shallot," in *Tennyson's Poetry*, ed. Robert W. Hill, Jr. (New York, W. W. Norton & Company, 1971), 15.

[77] Acts 1:11 (NIV).

How should one act in such a relationship? It is always a clutching of the invisible, reaching out with arms that are never filled.

There is some sense of satisfaction here, though. Sometimes the longing itself is so strong that it feeds me like bread. I can almost feast on desire, it is so utterly heartbreaking. Loneliness for God is unlike any other loneliness. It burns; it ravishes. I find myself so desperate to hear the voice of God that even regulations about mildew in Leviticus interest me. And I cry out to Jesus, "Tell me, please tell me how to find a Love Song in this warning about mold!"

Song of Solomon says that "His mouth is sweetness itself."[78] I want to gorge myself on his voice. I seek and read and search and pray, and still find myself hungry. Yet I have heard him say to me, "See! the winter is past; the rains are over and gone.... Arise, come, my darling; my beautiful one, come with me."[79] Indeed, "the rains are over and gone."

---

[78] Song of Songs 5:16a (NIV).

[79] Ibid., 5:11; 13a (NIV).

Tasting Famine

Sometimes my hunger for You
Is like bread itself
And I gorge myself on its crumbs
By desperate handfuls.
It seems Your presence teems so much
That even Your absence leaves
A trace, as of fragrant air,
And I gasp it in with greedy lungs.

Who are You,
That even Your shadow,
The brooding air of where
You are not,
Descends on me like dew
And I can binge on You,
Even while burning with thirst?

You are the first to kiss me thus,
With lips that are not there
And yet I always taste
The holy stain of wine.

No one can see You and live
And so You give us freely
Of Your invisibility,
Your silence
That is pregnant yet with melody.
You have reaped to the corners of Your field
And left us nothing,
But we find ourselves feasting
On what is not there,
For where You have lingered
There can never be famine.

I thought I felt You touch my hair,
Or brush the tips of Your fingers
Across my brow,
And yet I know now
It was only the ghost of contact,
A dream distilled from a dream.

For I am alone.

And yet something has grown
In the lack like loam:
A shoot, a stem
That bursts with heads of grain.

And now, not in Your arms,
I perish in abundance
From a drought that smells of rain.

I would lie in my bed at night and listen to worship music after everyone else had gone to sleep, pondering my longing for God. I would sense the weight of the presence of God pressing down on me, and I felt as if a deep well inside of me had opened, pouring out passion for God. One night I read the passage in Luke about Simeon, and how he said that the Lord could dismiss him in peace because he had seen God's salvation. I realized that I myself had held the infant Jesus in my arms; I had glimpsed salvation, the very face of God, and I could ask no more from this life except to immerse myself in His glory.

Myself as Simeon

(Luke 2:25-35)

In the badlands of my soul,
Embalmed in sand,
I quivered for the Consolation.
Sometimes there were date palms,
Or a bitter revelation
In a murky spring.
But mostly I was married to Despair,
My hair like fetters
Bound around my head,
Like strings that channeled
Only songs of regret.
But I gathered a prophecy
Like an ephah of manna,
A message spelled out in bones
On the desert floor:
There would be a Door
From another world
And One would migrate here
Like a mixed-up butterfly
Who would become a worm.
I would see him before I'd die—
My blood could not deny the voice from Another
That had settled on me in a desert storm.
A veil would be torn,
A curtain disarmed—
A Child would thunder in my arms.
The Word was certain.
Now his sword has pierced my heart
And I have learned the heavy art of joy.
The Boy's a Man now,
But He has never abandoned the embrace,
Although I don't quite know who's holding whom.

His face is always in bloom above mine,
And He is the trellis to my vine.
And now that I have known his joy,
Death is to me a brittle toy
That Life can break at will.
I am not afraid to be still.
So Master, lead me to the grave,
For death is but a surly knave,
A eunuch wasp denuded of the sting it had before.
Now Peace can lead me to the Door.

I longed for life to go on, because its consolations were now sweet and frequent, but I knew that I could give it up because the "child had thundered in my arms." Thus I had "learned the heavy art of joy"—heavy because unweighty things escape us into the empyrean without leaving behind a trace. But ponderous things are pregnant with a fecund fetus that in turn may give birth to others. But being taught such an art requires that we also gulp down gall and heartbreak. I was reminded of the verse in Isaiah that reads: "Your eyes will see the king in his beauty and view a land that stretches afar."[80]

I always thought of entering into Narnia or middle-earth when I read this. I had seen the King in His beauty, and the land had been laid open before me, a land I had glimpsed in moments of deep worship. It was not just heaven that lay before me, but a place in my heart where the Everlasting God meets the finite soul. The road to this land is littered with the bare skulls and bones of the self. Like Christian in *Pilgrim's Progress,* we can fall into the "Slough of Despond."[81] We can stumble through the Arctic for years, aching with cold, when suddenly one day the aurora borealis inflames the sky. Our eyes can sometimes glimpse a trick of light that illuminates for a moment the banks of the Jordan, but then it slips back into the penumbra of this life. This land is here already, but not yet. Everywhere we look we see the Kingdom storming the mundane, the broken and the sorrowful. The kingdom is among us, and we are the blind and the lame that have been invited to the feast.

In this land, beggars are princes; the wretched wear jewels. Tears are the currency with which we buy joy. The world is turned topsy-turvy. The foolish are wise. The weak are strong. Having seen this land, I can never turn back, no matter what the cost. I am drawn onward, inexorably toward my destination, and truly it seems that "our present sufferings are not worth comparing with the glory that will be revealed in us."[82] In fact, "our light and momentary troubles are achieving for us a glory that far outweighs them all."[83]

---

[80] Isaiah 33:17 (NIV).

[81] John Bunyan, *The Pilgrim's Progress* (Carlisle, PN: The Banner of Truth Trust, 1997), 8.

[82] Romans 8:18a (NIV).

[83] 2 Corinthians 4:17 (NIV).

And yet I could read "the land that stretches afar"[84] ironically, too. In contrast, the land could be the terrible terrain of depression which has marred the landscape for so many years of my life. It was a flat land with no vegetation or shelter—an occasional vine sprang up, but a worm always devoured it. For some reason this scenario reminded me of the children's book "Harold and the Purple Crayon," in which we find Harold on a blank page with nothing but a crayon. He is totally alone in a wasteland. The only reality he knows is the one he creates with his crayon. He sets out to decorate his blankness with the things he draws.

Like Harold, I was faced with a blank page, an oblivion, in my illness, and the only hope I had was to feebly draw some sort of meaning there with my purple crayon. There was no road there, so I was forced to create one. Only I didn't draw with my crayon—I wrote words. I wrote poems as altar stones to mark the journey. If life is, as Nietzche said, "a long obedience in the same direction,"[85] I had forced my feet, one in front of the other, to walk the path for nearly twenty years. And finally, I had found at least a glimpse of relief.

Occasionally I still felt my heart lapse into a blank stare, and the world would go gray, but those days were infrequent. I still experienced obsessions, too, and the strange restlessness caused by the medication. Once, for a whole month, I had adulterous images and thoughts repeat constantly in my mind, which caused a maelstrom of guilt and anxiety, but that, too, passed. During this time, I decided to try counseling again, so I began working with a woman named Billie, whom the girls called "Billie a billion" because I told them the therapy sessions were very expensive. First she told me to "repent" of my obsessive thoughts, and I wryly thought that I might as well try to repent for my heartbeat. She prayed over me constantly, concentrating on parts of myself that had, according to her, split off from the rest of my psyche.

One day I sat on her gray velour couch and she asked to speak with ten-year-old Nancy. I wasn't sure at all that "ten-year-old Nancy" was speaking, but I went along with it.

"What are you doing?" Billie asked the "child."

---

[84] Isaiah 33:17b (NIV).

[85] Friedrich Nietzsche, *Beyond Good and Evil,* Planetebook https:www.planetebook.com/free-ebooks/beyond-good-and-evil.pdf, accessed August 8, 2020.

"Hiding," I replied. I thought that answer sounded as good as anything else.

"Why are you hiding?"

"Because I'm bad." That seemed pretty appropriate too.

"Why are you bad?"

"Because I am."

"What have you done?"

"I don't know, but I'm bad."

"How do you know you're bad?"

"Because my mother shut the door and wouldn't speak to me all day."

"How did that make you feel?"

"Like an outcast."

"Do you want to forgive your mother?"

"Yes."

"Okay. Repeat after me: I choose to forgive my mother for shutting the door and not speaking to me all day, and for making me feel like I was bad."

"I choose to forgive my mother for shutting the door and not speaking to me all day, and for making me feel like a was bad." I began to play with a loose string on the couch. Billie kept her gaze fixed on me, her eyes like two sharp onyx stones. I stared at the floor.

Billie continued. "Ten-year-old Nancy, would you like to ask Jesus into your heart?"

"Yes."

"Okay."

"Can you ask Him now?" I tried to remember a salvation prayer, but I stumbled over the words.

"Uh, Jesus. I want…to belong to You. Please…come into my heart." I paused, then queried, "Is that good enough?"

"That's fine. How do you feel?" I wondered how I was supposed to feel.

"Okay, I guess."

"Now I'm going to pray for you to be integrated back into the rest of Nancy. Are you ready for that?" I stared at Billie as if she were an alien from Jupiter. I played some more with the couch string.

"I'm ready," I replied, wondering if the child would depart willingly, wondering if all this were bogus. Billie prayed that the child would be reconnected to the self, and I sat there motionless, mentally trying to figure how much Billie cost an hour. After all, wasn't it strange to pay people to pray for you?

In the subsequent sessions, Billie spoke to several other parts, asking them to accept Jesus, then praying that they would be integrated into the self. After all this, she proudly pronounced me a "whole" person. I felt myself mentally straining to piece together the fragments. She also said that she should pray for healing of my brain, so she put her hand on my head, right over my pink jeweled hair clasp, and began to pray.

"Do you feel anything unusual in any part of your head, heat or tingling?"

"I think I feel heat." In actuality, I felt nothing, but I desperately wanted to feel something.

"Good. Now I'm going to pray for the cerebral cortex." Billie spent a few minutes trying to remember where the cerebral cortex was located, then she placed her hand on what she thought was the appropriate area. She prayed again for healing, then asked me again if I felt anything. I lied again.

"Well, Nancy, your brain is healed, and you don't need the anti-psychotic anymore. Come back in three weeks and we'll see how you're doing." In three weeks, I was off the medication, and spending all day in bed. I started back on the medication.

Once Billie had me lie in a lazy boy chair for five hours straight while she constantly commanded different "parts" of my self to surface and tell us what they knew, that I myself did not consciously know. The parts were supposed to reveal secrets of significance, so I literally tried to squeeze my brain by tensing my facial and scalp muscles, in hopes of forcing out the surreptitious information. After five hours of struggling in the silence, I was emotionally battered, and Billie was mystified. She told me that she was going to call her mentor to see if he could shed some light on the mystery.

"This has never happened before," she confided sheepishly. Feeling incurable and traumatized, I went home and fell into a three-hour fitful sleep.

Billie also tried a form of therapy called "Heart Sync," in which she would ask me to close my eyes and enter into a memory, then imagine Jesus there. I shut my eyes and recalled the day on the kickball field when Jared had slapped me.

"Okay," said Billie after I told her I had entered the memory. "Can you see Jesus?"

"Yes," I whispered. I could see his long hair like the actor in Jesus of Nazareth, and his white robe was trailing in the mud on the field.

"Okay. What is He doing?" asked Billie.

"Nothing. Jared has just slapped me, and Jesus is staring at him."

"Ask Him what He wants to say to you, what He wants you to know."

I squeezed my brain like last time. Jesus's eyes fixed on me suddenly, with that intense, unnerving look that screamed *noli me tangere*. But He said nothing. I tensed up my whole body, willing Him to speak, screaming within my soul for at least a nod of acknowledgment. Nothing.

"I can't do this anymore," I muttered, then walked out even though we still had fifteen minutes left in the session. I felt officially reprobate. Although many people I knew had been helped by this type of therapy, I seemed to be stubbornly immune to it. My diagnostic testing report from the (Christian) psychologist had read, "Her condition has been significantly exacerbated by the attempted spiritual interventions."

At this time, I also became haunted by my unforgiveness toward my mother, which I knew had not simply vanished during my therapy session with Billie. I could still feel it pursuing me like the thunder of horses bearing hunters behind a hapless fox. Didn't God say that the unforgiving would be "handed over to the jailor to be tortured"?[86] I had consistently blamed her for all my ills and failings and had thus given her no access to my heart.

She had read of my poems that seemed to indict her in this area, and she had wept over it and told Edith about it. Edith had looked her squarely in the eye and stated firmly, "You were a good mother, Mrs. Craig." I felt deep regret when my mother told me about this conversation, but I could not find the numerical combination to the giant safe inside me where I kept my heart. Otherwise, I would have gladly let my mother in to share in the intricacies of the emotions that defined me. I prayed unceasingly that my anger would dissipate like a poisonous fog so that I could love my mother in the way she deserved. But every time I saw her my whole

---

86 Matthew 18:34 (NIV).

inner being solidified into a living but stony accusation against her. The bitterness lodged in my throat like a fishbone, and I cried out repeatedly for the grace to embrace the one who had borne me and faithfully cared for me from birth to adulthood.

God answered this prayer with a sentence from a seventy-year-old letter. My mother had recently been moved into an Alzheimer's unit several years after the death of my father, who had also suffered from dementia and been institutionalized in the last years of his life. He had been a wonderfully kind, funny, intelligent person, and I missed him and his constant, wide grin. Before moving my mom into her new facility, my brothers and I had sorted through her belongings in her apartment to dispose of them properly. Among her papers we found a box of old letters, some of which she had written to my father when they were engaged. I came downstairs one day to find Eva engrossed in these letters, and she abruptly waylaid me as I walked by with a cry of "Hey, listen to this!" Eva read me one sentence from what amounted to a passionate love letter my mother had written to my father: "It has been too long since we were together, and I want—no, I need—to see you desperately."

At that moment the cruel and ungodly lie that she could not possibly have loved me collapsed and exposed itself as evil. My mother had become flesh and blood before my eyes, no longer a prudish, cool-hearted woman that I had always addressed with the awkward and bloodless title of "Mother" when I spoke to her. I gasped with joy and regret—my mother had a secret self, just as I did, that pulsated with vivid colors and ran red with blood. But I knew that my epiphany had come too late to enable me to coax out of her all the thoughts and experiences that had led to the writing of such a letter; my mother's memory had become now like a disordered box of puzzle pieces that would never be put together again in this life.

Soon after this breakthrough, Issa and I visited my mom at her new residence. In the fog of dementia, she thought I was her sister, but it didn't matter. She had become suddenly dear to me. I leaned over her wheelchair and kissed her on her wasted, wrinkled cheek— "I love you, Ma," I murmured. It was the first time that I had ever kissed her or initiated a word of endearment. She was wearing a Christmas sweater with a reindeer on it (it was August), and her hair stood up in gray tufts on her scalp.

"I love YOU," she said, and in her eyes, I caught a glimpse of cognizance, as if she knew that something dark and dreadful between us had been exorcised.

After this spiritual triumph I soon forgot that I had ended up in bed when I tried to get off my medicine, and I was lulled into thinking that my brain was almost normal. My doctor told me about a new drug that might help me without causing metabolism changes, and I was eager to try it. A few days after the change, I began to feel rather emotional and strange, but I thought the feeling would pass. We had gone up to the mountains for vacation. The next day I woke up in torment. The feeling was indescribable. I felt as if two hands had reached inside my skull and were squeezing my brain with incredible force. I tried to put on a good front for the girls, especially since we were on vacation, and it was Moriah's birthday. She was turning twelve years old. But every moment was torture, a restless sea of anguish. I was not depressed, or I didn't think so. I only knew that the new medicine was not working, and that without the proper chemicals, my brain was a murderer bent on my destruction. Indeed, in my mind I thought of how I would be forced to end my life if such feelings continued.

The day passed in a blur. We ate lunch at Verandah, a quaint, feminine restaurant that the girls found delightful. I was momentarily distracted by the chef salad I ordered. Next we went to peruse the street fair that was set up for the weekend. For reasons that I still don't fathom, I bought a ring made of silver and freshwater pearls. Abigail and Moriah bought glittering stuffed snakes, and Eva bought a stuffed dragon. Meanwhile my own personal dragon was breathing fire in my brain, leaving it a scorched ruin.

We moved on to the mall, where I attempted to become interested in clothing or trinkets, but I could not distance myself from the slow squeezing of my brain. Finally, we returned to the house, and the girls wanted to watch the *Veggie Tales* Esther video. I agreed to watch with them, trying to distract myself. When the two villains who tried to kill the king were sent to the "island of perpetual tickling," I was horrified. What had always seemed funny before became suddenly perverse. I imagined being tickled forever, and it bore too much of a resemblance to what I was feeling. I shuddered. Finally, I went into the bedroom and pulled out my Bible. I lay on the bed and very slowly read Psalm 119 out loud, sobbing between verses. I felt that God had abandoned me, that He had already assigned me to a hell on earth, but I still found some power in declaring the word of God out loud. Issa lay by my side, faithful as ever. That night I started my previous medicine again, and mercifully, it soon put me into a restful sleep.

The next day I woke up feeling completely normal, as if nothing had happened. However, a dreadful fear had taken root in my mind, a fear that someday, for some reason, I would not have medicine, and that I would have to endure a life of mental agony. I was afraid that I would not be able to face it and that I would end my life in suicide. This fear became an obsession that gnawed at me day and night. Eventually, the thoughts subsided somewhat, but they still haunted me. Soon I began having panic attacks again. I would feel as if my whole body were about to explode or spontaneously combust. Sometimes I would play worship songs on the guitar to try to calm myself down. My voice, weak and strained, would call out:

> Falling on my knees in worship,
> Giving all I am to seek your face,
> Lord all I am is yours.
> My whole life I place in your hands
> God of mercy, humbled I bow down
> In your presence, at your throne.
> I called, you answered,
> And you came to my rescue and I
> Wanna be where you are.[87]

Sometimes the Xanax would not relieve my symptoms and I would curl up in bed, squeeze my eyes shut, and pray the Jesus Prayer while inhaling and exhaling slowly: "Lord Jesus Christ have mercy on me." Eventually the panic would die out like a raging fire whose fuel is spent, and I would sleep. Over one ten-day period, I had panic attacks every other night, usually while everyone else was sleeping.

Sometimes Moriah would be awake, and she would make me a cup of hot herbal tea. Her sweet, gentle presence often comforted me. I finally

---

[87] "Came to my Rescue," Hillsong United, written by Dylan Thomas, Joel Davies and Marty Sampson, Copyright 2005 Hillsong Music Publishing.

began taking medication for the panic attacks, and found relief, but the obsessions were cured by supernatural means. Taking a suggestion of Beth Moore, I wrote encouraging verses on note cards and read them out loud every day. I bought a cute pink box to hold them, and soon I had filled it up with over one thousand cards. I meditated on these verses so often that soon the fears had vanished and were replaced with faith.

But once in a while, when I took my medicine at night, I would remember that day in the mountains and a haunting anxiety would overtake me momentarily, but my mind had stopped roaring like a jackhammer with fear. So I was left with the realization that I was not healed, that in fact, my brain was worse than it had ever been, although I felt normal with medication. I was faced with the question of why God had not healed me. Was it lack of faith? Was it because He wanted me to be dependent on Him? God showed me that I was like the Israelites crossing the Red Sea. I imagined the fear they must have felt, crossing on dry ground with enormous walls of water on either side, with fish mouthing at them. I realized that they had to trust God to hold back that water until they had reached the shore. If He did not, they would be swept away. I saw that God was holding back the water and allowing me to cross on dry ground, but I had to trust Him not to let me drown. I could see the water looming, towering above me, and the silver bodies of fish. But I had to keep on walking.

How many people get to exercise faith for their sanity? How many know, that but for the mercy of God, madness would overtake them? Indeed, it is a unique road I have traveled. I have opened Pandora's box and found all manner of evils escaping into my life, and yet hope has always held me in its arms like a faithful lover. "[E]very new day he does not fail,"[88] says the Bible of the Lord, and every day He gave me at least a crust of sustenance, a morsel of manna to feed my spirit. It was the bread of affliction, but it nourished me in the Badlands. Sometimes even the minutest consolations would comfort me. When I was in the throes of obsessions, I used to stare at a picture of a green tree in a vinyl bathtub book one of the girls had played with as a toddler. I wasn't sure why I had kept it for so long. It was a book on colors, and the page for green showed a magnificent oak, the vibrant color of which seemed to

---

[88] Zephaniah 3:5b (NIV).

render it worthy of paradise. It gave me a glimpse of otherworldliness, to remind me of "the land that stretches afar." During this time, I also had an awakening to the power of the Holy Spirit and began to believe that God might miraculously heal me.

After our strange experiences from years ago, we had backed away from the miraculous and almost ceased to believe in it. But we met a family who had been missionaries overseas, and they told us bizarre and wonderful stories of miracles that the Lord had done. We began attending a small group at their house, where we had a time of worship, and then our neighbor, Samuel, would talk about the prophetic gifting. One night they wanted to go out on the street and pray for people for healing. We were excited, but scared. We met at Starbucks that night, and I ordered my usual Earl Grey tea. Samuel told us a few more stories, then he said, "I feel a pain in my lower back. Is that where the kidney is?" Issa told him that it was, and he told us he believed he was receiving a word of knowledge for the couple sitting across from us. Samuel got up, walked over to the couple and introduced himself.

Meanwhile, Issa and the girls and I glanced at each other nervously, careful not to look in the direction of the couple. Samuel proceeded to tell them that he believed God had given him a word of knowledge for them that someone in their family had a kidney problem. The couple, who was Muslim, told him that the wife was pregnant, and that an ultrasound had revealed that the baby had only one kidney. The couple would not let Samuel pray for healing for the baby because they were Muslim, but they said they may call him after the baby was born. Samuel gave them a business card. I was overwhelmed by what happened. My past experiences with prophecy had been bad ones. I believed that the people making the prophecies were deluded. But here, right before my eyes, was an example of God's power at work. I began to seek the Holy Spirit in my life and eventually started to pray in tongues again, a gift that had ceased for me years ago. At this time, we also went to the winter conference for our denomination, and we attended a healing service. By the time it was over, Issa, Moriah, and Abigail had gotten prayed for and ended up on the floor, and Eva felt warm and tingly. I experienced a deep, melting peace that made my knees turn to rubber.

With this increased emphasis on the Holy Spirit in our lives, the question of why I had not been healed gnawed at me even more, and all I could conclude was that at the heart of life lies mystery. We live in a place of shadows, inconsistencies, and paradoxes. Although at the center of the universe is a Word—Christ—whose very body is speech, yet somehow there is also a great and holy Silence there. Before the seventh seal was opened in heaven in Revelation, there was silence in heaven for half an hour. Some things are too holy to be spoken, or to be answered, and I believe that suffering is one of these. We cry out for explanations, we ask the eternal "Why?", and we are faced with silence. Yet God has given us his wounds, and He bids us to put our fingers inside them. It is no accident that Thomas said "My Lord and my God"[89] after touching Christ's wounds. We can say no to God's goodness, holiness, and power, but we are all compelled to worship when we see his scars. No one can argue with a suffering God. And, as Deuteronomy 29:29 states, "the secret things belong to the Lord our God."[90]

Interpretations also belong to God, as Joseph says in the Genesis 40:8. This idea is echoed in William Cowper's hymn, "God Moves in a Mysterious Way." He tells us that "God is his own interpreter."[91] Secret things do not belong in a neat, pretty box of explanation; they belong in the throne room of God, burning among the coals on the altar. Eliot says that "what you do not know is the only thing you know."[92] He goes on to say that "you are not here to verify, instruct yourself, or inform curiosity or carry report. You are here to kneel where prayer has been valid."[93] This is all we can do: to "kneel where prayer has been valid."

Later, I began to meditate on the scripture in Romans that states that God "calls things that are not as though they were,"[94] and I realized that

[89] John 20:28 (NIV).

[90] Deuteronomy 29:29a (NIV).

[91] William Cowper, "On the Receipt of My Mother's Picture out of Norfolk," *The Poetical Works of William Cooper,* ed. William Michael Rossetti (London: William Collins, Sons and Co., n. d.), 292.

[92] T. S. Eliot, "Four Quartets: East Coker," in *T. S. Eliot: The Complete Poems and Plays* (San Diego: Harcourt Brace Jovanovich, Publishers, 1980), 127.

[93] T. S. Eliot, "Four Quartets: Little Gidding," in *T. S. Eliot: The Complete Poems and Plays* (San Diego: Harcourt Brace Jovanovich, Publishers, 1980), 139.

[94] Romans 4:17b (Lexham English Bible).

sometimes He gives us the spiritual eyes to see the world this way. In the midst of mental illness, this means choosing to believe in peace where no peace exists and choosing to hope where no hope exists. The Bible says that "against all hope, Abraham in hope believed."[95] Everything that we see is against hope. Suffering is against hope, meaninglessness is against hope. Sometimes the only peace we can have is the peace of choosing to love God in the face of no peace, in the face of blinding fear. When Satan's voice screams at us to "curse God and die,"[96] we falter forward, crawling on our knees toward an absent God. This is the highest form of worship: when no-peace and no-hope hound us though God has promised both peace and hope, and we choose to "call things that are not as though they are."[97] Perhaps it is in believing, in the face of no healing, that in God's economy we have indeed been healed. This screams against reason. It is insane. But this kind of insanity is the highest form of sanity. God's world turns everything upside down. Happy are those who mourn. The only way to live is to die.

And so, God's world is a kind of Alice-in-Wonderland existence where rabbits carry pocket watches and caterpillars smoke hookahs. All we can say is "curiouser and curiouser."[98] Reason becomes non-reason. Logic breaks down. What is not, is. To believe this is the faith God requires. Perhaps only the insane can accept this, for it is foolishness in the eyes of the world. This is why God has chosen the foolish things of the world, the things that are not.[99] Only the people who are not can believe in the things that are not. "[T]he sleek and the strong"[100] are destroyed because they cannot accept the foolishness of the cross.

And so, I considered my situation, but found no answers. I remembered reading *Lord Jim*, by Joseph Conrad, many years ago, and one sentence stood out to me: "In the destructive element immerse."[101] I wondered if I should immerse myself in the illness by accepting it, or if I should fight

[95] Romans 4:18 (NIV).

[96] Job 2:9b (NIV).

[97] Romans 4:17b.

[98] Lewis Carroll, *Alice in Wonderland* (London: MacMillan and Co. Limited, 1912), p. 13.

[99] 1 Corinthians 1:27.

[100] Ezekiel 34:16.

[101] Joseph Conrad, *Lord Jim* (New York: Doubleday & Company, 1920), 157.

it with everything in me. My counselor at the time said: "The answer is both." Someone told me that mental illness was a "calling" on my life, and I didn't know whether to agree with her or to be angry. Eliot says "our only health is the disease,"[102] and I wondered if my illness were somehow necessary to my spirituality, and I knew that, if it were, I would embrace it as if it were a lover. But I wasn't sure.

But as we began attending our neighbor's church, my view of God and suffering began to radically change. All my life I had harbored a deep fear that God wanted to judge me and to hurt me. When I became a Christian, I simply transferred that fear into the idea that God wanted to crush me to a bloody pulp until I was half-dead but good and holy. I saw God as someone who loved with a love that wounded, seared, dismembered, and maimed until it could no longer be recognizable as love. I could relate to Andrew Peterson's song, "Love is a Good Thing":

> It knocked me down, it dragged me out
> it left me there for dead
> It took all the freedom I wanted
> and gave me something else instead
> It blew my mind, it bled me dry
> It hit me like a long goodbye
> and nobody here knows better than I That it's a good thing.
> Love is a good thing, it'll fall like rain on your parade
> Laugh at the plans that you tried to make
> it'll wear you down till your heart just breaks
> And it's a good thing, love is a good thing
> It'll wake you up in the middle of the night
> It'll take just a little too much
> it'll burn you like a cinder
> till you're tender to the touch, it'll chase you down
> swallow you whole, it'll make your blood run hot and cold
> like a thief in the night it'll steal your soul
> and that's a good thing, love is a good thing.[103]

---

[102] T. S. Eliot, "Four Quartets: East Coker," in *T. S. Eliot: The Complete Poems and* Plays (San Diego: Harcourt Brace Jovanovich, Publishers), 127.

[103] Andrew Peterson, "Love is a Good Thing," from the album *Resurrection Letters, volume two,* released 2008.

Even though Petersen went on to glibly say, "do not fear," I did fear. I bought into the idea that C. S. Lewis almost began to believe in when his wife died: God is a vivisectionist, and we are the hapless laboratory rats. We are wounded, starved, experimented on, and given thorns in the flesh until we are oozing pus and righteousness. I felt guilty that I was not considering this view of sanctification as pure joy, but I could not. I wanted to embrace a God who tormented people to make them dependent and saintly, but I couldn't do that either. And yet when I felt the glory of God seeping into my pores and turning my blood into wine, when I felt dizzy and breathless from the heavy presence of a God who is pure love, I knew that such theology was flawed. I had experienced God as a lover who was tender and gentle, but also wild and exhilarating.

One day during this time of seeking to discover who God is, I was in the mountains with my daughters shopping at Kohl's. They were trying on bikinis because I had decided that even girls who wear bikinis can go to heaven. I was sitting in the entryway to the store on a white bench railing at God. I had been having horrible attacks of torment and fear. I really wanted to just start walking toward the woods until I found a cave or a hole or a gorge where I could curl up in a ball and stay there till kingdom come or until a bear dismembered me, whichever came first. I finally cried out, in my head of course, *Okay, God, just what can I expect from You: blessing or torment? Which is it?* What I did not expect was an answer, but I dragged myself off that bench to go in and see how the great bikini search was going, hoping that none of it involved strings or fringe. I skulked past the cash registers and stopped in my tracks. Right there in front of my face stood a display of green cloth shopping bags for sale, which was of course not extraordinary. But as I took a second glance, I noticed that the bags were printed with three words above a raindrop design: "Expect Great Things." I was more than shocked. I bought the bag for ninety-nine cents and hugged it to my chest as if it were a baby. I found my daughters and bought three bikinis without even grumbling.

The journey was far from over, however. Once I got home, I began to doubt the legitimacy of my Kohl's "coincidence," and the question of whether it was God's will for me to suffer this agony continued to harass me like a hornet trapped inside my head. One day I was reading *Streams in the Desert,* a popular devotional given to me by my mother-in-law, and one that seemed to address on every page the importance of suffering to the believer. I turned to July ninth, and read the following poem that was part of the day's reading:

> Pain's furnace heat within me quivers,
> God's breath upon the flame doth blow;
> And all my heart in anguish shivers
> And trembles at the fiery glow;
> And yet I whisper, "As God will!"
> And in the hottest fire hold still.
>
> He comes and lays my heart, all heated,
> On the hard anvil, minded so
> Into His own fair shape to beat it
> With His great hammer, blow on blow
> And yet I whisper, "As God will!"
> And in the hottest fire hold still.[104]

My heart began to vomit up emotion. I threw the book down and began to imagine God the Father as a dark and sinister robed monk in the Inquisition, armed with hammers and racks and screws ready to torture the heresy out of all His recalcitrant, but of course, well-loved, children. I began fuming at God again and demanding that He give me an answer about my suffering. I decided to gather up my commentaries on various verses on suffering and do some research. I picked up my *New International Commentary* on First Peter and began reading the introduction:

Although in Hebrews suffering can be viewed as divine discipline, God is rarely seen as the one who brings suffering. Tests of faith come, but God does not bring them, argues James. Rather...testing comes from two causes (1) the internal drive to evil, which must be resisted, or (2) the devil. In other words, the setting of the church is...one of cosmic conflict in which there is an Evil One who seeks the destruction of the Christians and rules in the nations of this world. God is in relative control, so we pray,

---

[104] anointing.files.wordpress.com. Julius Sturm, quoted in *Streams in the Desert,* by L. B. Cowman, edited by James Reimann, 264-265. Date accessed August 11, 2020. https://anointing.files.wordpress.com/2013/01/devotional-streams-in-the-desert.pdf.

"And keep us from the test, and deliver us from the Evil One." Yet this prayer does not guarantee that we will not come into a testing situation, but there is a real power that works against believers. While God does allow suffering for his purposes and our good, he is generally presented as the one who is on our side in arming and delivering us and limiting the ability of the devil to cause suffering.[105]

The commentator went on to prove, through looking at the original Greek words, how the suffering that comes to believers and refines them is persecution, not illness. As I read these words, I became more and more agitated. I could literally feel neurons firing in my brain as God breathed revelation into me. I began reading some of the footnotes, and I noticed that the commentator referenced a book by Morton Kelsey called *Healing and Christianity*. Another incandescent bulb sputtered alive in my head. By "coincidence," I had just bought that book from the used book sale up at Montreat the previous week. I ransacked the house looking for it, and when I found it, I began to read:

> If Jesus had any one mission, it was to bring the power and healing of God's creative, loving Spirit to bear upon the moral, mental, and physical illnesses of the people around him. It was a matter of rescuing man from a situation in which he could not help himself. Jesus disclosed a new power, a ladder to bring him out of the pit of his brokenness and sin. Leaving man in his wretched condition so as to learn from it makes no sense in this psychological framework. Judgment and punishment only add to a burden already intolerable....[106] He made clear in various ways the destructive and deteriorating effect of sickness on human beings: that it tears life down rather than building it up....It is well and good to talk of the brave, patient souls who have developed through suffering, but the fine border-line at which disease ceases to be a destructive force and becomes a blessing is very hard to see. Perhaps

---

[105] Peter H. Davids, *New International Commentary on the New Testament: The First Epistle of Peter* (Grand Rapids, MI: William B. Eerdmans Publishing Company, 1990), 36-37.

[106] Morton Kelsey, *Healing and Christianity* (New York: Harper and Row Publishers, 1973) 67.

> God can turn evil to good, but this does not change the fact
> that many are simply destroyed by illness. For instance,
> the mentally ill who have disintegrated as egos cannot
> possibly benefit....The "Christian" attitude that glories in
> sickness is completely alien to that of Jesus of Nazareth;
> it is aligned on the side of what he was fighting against. I
> very much suspect that anyone who glories in the benefits
> of illness has either known little of it in himself or those
> dear to him, or else has serious masochistic tendencies.
> Sickness is a destructive and evil phenomenon, and Christ
> as the incarnation of creativity was dead set against it.[107]

I was ready to tear out every page from *Streams in the Desert* and feed them to my guinea pig. "Streams in the Desert" was really "Screams in the Desert." I ventured on in my search, beginning to read books by Gregory Boyd such as *God at War* and *Satan and the Problem of Evil.* I began to grapple with the question of whether all of life has been predetermined from the beginning of time, or if the future is somehow open in some sense. If it is all predetermined, then of course everything that happens is actually God's will. But this conclusion leads to egregious difficulties. Boyd begins one of his books with a story about how the Nazis gouged out a young girl's eyes in front of her mother because they thought her eyes looked like beautiful black diamonds. How, argues Boyd, does an event such as this fit into some predetermined, beautiful plan? And why should we even bother to pray if everything that happens has been predetermined and if everything that happens is already God's will? As I grappled with this however, I began to be obsessed with these questions and my mind began to race abnormally. Finally, in no uncertain terms, God told me to stop. He had given me some answers, but I was to stop fixating on unanswerable questions. God gave me a verse from Second Corinthians: "For I resolved to know nothing among you but Jesus Christ and him crucified."[108] I got the point. I had to let go of the need to know, my need to eat of the tree of knowledge of good and evil, thereby trusting in my own reason and intelligence to figure out the universe. But I had

---

[107] Morton Kelsey, *Healing and Christianity* (New York: Harper and Row Publishers, 1973) 67.
[108] First Corinthians 2:2 (NASB).

seen a glimpse of God's heart. He was on my side. He was gentle. He was a protector, not the Divine Inquisitor ready to throw me on the rack.

I began to see dramatic answers to prayer as I suffered from various mental states. For example, at one point my medication had stopped working well. I had a day when my mind was very disordered, so I decided to increase the dose, but this time I did not get better. In fact, my mind was tormented with that indescribable feeling, and I became afraid that my medicine would stop working and I would have to suffer indefinitely. I felt as if worms were gnawing on my brain. I began to descend into a pit of unbelief and despair. I felt completely hopeless, alone, and frightened. My daughters wanted to watch *The Lion, the Witch and the Wardrobe*, so I sat there in anguish, hoping to distract myself with the movie. I was moved by the awesome power of good over evil portrayed in it, although I had seen it many times.

I said to the Lord in my mind, *I trust You,* although I didn't really feel that way at all. I just wanted to declare it anyway.

A few moments later I heard the Lord say to me, as clearly as He had ever spoken, "The Lord is with you, mighty warrior."[109] The words were taken from the story of Gideon, which is one of my favorites. Suddenly I knew that the Lord was indeed with me, and that He had seen my terrible struggle to survive all these years. I felt that He appreciated my pain and my perseverance. At once the torment lifted, along with all the unbelief and despair. I felt completely normal. I learned that day the power of a word from God and that my fate is not dependent on medicine, but rather it is in the hands of God.

During this time I began to consider if God really does speak to us personally with words other than Bible verses. The church we had been attending focused heavily on how we can hear the voice of God, but my feelings about the matter swung back and forth like a dizzying pendulum. At times I felt that I had received divine revelation, but I wondered if God ever spoke in clear phrases or sentences. And if I did hear from Him in this way, how could I be sure I wasn't just entertaining an overactive

---

[109] Judges 6:12b (NIV).

imagination? I had believed for years that God spoke to me, but I was always uneasy about believing that what I heard really came from God.

One night I experienced a rather extraordinary confirmation that God does indeed communicate actual sentences to our minds or spirits. I was at church "soaking," which for me usually consisted of lying across three sanctuary chairs with a mini pink and purple unicorn pillow under my head, staring absently at the ceiling configurations while soporific music wafted around me, mixed with an occasional snore from my fellow soakers.

Suddenly I thought I heard God say, "You make Me cry." This didn't sound promising, but I decided to ask for clarification.

"What do You mean, Lord?" I asked.

"You make Me cry with joy," He replied.

I was touched by that, but I wasn't sure that I could trust what I had heard. I pondered this until soaking ended and the participants filed into a classroom to give testimonies. I clutched my unicorn pillow and followed them, then slipped into an unobtrusive seat in the back row. At the invitation of the teacher, another student described how he had been ushered into the throne room of God during the soaking time.

"I looked up and there was God the Father," he continued, "and I saw tears running down his cheeks. I asked him what was wrong, and He told me, 'I'm crying for joy over you.'"

I was startled. What a strange coincidence! But my post-Enlightenment mind was reluctant to accept what I had heard. The whole process felt terribly questionable and subjective. After all, a plethora of preachers had reminded me in my lifetime that the heart is "deceitfully wicked." So, I packed up my deceitfully wicked heart and drove home. But that same heart was still longing to be assured that I had indeed heard from God. I walked through my front door, my inner being stirred, and marched upstairs to tell my husband what happened and ask for his opinion.

As I spoke, his eyes developed a puzzled expression, then he spoke: "Tonight I was praying for a man using inner healing techniques, and suddenly I had a vision of Jesus standing over him weeping tears of joy just from being in that man's presence." I was speechless. I had never heard anyone mention Jesus crying tears of joy over us, and now suddenly I had heard about it three times in succession on the same night. Coincidence? I doubted it. I felt I had to believe in the word's authenticity after all the confirmation, but I struggled to accept it. Could Jesus really love me, let alone like me, that much? Was He really so tender? This didn't fit with the "policeman in the sky" image of God that many a speaker and writer had hurled at me like hailstones on the delicate tendrils of my faith. Yet obviously God had to be in the night's events…or was He? It was a conundrum I could not answer, but as scripture says of Mary, I "treasured these things and pondered them in my heart."[110]

Many other apparently divine episodes such as this one followed, and I began to toy with the idea of getting off my medicine. I went through several cycles of dropping the drugs, demanding God to take care of me without medicine, crashing emotionally, getting angry and traumatized, then beginning the agonizing process of trying to get stabilized again. I wanted to get off drugs not just to avoid side effects, but so that my disgrace would be taken away. I was still bombarded with all the opinions of "Christian amateur psychiatrists," of whom there are many, who would humiliate mentally ill people from the pulpit in various ways. For example, one speaker compared the sufferer to the "Dead Sea," because "[t]he Dead Sea is a place where water flows in, but nothing goes out."[111] Later, when I was actually privileged to go to the Dead Sea, I felt the sting of his remark. Surely my heart could not be as stagnant and poisonous as the watery cauldron that lay before me! I had been on antipsychotic drugs for so long I felt like Hester Prynne with a huge embroidered "C" for "crazy" on my chest. Often I prayed that one day God would vindicate me in the eyes of all who blamed me and heaped shame on me. And every time I had an unsuccessful attempt to get off medicine I would go limping back to my godly, longsuffering psychiatrist who would patiently suggest, without a hint of censure, that I start taking my meds again.

Reader, I am *still* not healed! But now I truly believe that God desires healing for me and not sickness. But even if He does not heal me, I will never stop believing that Jesus is exquisite, magnificent, and perfectly good. He frequently embraces me and I feel passionate waves of a love that is explosively ardent and yet infinitely tender. My heart belongs unequivocally to Jesus of Nazareth, even when I can't breathe from anxiety, or thoughts gnaw my brain like worms, or emotional pain sears

---

[110] Luke 2:19 (NIV).

[111] Bill Johnson, "Taking Flight from the Dead Sea," sermon dated September 16, 2019.

my gut. I am impossibly drawn to Him, and even when I am pummeling my fists against His chest in anger, I am so intoxicated just to be touching Him that I unclench my hands and fall weeping into His embrace. Even, even, even – I can say no more. God is a Lover.

And now all that remains is to tell my story. God is at his heart a voice, a Word. His words called the worlds into being. For us, silence is the realm of Satan. He threatens to choke us so we cannot speak or make us deaf so we cannot hear the words God speaks. Words are power. I was struck by the verse in Revelation that reads that Satan was overcome "by the blood of the lamb and the word of their testimony."[112] I decided that I must speak. Words become stories, and stories pour one by one into his story, the marvelous tale of redemption. Stories heal the reader, and they heal the writer. Every word written closes a wound in my heart. My story is myself. When I write, I create myself anew. Like Christ, I am made of words. We are all stalked by silence, by words that want to emerge but never do. If we remain silent, the stones will cry out.[113]

Silence, other than the silence of mystery, is a kind of death. It erases our footprints before we have made them. Christ's word was written in blood, and so is mine. To write the story is to enter into it again, as a grown man back into the womb, which is a kind of gestating death that we must be born out of anew. To write one's story is to enter into a fierce reincarnation in which nightmares assail again, and yet the travail leaves us squirming and bloody on the breast of God, ready to begin life over again, yet with new eyes.

Eliot says that "old men ought to be explorers,"[114] that "we shall not cease from exploration and the end of all our exploring will be to arrive where we started and know the place for the first time."[115] And so, I vowed to revisit my past, to arrive where I started, in hopes that I would know the place for the first time. As John says in 1 John1:4, "We write this to

---

[112] Revelation 12:11 (NIV).

[113] Luke 19:40.

[114] T. S. Eliot, "Four Quartets: East Coker," in *T. S. Eliot: The Complete Poems and Plays* (San Diego: Harcourt Brace Jovanovich, Publishers), 129.

[115] T. S. Eliot, "Four Quartets: Little Gidding," in *T. S. Eliot: The Complete Poems and Plays* (San Diego: Harcourt Brace Jovanovich, Publishers, 1980), 145.

make our joy complete,"[116] the joy that is a heavy art. But I was troubled about how to end such an account, when I had no answers and the story was still unfolding. I wanted to go back to that neat box of explanation, with the pretty bow on top. Have you ever noticed how, when you buy something and want to return it, it will never fit correctly back in the box? Such is my life. It won't fit into what I think is the proper box, and there is no pretty bow.

But as for an ending, I decided to look again to Eliot, who said "In my beginning is my end."[117] The present circles back into the past, as waves constantly break on the shore. What we have been is rebirthed in what we are. So, I will make my story perfectly round, to mirror eternity, to mirror my circuitous thoughts as I seek after answers. And so, after much deliberation and anguish, I picked up, incongruously, a pink gel pen and a leather-bound journal that would open its mouth to receive my story and wrote my first sentence: "It has been twilight all day long."

"In my beginning is my end."[118]

---

[116] 1 John 1:4 (NIV).

[117] T. S. Eliot, "Four Quartets: East Coker," in *T. S. Eliot: The Complete Plays and Poems* (San Diego: Harcourt Brace Jovanovich, Publishers, 1980), 123.

[118] Ibid.

Incident at Bethany

Lord, the one You love is sick.
And You are dallying in doorways elsewhere,
The Spirit feathering above Your head
Like a fire bound phoenix
While we are dark in the gullet of the grave
Worms dotting our grave clothes like seed pearls.
The perfume I smeared on Your body
Now caresses my corpse
But we are dark with a decay
That can wear no mask.
But even now
You can come to Jerusalem and die, my Love.
We are all hungry for Your blood,
Leaning over Your wounded well
To pull up life in this tenuous flask.
Go deep into the belly of the world
And give birth to us there.
Unswaddle us from graveclothes
And we will stand uncovered as Eve
In her orchard where the rivers run with gold.
Marry us here in Hades.
The stone that sealed us will become an altar
In this crooked cathedral.
But You will turn it into bread
And we will all eat our way out
And die in a childbirth
That will never cease screaming out life.
Four days dead.
But I still see an always in Your eyes.
So let me drink You down
And watch death undo itself.
Let me hide myself in the holes in Your hands
As I am coughed up from the crypt to the cross.
Marry me and wear me like a ring in this tomb

That is now the womb
Of a scandalous, sacred emptiness
That now fills all that is
And all that is not.

The Woman at the Walmart

Her hands move so mechanically
That I think she could scan cans
Or even Velveeta cheese
With her bare fingers,
And $3.50 would appear
On the display.
For her, the day crawls with the ordinary—
Armies of milk cartons, beer, and Cocoa Puffs
March across the conveyor belt,
Ending up in the trenches
Of the revolving bag holder—
An Armageddon of processed food.
She is bolder than some,
Her body crucified with piercings—
Ears, lips, a cubic zirconium in the nose.
Her eyes are painted like peacock feathers,
And her mouth is a scarlet ibis
That got blown by the trade winds
From Madagascar or somewhere
Into the Walmart.
I avoid her eyes,
Afraid that they will scan her heart
And the price she's paid in pain
Will pop up with digits in her pupils.
I notice vague creases on her wrists
Like mouths that once spoke blood
But were stitched silent.
I am appalled by the stench of violence,
So I stare at the mylar smiley face balloon
Lolling from a string tied to the register light.
I am about to take my welcome flight,
When Jesus walks up to the conveyor belt
In a seamless tunic with a ragged bloodstain
Over the rib cage.

He is buying a box of penny nails,
Whole mustard seed and some Pop Tarts,
Perhaps to multiply for the homeless.
He eases up to the woman,
Who quivers and forgets the seven other men
Probably on her mind.
He's not really my kind.
But He brushes her hand with His fingertips
As if it were a jewel.
She must think Him a fool,
To notice a girl like her,
But I swear she feels His gaze
As if He were binding a lesion in gauze.
He pays.
Then His eyes cradle her with chaste delight,
And He sees that her own are deep,
Perhaps bottomless, hungry wells
Where grief like a jagged stone sinks.
He sighs deeply, and asks her for a drink.

Lament from a Jesus Girl

I met you at a bar
And your hands bled all over your margarita
And all over my fingers starving to trace words
Like whip-poor-will calls
On the nape of your neck.
We danced to "Hotel California" very slowly.
The music gathered around us like a sapphire mist.
In your arms I turned inside out
And my heart hung there in my ribs
Like a panther in a cage.
I don't know who you are
But you told me you're my Lover.
You handed me some poems I don't understand
Scribbled down on paper grocery bags,
And then you ascended from the road in your gleaming
white sedan.
You told me you'd come back for me
But all your shiny policemen did nothing
But hand out parking tickets
While silence raped me in this ghetto.
You have let your cell phone die
And I have begun to believe I hallucinated your lips
That seared my face, urgently, secretly
On that day I died so I could tattoo myself over your heart.
Remember me, Lover,
Who left me with nothing
but a longing like Vesuvius and a ticket stub.
I am barefoot with a body like paper
But when you held me
Your scars were born again in me.
My side gapes and the wind insinuates carnage,
Molesting me through the green parka you gave me.
I tore out my eyes
And left them at the stop sign

Where you told me goodbye,
Black pupils swallowing up the blue
As they scour the road for a trace of you.
My body moves on sightless,
Tears oozing from empty orbs.
I hitchhike to Walmart to buy Kleenex,
Groping down the aisles with hands
Still tinctured with the scent of your hair.

Christmas in the Alzheimer's Unit

For my parents: HBC and DMC

In the dusky evening of disease
That empties men to husks,
Tongues that once wagged
Wax still;
Mouths gape
And nurses like hovering spirits
Fill them with pills.
It is the very rape of reason,
Absurdity in the bitterest of seasons.
Now burns the chill of approaching dark,
Like an unwanted lover one can never spurn.
Who are they,
Those who slouch in contraptions
Of steel and wheels,
Ironic thrones earned with age?
Where is the sage
Who can interpret the sign
Of plastic plants (the non-toxic kind)
On every rudimentary dining table?
And where is the platitude
That is able to redeem
The gleam of drool
On the chin of a Ph.D.?
I wish I had no eyes to see such things.
Perhaps I should blind myself
With someone's brooch
So I would be no witness
To the wicked hand that encroaches
On all that is fair.
I feel the singularity
As their vacuous sockets stare at me.
When they speak,

Is it with the tongues of men or angels?
Where is the place in them
The serpent has not stung,
And how can we mourn
Now that our eyes have been wrung dry of tears?
A career has been thrust upon them,
A vocation allowing for no resuscitation.
But what if one of them should suddenly remember
How to decode the elevator?
Perhaps one snowy December
There will be a collective revelation
Like a hallucinated angel choir
Or radiant beams from the tree's plastic star,
And they'll all march out in formation
Into the city streets.
The cops on their beat
Will find it hard to know
Just who needs to go back in the ward,
Because we all lean a little toward madness.
Others will join them,
(wanting to be in on the secret that normal men have lost)
As they shuffle in their walkers
Toward Bethlehem,
Beneath the flashing reindeer atop the streetlights.
They will halt at the Nativity scene,
Then remembering every word of "Silent Night,"
Will gurgle it out
To the cardboard donkey and sheep.
All this, while the rest of us sleep.

Epilogue

The Still Point of the Turning World[119]

I HAVE FINALLY BEGUN to see that what we believe about God is a choice, an act of the will erupting, often violently, from our own convictions based on Scripture and experience. In this universe of apparent contradictions and certain uncertainty, belief cannot be a phenomenon that is inevitably imposed on us by our minds in the face of incontrovertible evidence. The world, which appears solid and rooted in some kind of scientific objectivity that should lead us all to the same conclusion, is really murky and molten as quicksand. Evidence gives us no sure footing. Eventually we have to exercise faith in something in order to prevent insanity, in order to live practically in this life. For example, one can reach at least two logical conclusions about God based on circumstances and the created order. If one focuses on all the beauty, harmony, and even humor evident in creation, one sees a God worthy of worship, a God whose perfect creation has been vandalized by the lying graffiti of Satan. Satan has spray painted foul words across the Mona Lisa of the universe. If, on the other hand, one focuses on the Holocaust, babies with spina bifida, and volcanoes that roast alive entire cities, one could conclude that God is a sadist of the most perverse type. Both are reasonable conclusions. Evidence does not sweep our minds toward an inexorable worldview; we participate, choosing one path based on, perhaps,

---

[119] T. S. Eliot, "Four Quartets: Burnt Norton," in *T. S. Eliot: The Complete Poems and Plays* (San Diego: Harcourt Brace Jovanovich, Publishers), 119.

some gut instinct that leads us one way or another, or even based on a personal preference or practicality.

The Bible, of course, in a sense gives Christians an anchor, some type of sure footing to stand on, and yet even it is not straightforward; theologians and laypeople alike reach opposing conclusions based on the same verses. The Bible is like the universe: interpreting it one way or another is a choice based on our own gut instincts about God. Gregory Boyd, in his sermon called "The Rorschach Test," shows how people throughout history have used the Bible to justify evil by choosing specific verses out of context and applying them."[120] He says that the Bible functions as a psychological test, such as the famous inkblots, that reveals much about the person drawing the conclusion. Men who desire violence can find multiple verses to justify their behavior. People motivated by love conclude that the Bible tells us to shun violence. This is not to say that the Bible is contradictory or teaches us that truth is only a personal preference, but its obvious ambiguity, subtlety, and complexity serve to bring out the character and tendencies of a person.

We are all like the traveler in the famous Robert Frost poem "The Road Not Taken," who sees two roads and has to make a choice. He wavers between the two, thinking to himself about the advantages of each, and in the end he chooses one that he tells himself is "less traveled," and that his choice has "made all the difference."[121] However, the bulk of the poem implies that the roads actually look equal; three times the speaker tells us how there seems to be no difference in the roads. Yet a choice must be made, so the speaker chooses according to his desire, which is to take a path that seems to turn him into a trailblazer of sorts, a pioneer in a world where most people take the well-worn paths of mediocrity. He justifies his choice in his mind using the evidence, so he tells himself, although the evidence could just as easily lead him down a different road. Yet to admit that there is no obvious basis for one's choice, that either option can be supported, is to reach a frightening conclusion about the universe: namely, that we don't know anything with surety, that we are afloat in a strange sea that is over our heads and devoid of solid footholds that we can see. Yet most of us think and act like our view is the only

---

[120] Gregory Boyd, Woodland Hills Church, sermon titled "The Rorschach Test," July 4, 2010.

[121] Robert Frost, "The Road Not Taken," in *The Norton Anthology of American Literature, volume 2*, 2nd edition, ed. Nina Baym (New York: W. W. Norton and Company, Inc., 1985), 1020.

reasonable one and that everyone else is simply disregarding what should be irrefutable evidence.

What does this have to do with my journey through the emotional wasteland? Everything. I realized that every time I read or heard an argument that seemed to support a frightening conclusion about myself, the universe, or God, I would spiral down into a noxious bog of shame, guilt, and fear. On the other hand, when I was presented with an argument that lined up with ideas that gave me hope, I would burst forth into glorious bliss. Thus, the violent mood swings made me appear bipolar, although I am not. But recently I discovered that I can actually choose what to believe, that I am not a helpless tree swayed back and forth by the winds of a mind beyond my control. I have long seen my psyche as my master, and a cruel one at that, one who is trying to destroy me by malevolent design. But now I see that my mind is actually the slave of my will and that if my theology makes me critically ill, I can simply refuse to believe it, even though there may be some evidence that seems to support it.

The truth should set us free. If our beliefs bring about the fruit of bondage, can they really be true? If they cast a dark shadow on the character of God, should we harbor them? Even if we suspect so, we should reject them. This is not so shockingly close to relativism as it seems. We can know nothing for sure, as Descartes observed—other than our own existence. Every other belief we hold, we have chosen to believe it out of an infinity of alternatives, many of which may be equally supportable by evidence. Those of us who believe in absolute truth believe in it because we have chosen to, because we desire to, because relativism leads us to conclusions that frighten or disgust us. No one can prove that absolute truth exists through philosophical mind games. Ultimately, we don't know anything with certainty.

Jesus Himself upholds a worldview in which faith matters tremendously. "Your faith has healed you,"[122] He says to people who sought Him out for relief. But I thought it was Jesus who healed people! Maybe they are one and the same. Certain beliefs unlock the power of God while others quench it. And so I dismiss the ambiguity by exercising my will to believe what my heart tells me must be true. I must assume that the world is for everyone (if everyone

---

[122] Mark 5:34a (NIV).

else actually exists!) as it is for me: a shapeless mass of sensory and psychological phenomena fraught with the most disconcerting ambiguity and apparent or real contradictions. I have finally realized that I have power over this ambiguity. I can shape it and form it into a vessel that honors Christ, a vessel that the sight of which does not send me running for tranquilizers. Perhaps God has designed life as apparently ambiguous for the sole purpose of allowing us to choose what to believe, to exercise our faith muscles so that the whole world becomes a Rorschach test.

I did not think such things were possible. I believed we had to wait passively for faith to come from God (although, strangely, faith is a gift of God, and yet still our own!), or to pop magically out of the evidence like a dancer from a giant birthday cake. I thought faith controlled me and not vice versa. But indeed, faith did control me, because I was not exercising my power over it. By default, faith wanders around like a horse with no one to apply the reins if the rider sits like a dead man on its back. I have suddenly found that I am not a victim, that I have the power of life or death in my will, and that choosing wisely will bring the promised peace, while letting myself be "carried about by every wind of doctrine,"[123] as the Bible says, leads to severe neurosis in which the world becomes uninterpretable to the point of madness. Now I sometimes strongarm myself out of the anxiety that I was catapulted into by some book or preacher, and I choose a beautiful and healing interpretation of Scripture. Almost magically, my peace is restored. I have suffered immensely from the repercussions of other people's beliefs, and I have believed that I had no power to say "no," no power to take up my sword and cleave in pieces that serpent that was strangling my soul.

Some people find beliefs such as five-point Calvinism tolerable or even invigorating, but to me they have brought torment and death. Most problematic, however, is Calvinism's incompatibility with God's love, not to mention its clash with the scriptural principle that God "...desires all people to be saved and to come to the knowledge of the truth."[124] Others find Arminianism more palatable—God does not sovereignly decree who goes to heaven or hell based on His own good pleasure, but

---

[123] Ephesians 4:14b (ESV).

[124] 1 Timothy 2:4 (ESV).

He gives man the choice to accept or reject Him. However, an Arminian can be prone to wonder obsessively if his faith is "genuine" or if he has lost or will lose his salvation at some point. Furthermore, and again most problematic, Arminianism renders humanity in a sense in control of his own salvation, since it partially depends on human choices rather than on the sovereign, objective act of God. Thus, neither view is satisfactory. And so I have chosen to believe, based on my heart's convictions about the character of God and certain straightforward Scriptures, that Christ's blood is all-sufficient, and His love is efficacious, all-encompassing, and everlasting. Period. All the "buts" that inevitably follow such a statement for many people have been eradicated in my thinking. "By their fruits you will know them."[125] Rot and decay were the fruit of my dark and confused theology, but I will no longer be a victim of the Cosmic Ogres created by heartless and myopic theologians. Indeed, there will be consequences for sin and unbelief—"everyone will be salted with fire,"[126] and "there will be weeping and gnashing of teeth."[127] But the same God who warns of judgment for the wicked also promises that "mercy triumphs over judgment."[128] Thus my predicament has driven me to cling obsessively to the Cross alone—a Cross that is quintessentially a trinitarian act of selfless love, not a ransom of blood paid to an angry father.

It has been quite a few years since I wrote the above account. I have been waiting for the happily ever after, slain in the Spirit, never depressed again, threw my pills down the toilet and didn't go down screaming after them scenario. But that hasn't happened yet. I have not been given the respectable Christian life package A, the never-doubting, mission-trip guru, Proverbs 31 woman, Sunday School teaching, joyful, victorious, evangelical believer. I have accused God of abandoning me. I have told Him I was so angry that I wanted to kill Him. (Then He reminded me that I already had.) I have doubted His goodness at least on every third Saturday. I have feared in the dankest dungeon of my psyche that God is an egotistical, maniacal, child-killing, sinner-roasting control freak who sets impossible standards. Then when we can't deliver, He squashes us

---

[125] Matthew 7:16 (NKJV).

[126] Mark 9:49 (NIV).

[127] Luke 13:28a (NIV).

[128] James 2:13b (NIV).

like blood-filled ticks while we desperately try to suck life from our idols. But the great Church Father Origen said that if the "surface" meaning of a Scripture appears to be "[un]worthy of God," the reader should "[investigate]…that truth which is more deeply concealed" until a more praiseworthy interpretation can be found.[129] Thus we should only believe what is befitting of God, and so I choose to believe the Word that is Christ, who indeed has blood on his hands, but it is his own.

I am about to embark on my one hundred and first medicinal exploration: starting on a new drug. (The number may be literal.) Last month I enjoyed a cocktail of four and sometimes five drugs, and still I spent much of my time disassociated and despondent. I have wanted to flush my religion down that toilet instead of my pills. But the reality of God has haunted me delightfully, dangerously as if I were in some strange hall of mirrors in which every panel reflected an infinity of His face, His body, His corporeal love.

I am certifiably crazy. I don't cook. I exist on trail mix and Belvita cookies. My house has cobwebs on its cobwebs. I study Greek, Hebrew, and theology obsessively. But I am in a tangled-up love affair with the Invisible Man who nevertheless appears everywhere. I am terrified and tantalized by Him. I feel Him breathing down my neck and I don't know whether to scream in gut-twisting fear or turn around and find His lips. I have unashamedly read books on Universal Reconciliation and annihilationism. I have prayed for the dead. I have become at last unafraid of critical thinking in regard to God, faith, and the Bible; I have plunged into hotbeds of controversy without quivering like my terrier during a bath. My faith has long consisted of a passive assimilation of other people's theology and rules, much of which led to feelings of fear, guilt, condemnation, and despair. I swallowed my questions and tried desperately not to vomit them up. No more. I make no apologies. I have become one of Eliot's "old men" engaged in exploration. Old women, rather, I say, as I have lived now for over half a century. I began as a girl with her God many years ago, and now it's as though I have been born

---

[129] Origen, *De Principiis* 4.1.18, in *Fathers of the Third Century: Tertullian, Part Fourth; Minucius Felix; Commodian; Origen, Parts First and Second*, vol. 4, ed. S. Roberts, J. Donaldson, and A. C. Coxe, trans. F. Crombie (Buffalo, NY: Christian Literature Company, 1885), 364, Logos Bible Software.

into Him as an infant again. My mind is yet a churning quicksand, but I sometimes reach

> "…the still point of the turning world;
> Neither flesh nor fleshless;
> Neither from nor towards; at the still
> Point, there the dance is…
> Except for the still point, the still point
> There would be no dance, and there is only dance."[130]

There I have danced in the light waves of mercy, love, and joy that shimmer from the body of the crucified yet risen Christ. There He has left me breathless. In *Repenting of Religion*, Gregory Boyd illustrates how this battle in the mind over the trustworthiness of God has been smoldering since the Garden of Eden, when Satan wormed his way into Eve's psyche with the larva of doubt about the character of God. He writes:

> Adam and Eve's story is not just a "once upon a time" story;
> it is also the story of every human being. The beginning of
> all sin—the origin of all that is unloving—is a judgment
> about God. We embrace a picture of God that is less
> loving, less beautiful, less full of life, less gracious, and
> less glorious than the true God really is."[131]

I have ditched my paranoid passion to have perfect doctrine; I only want to throw my body upon the pyre of the consuming, holy love of God. My theology, like everyone else's, will continue to evolve, but I will proclaim with my dying breath the reality of one Person: Jesus Christ and Him crucified. He is the only Word with meaning that has ever been spoken. All other speech is just babbling into a vacuum compared with Him. His voice commands the void to part like a sea before us and we walk through into Canaan as the black hole sucks up our enemies at last.

---

[130] T. S. Eliot, "Four Quartets: Burnt Norton," *in T. S. Eliot: The Complete Poems and Plays*, (San Diego: Harcourt Brace Jovanovich, Publishers), 129.

[131] Gregory A. Boyd, *Repenting of Religion: Turning from Judgment to the Love of God* (Grand Rapids, MI: Baker Books, 2004), 127.

My emotional illness may grow worse. I may become suicidal. Occasionally I am swallowed up by agonizing fears of being one of the "reprobate." I have been diagnosed with PTSD, compulsive anxiety, panic disorder, major depression, and probably a myriad of other strange disorders that I am unaware of, because my doctor told me I probably should not read the report written about me based on my diagnostic testing. I have flunked out of nearly every method of therapy and inner healing. Every once in a while, I wake up screaming with images of shadowy, hostile faces still hovering in my mind. As I read my own story I am overwhelmed by my egotism, selfishness, greed, unfaithfulness, pride, and God knows what else. But even more than that, I am astounded by the hovering, paternal, inexplicable graciousness of God. I know that welling up inside me is a brilliant light that defies both reason and medical science and abysmal serotonin levels. I am immortal. My God is my L.over, and I am His clumsy, sinful, underachieving, psychotic but somehow strangely beautiful-to-Him bride.

There are many stories in the universe, but for every human being that has ever lived, this is the only one that matters: a love that burns us into beauty if we embrace it will come to us on some unfathomable night, and we must whisper or shout or gesticulate "Yes, yes, yes," to Him, or find ourselves raped by our own "no." God promises that all things will be reconciled, that every tongue will gladly confess His Lordship. I pray it may be so, and I will betroth myself to hope until He comes at last to say, (I hope!) "Well done," and I put out His words with a kiss.

I do not believe I am alone in my tortured wanderings. Most of us in the Western church have been left like Mary Magdalene outside the tomb of our faith, weeping. Why are so many churchgoers wounded, depressed, and anxious people? Because the church has taken our Lord and we don't know where they have put Him! Surely this caricature they have presented us with is nothing like the Jesus who is love incarnate. This god chooses people to torment in everlasting hell, for His own glory. This god is a slave to the blind goddess Justice, who weighs our hearts and our deeds on a balance and declares that someone must be punished for our failures, that someone must placate her wrath. Or this god commands us to muster up and keep our own faith in him, or else we will be cut off and burned like useless branches. All we can do is mourn in our grief and confusion: "They have taken my Lord away,…and I don't know where they have put him."[132] The Western church has left us weeping, and when, as to Mary, the real Jesus appears to us, we cannot recognize Him! We think He is the gardener because He is not afraid of our dirt, the dark loam of our sin, and He even causes blooms to burst out of it! But what God gets dirt under His fingernails? Surely not the god who has blind justice as a concubine. We think He is the gardener because He is a servant who takes off His garment, dresses Himself in a towel and washes our feet! We think He is the gardener because He causes us to flower, because He says "yes" to us rather than a cacophony of thou shalt nots. And when we finally give up on our religion and say we'd rather be married to the gardener, we rot in shame and guilt. The theology that the church presented to us as truth and made us kiss like the skull of some dead saint haunts us like a specter day and night, and our own brainwashed minds declare us heretics. Until at last Jesus Himself whispers to us "Mary," and our toxic theology explodes like a supernova, and our blind eyes are burned into sight from the cataclysm. Then we finally find our stolen voices again, and in the fever of recognition anoint His gloriously human feet with kisses, and our unfettered *imago dei* crys out, "Rabboni!"

"For God was pleased to have all his fullness dwell in, and through him to reconcile to himself all things, whether things on earth or things in heaven, by making peace through his blood shed on the cross." Colossians 1:19-20[133]

"And I, when I am lifted up from the earth, will drag everyone to me." John 12:32[134]

"Amen. Come, Lord Jesus." Revelation 22:20b"[135]

---

[132] John 20:13b (NIV).

[133] Colossians 1:19-20 (NIV).

[134] John 12:32, in David Bentley Hart, *The New Testament: A Translation* (New Haven: Yale University Press, 2017), 200.

[135] Revelation 2:20b (NIV).

Altar Stones

I found the stones in unexpected places,
Neglected shacks, deserts, furrows;
Cracks and burrows in the ground.
They seemed to have faces,
All of them, uncut as they were by human hands.
They sometimes demanded more than I could give,
Since I had already lived so long,
And toting them was slow.
But I grew strong as I carried them,
Though the journey sometimes seemed hollow.
At times, I tarried.
But I blessed each one,
Often with tears that glazed
The creases of my face.
Each stone has its place now,
And I have built as He requires.
And now, heavy with desire,
I will crown my burden with a lamb
And plunge my knife into its hilt
Until the blood erupts and finally wanes
And it is finished.
I am always stunned,
Perplexed by the pain that adorns such acts,
And I wonder that I come
Back to it again and again.
Sometimes it seems a game that one can never win,
And yet I have grown to love
The dragging and the building,
And even the dangerous sting of blood.
I succumb to days as to a flood—
Each one like a bell that rings
And is then forever silent.
I mark them with stones.
And I have found that the altar

Is a kind of throne,
Though I never hear the voice of the King
In times like these.
Silence is His holy choice,
Yet I pray that He is pleased.
Somehow, my wounds are always eased;
In the vicarious flowing they are staunched.
And now, though I have been calling
Half the night and begin to tire,
I know my God will answer me with fire.

Works Cited

Abrams, M. H., ed. "William Cowper," in *The Norton Anthology of English Literature,* vol. 1, 4th edition. New York: W. W. Norton & Company, 1979.

___. "Christopher Smart," in *The Norton Anthology of English Literature*, vol. 1, 4th edition. New York: W. W. Norton & Company, 1979.

anointing.files.wordpress.com. Julius Sturm, quoted in *Streams in the Desert,* by L. B. Cowman, edited by James Reimann, 264-265. Date accessed August 11, 2020. https://anointing.files.wordpress.com/2013/01/devotional-streams-in-the-desert.pdf.

Athanasius. *On the Incarnation.* In *The Christology of the Later Fathers.* Edited by Edward R. Hardy. Louisville, KY: The Westminster Press, 1954.

Bono. "I Still Haven't Found What I'm Looking For." From the album *The Joshua Tree.* Released 1987.

Boyd, Gregory. *Repenting of Religion: Turning from Judgment to the Love of God.* Grand Rapids, MI: Baker Books, 2004.

___. Woodland Hills Church. Sermon titled "The Rorschach Test." July 4, 2010.

Bunyan, John. *The Pilgrim's Progress.* Carlisle, PN: The Banner of Truth Trust, 1997.

Conrad, Joseph. *Lord Jim.* New York: Doubleday & Company, 1920.

Carroll, Lewis. *Alice in Wonderland.* London: MacMillan and Co., Limited, 1912.

Cowper, William. "The Castaway." In *The Norton Anthology of English Literature,* vol. 1, 4th edition. Edited by M. H. Abrams. New York: W. W. Norton & Company, 1979.

Cowper, William. "On the Receipt of my Mother's Picture out of Norfolk." *The Poetical Works of William Cowper.* Edited by William Michael Rossetti. London: William Collins, Sons and Co., n. d.

Cowper, William. "There is a Fountain Filled with Blood." In *Conyer's Collection of Psalms and Hymns,* 1772.

Crosby, Fanny. "Blessed Assurance," 1873.

Curtis, Brent and John Eldridge. *The Sacred Romance.* Nashville: Thomas Nelson Publishers, 1997.

Davids, Peter H. *New International Commentary on the New Testament: The First Epistle of Peter.* Grand Rapids, MI: William B. Eerdmans Publishing Company, 1990.

Donne, John. *"Holy Sonnet 10." In The Norton Anthology of English Literature,* vol. 1, 4th edition. Edited by M. H. Abrams. New York: W. W. Norton and Company, 1979.

Dylan, Bob. "All I Really Wanna Do." From the album *Another side of Bob Dylan.* Released August 8, 1964.

___. "Like a Rolling Stone." From the album *Highway 61 Revisited.* Released June 15-16, 1965.

Eagles. "Hotel California." Written by Don Henley and Glenn Frey. From the album *Hotel California*. Released December 8, 1976.

Eliot, T. S. "Four Quartets: Burnt Norton." In *T. S. Eliot: The Complete Poems and Plays*. San Diego: Harcourt Brace Jovanovich, Publishers, 1950.

___. "Gerontin." In *T. S. Eliot: The Complete Poems and Plays*.

___. "Four Quartets: The Dry Salvages." In *T. S. Eliot: The Complete Plays and Poems*.

___. "*Four Quartets*: *East Coker*." In *T. S. Eliot: The Complete Plays and Poems*.

___. "Four Quartets: Little Gidding." In *T. S. Eliot: The Complete Plays and Poems*.

___. "The Love Song of J. Alfred Prufrock." In *T. S. Eliot: The Complete Plays and Poems*.

___. "The Waste Land." In *T. S. Eliot: The Complete Plays and Poems*.

Frost, Robert. "Nothing Gold Can Stay." In *New Enlarged Anthology of Robert Frost's Poems*. New York: Holt, Rinehart and Winston, 1951.

___. "The Road Not Taken." In *The Norton Anthology of American Literature,* vol. 2, 2nd edition. Edited by Nina Baym. New York: W. W. Norton and Company, Inc., 1985.

Hart, David Bentley. *The New Testament: A Translation*. New Haven: Yale University Press, 2017.

Hillsong United. Written by Dylan Thomas, Joel Davies and Marty Sampson. "Came to my Rescue. Copyright 2005 Hillsong Music Publishing.

Hopkins, Gerard Manley. ("Carrion Comfort."), in *The Poems of Gerard Manley Hopkins*, 4ᵗʰ edition. Edited by W. H. Gardner and N. H. Mackenzie. New York: Oxford University Press, 1967.

___. ("No Worst, there is None"), in *The Poems of Gerard Manley Hopkins*, 4ᵗʰ edition.

___. ("Thou Art Indeed Just, Lord."), In *The Poems of Gerard Manley Hopkins*, 4ᵗʰ edition.

Kelsey, Morton. *Healing and Christianity*. New York: Harper and Row Publishers, 1973.

Leitch, Donovan. "A Soldier's Dream." From *Brother Sun, Sister Moon*. Produced by Franco Zeffirelli. Released December 2, 1972.

Marquez, Gabriel Garcia. "A Very Old Man with Enormous Wings." Translated by Gregory Rabassa. In *Literature: Reading Fiction, Poetry and Drama*, 2ⁿᵈ edition. Edited by Robert DiYanni. New York: McGraw-Hill Publishing Company, 1990.

Merton, Thomas. *The New Man*. New York: The Noonday Press, 1961.

Nietzsche, Friedrich. Beyond Good and Evil. Planetebook https:www.planetebook.com/free-ebooks/beyond-good-and-evil.pdf. Accessed August 8, 2020.

Origen. *De Principiis* 4.1.18. In *Fathers of the Third Century: Tertullian, Part Fourth; Minucius Felix; Commodian; Origen, Parts First and Second*, vol. 4. Edited by S. Roberts, J. Donaldson, and A. C. Coxe. Translated by F. Crombie. Buffalo, NY: Christian Literature Company, 1885. Logos Bible Software.

Plath, Sylvia. *The Bell Jar*. New York: Harper and Row, 1971.

Peterson, Andrew. "Love is a Good Thing." From the album *Resurrection Letters, Volume Two*. Released 2008.

Poe, Edgar Allen. "Annabel Lee." In *The Norton Anthology of American Literature*, vol. B. Edited by Nina Baym. New York: W. W. Norton & Company, Inc., 2012.

Prince and the Revolution. "Purple Rain." From the album *Purple Rain.* Released June 25, 1984 by Warner Bros. Records.

The Project Gutenberg. 1996. Emily Bronte. Wuthering Heights. Accessed August 7, 2020. https://www.ucm.es/data/cont/docs/119-2014-04-09-wuthering%20heights.pdf.

The Rolling Stones. "(I Can't Get No) Satisfaction." From the album *Out of our Heads.* Released June 5, 1965.

Shakespeare, William. *Hamlet.* In *The Norton Shakespeare*, 2nd edition. Edited by Stephen Greenblatt. New York: W. W. Norton and Company, 2009.

___ MacBeth. In *The Norton Shakespeare*, 2nd edition.

___. King Lear. In *The Riverside Shakespeare.* Edited by G. Blakemore Evans. Boston: Houghton Mifflin Company, 1974.

Saint John of the Cross. *The Collected Works of Saint John of the Cross*, revised edition. Translated by Kieran Kavanaugh and Otilio Rodriguez. Washington, D. C.: Institute of Carmelite Studies, 1991.

Styron, William. *Darkness Visible: A Memoir of Madness.* New York: Vintage Books, 1990.

Tennyson, Alfred. "The Lady of Shallot." In *Tennyson's Poetry.* Edited by Robert W. Hill, Jr. New York: W. W. Norton & Compnay, 1971.

Thomas, Dylan. "Love in the Asylum." In *The Poems of Dylan Thomas.* Edited by Daniel Jones. New York: New Directions Publishing Company, 1971.

Thomas, Dylan. "The Force that through the Green Fuse Drives the Flower." In *The Poems of Dylan Thomas*. Edited by Daniel Jones. New York: New Directions Publishing Company, 1971.

Wesley, Charles. "And Can it Be, that I should Gain?" In *Hymns and Sacred Poems*, 1739.

Zarzar, Nancy Craig. "Burial." In *Waiting for Pentecost*. Charlotte, NC: Main Street Rag, 2007.

Zarzar, Nancy Craig. "Pieta." In *Waiting for Pentecost*. Charlotte, NC: Main Street Rag, 2007.